A History of the Armenian People

Volume II:
1500 A.D. to the Present

George A. Bournoutian

MAZDA PUBLISHERS

Costa Mesa, California

The publication of this volume was made possible by a grant from the AGBU Alex Manoogian Cultural Fund

Library of Congress Cataloging-in-publication Date

Bournoutian, George A.
  A History of the Armenian People / George A. Bournoutian.
      p.   cm.
  Includes bibliographical references and index.
  Contents: v. 2. 1500 A.D. to the present
      1. Armenia – History.
  DS175.B65   1994

ISBN: 1-56859-032-6
10 9 8 7 6 5 4 3 2 1

A History of the Armenian People

In memory of my great-uncle, Nazaret Bournoutian,

a khmbapet *in the defense of Van,*

April-May 1915

Contents

MAPS

TIME-LINES

PLATES
(pages 203-210)

1.   Mekhitarian Center, San Lazzaro, Venice
2.   Armenian Cathedral, New Julfa, Iran
3.   Gandzasar Monastery, Mountainous Karabagh
4.   The Armenian Church, Madras, India
5.   The Armenian Church, Singapore
6.   The Armenian Church, Dhaka Bangladesh
7.   The Armenian Church, Cairo, Egypt
8.   The Armenian Church, New Nakhichevan (Rostov, Russia)
9.   The Armenian Church, St. Petersburg, Russia
10.   Lazarian Institute, Moscow, Russia
11.   An Armenian Church, Tiflis, (Tbilisi) Georgia
12.   Samuel-Murad Armenian School, Sèvres, France
13.   Murad Raphaelian Armenian School, Venice, Italy
14.   Armenian Church (Czernowitz, Moldavia), Chernovtsy, Ukraine
15.   Holy Cross Monastery, Crimea, Ukraine (photo C. Mutafian)
16.   View of Zeitun, 1912 (courtesy of ALMA)

Preface

This second volume of *A History of the Armenian People* focuses on the modern period, that is, from 1500 A.D. to the present. This work, like its predecessor, is not based on original research, but it does contain some fresh interpretations and has utilized numerous sources. It is a survey which places the last five hundred years of Armenian history in the context of world history. The maps and timetables have been especially prepared to aid in this endeavor. The work is intended for college undergraduates, select high school seniors, and the general public. Its main purpose is to acquaint Armenians and non-Armenians with a history which is absent from most academic texts. The bibliographical guide cites the majority of works available in English on the period covered in this volume, as well as a few works in other languages. As in volume I, the study strives to be brief and concentrates on political events, glossing over the arts, literature, and socioeconomic issues. Some topics have been simplified or condensed, and others left out altogether.

I have been fortunate to have had the assistance of many colleagues and friends whose advice and support has been invaluable for the realization of this undertaking: Avedis Sanjian of the University of California at Los Angeles; Robert Hewsen of Rowan College; Khachik Tololyan of Wesleyan University; Aram Arkun of the Zohrab Center of the Armenian Diocese; Barlow Der Mugrdechian of California State University at Fresno; Stephan Astourian, Arman Grigorian, Carol Aslanian, Pergrouhi Svajian, and Mark Malkasian, all read the various drafts and made valuable suggestions. Without the financial and moral support of Louise Manoogian Simone, the President of the AGBU, who despite her busy schedule took time to devote her attention to this project, and Edmond Azadian of the AGBU Alex Manoogian Cultural Fund, this volume, like its predecessor, would have never been produced. A last minute research grant from Iona College aided in obtaining relevant data for the final chapter. Lois Adams edited the text, Greg Kazarian and Robert

Hewsen prepared the maps, and Armen Garabedian designed the layout. Finally, my wife Ani, as always, was an invaluable partner in this undertaking.

George Bournoutian
Associate Professor of History, Iona College
Summer 1994

Explanatory Notes

To conform with the dialect spoken in the Republic of Armenia, Armenian words, with few exceptions, have been transliterated according to the sounds of Eastern Armenian. Persian words, with some exceptions, have been transcribed to reproduce the sounds of modern Persian. Russian words have been transliterated according to a simplified version of the Library of Congress system. Diacritical marks and ligatures have been omitted in all instances. Some foreign names and terms, particularly those included in *Webster's Unabridged Dictionary, Third International Edition*, have been Anglicized. Finally, present-day geographical place names and foreign terms appear in parentheses.

It is important to remember that various cultures have different calendars. Religious and secular calendars can also be different. Although no longer used, the Armenian Church calendar was 551 years behind the Church calendar previously used in the West. Chinese, Hebrew, Arab, Iranian, and prerevolutionary Russian calendars, among others, also differ from the Western, or Gregorian, calendar used today. To simplify matters, all dates, except for those in prerevolutionary Russia, have been converted to the Gregorian calendar. Dates before February 1, 1918, which refer to events in Russia or Transcaucasia, are given in the Julian calendar, which was thirteen days behind the Gregorian calendar in the twentieth century, twelve days behind in the nineteenth century, eleven days behind in the eighteenth century, and so on. All dates following the names of rulers, popes, and catholicoses refer to their reigns; after all other names, the paranthetical dates refer to lifespans.

Geographical terms can be confusing. *Arab lands* or *Arab world* refers to lands in North Africa and the Middle East which are inhabited by Arabs. *Middle East* is the modern Middle East -- or all the lands inhabited by Muslims, Christians, and Jews which lie between the Mediterranean and Pakistan, including Iran, Turkey, Sudan, Egypt, and Ethiopia. *Transcaucasia* or *Transaraxia* is the region occupied by the present-day republics of Armenia, Georgia, and Azerbaijan. *Mesopotamia* refers to the territory of present-day Iraq; the *Levant* to Lebanon and parts of coastal Syria; and *Greater Syria* to present-day Lebanon, Syria, and parts of Jordan, Palestine, and Israel. *Iranian Azerbaijan* is the province in northwestern Iran below the Arax river; while *Azerbaijan* is the republic of Azerbaijan (1918-present). The *Balkans* are the present-day states of Greece, Albania, Bulgaria, Romania, and most of the former Yugoslavia. *Asia Minor* or *Anatolia* is the territory of present-day Turkey. *Eastern Europe* encompasses the former Soviet Block (excluding East Germany), Yugoslavia, Greece, and Cyprus; *Western* and *Central Europe* encompass the rest of that continent. *Western Armenia, eastern Anatolia* or *Turkish Armenia* refer to the Armenian-populated provinces in eastern and southwestern Turkey; and *eastern Armenia, Russian Armenia*, or *Transcaucasian Armenia* refer to the Armenian regions which lie between the Arax, Kur, Khram, and Arpachay (Akhurian) rivers.

The names of some national groups are another source of confusion. *Turk* refers to both the Ottomans and present-day Turks. Prior to the twentieth century, the Turkic groups who inhabited Transcaucasia were referred to by most sources as *Turko-Tatars*. In this century they are called by their newly adopted name, *Azeri* or *Azerbaijani. Persian* will denote the written and spoken language of Iran; *Iran* and *Iranian* will refer to the land and its people.

In addition to the sources listed in the bibliographical guide, I have referred to my lecture notes and have benefited from the seminars on modern Armenian history and literature taught by Richard Hovannisian and Avedis Sanjian at UCLA. Moreover, I have consulted the following world history texts, art histories, encyclopedias, and atlases for the preparation of the timetables and maps:

WORLD HISTORY TEXTS

The New Cambridge Modern History, 12 vols. Cambridge, Cambridge University Press, 1967-1977.

A. M. Craig, W. A. Graham, D. Kagan eds., *The Heritage of World Civilizations*. New York, Macmillan, 1990.

A. Esler, *The Human Venture: A World History from Prehistory to the*

Present. Englewood Cliffs, New Jersey, Prentice Hall, 1992.

R. L.Greaves, R. Zaller eds., *Civilizations of the World.* New York, Harper-Collins, 1993.

J. P. McKay, B. D. Hill, J. Bucler eds., *A History of World Societies.* Boston, Houghton Mifflin, 1992.

W. H. McNeill, *A History of the Human Community.* Englewood Cliffs, New Jersey, Prentice Hall, 1990.

P. L. Ralph, R. E. Lerner, E. M. Burns eds., *World Civilizations.* New York, W.W. Norton, 1991.

L. S. Stavrianos, *A Global History.* Englewood Cliffs, New Jersey, Prentice Hall, 1991.

J. Upshur, J. Terry, J. Holoka eds., *World History.* Los Angeles, West Publishing, 1991.

T. W. Wallbank, A. M. Taylor eds., *Civilizations Past and Present.* NewYork, Harper-Collins, 1992.

R. W. Winks, C. Brinton eds., *A History of Civilization.* Englewood Cliffs, New Jersey, Prentice Hall, 1992.

ENCYCLOPEDIAS

An Encyclopedia of World History (W. L. Langer, ed.). Boston, 1972.

The Columbia History of the World (J. A. Garraty and P. Gay, eds.). New York, 1981.

Encyclopaedia Iranica (E. Yarshater, ed.). London & Costa Mesa, 1985- .

Encyclopaedia of Islam. (New Edition) Leiden, 1960- .

Soviet Armenian Encyclopedia (in Armenian, Academy of Sciences of Armenia). Yerevan, 1974-1987. A new 4 volume edition is in preparation.

The Timetables of History (B. Grun, ed.). New York, 1991.

ATLASES

Historical Atlas of Armenia (Z. Armen, V. Artinian, H. Abdalian, eds.). New York, 1987.

Hammond Historical Atlas of the World. New Jersey, 1989.

The Penguin Atlas of Modern History : To 1815 (C. McEvedy, ed.). New York, 1972.

The Penguin Atlas of Recent History: Europe since 1815 (C. McEvedy, ed.). New York, 1982.

Historical Atlas of Iran (`A. Mostowfi, ed.). Tehran, 1971. *(in Persian)*

The Anchor Atlas of World History, Vol II : From the French Revolution to the American Bicentennial (H. Kinder and W. Hilgemann eds.). New York, 1978.

Historical Atlas of the World (O. Bjorklund, H. Holmboe, A. Rohr, eds.). New York, 1972.

An Atlas of Russian and East European History (A. E. Adams, I. M. Matley, W. O. McCagg, eds.). New York, 1967.

Atlas of Soviet Armenia (in Armenian, Academy of Sciences of Armenia). Yerevan, 1961.

Introduction

Armenia's geographical location, as well as the adaptability of its people,
gave rise to a unique language, literature, art and architecture, all of which,
combined with its ardent Christianity, maintained Armenian culture for over
two millennia. During that time Armenia was ruled by a number of native
dynasties and served as a corridor for goods and ideas from the East to the
West. At the end of the Middle Ages, however, Armenia had not only lost its
independence, but four centuries of Turko-Mongol invasions had altered its
demography. Destruction, death, and emigration had turned the Armenians
into a minority in parts of their homeland. Most Armenian urban centers
were left in ruins and many villages and farms had reverted to pastureland.
Isolated villages, mountain strongholds, few trading centers, and a handful of
monasteries struggled to maintain Armenian culture and traditions. Unlike
the ancient, classical, and medieval periods, therefore, the history of the
Armenians in modern times lacks dynastic continuity and, with the exception
of several short periods and isolated pockets, independent rule.

Since Armenia's military, administrative, commercial, and cultural
leadership was either destroyed or relocated (voluntarily as well as forcibly)
to urban centers in Europe and Asia, it was in the diaspora that the Armenians maintained much of their heritage and, in time, began their cultural and
political revival. The history of the Armenians in modern times, therefore, is
concerned with two different groups. In the first group are the various
Armenian communities of the diaspora, called *spiurk* in Armenian, which
formed, increased, or diminished as a result of invasions, massacres, revolutions, attempted genocide, colonialism, and nationalism. In the second group
are the Armenians who remained in historic Armenia, which was itself first
partitioned between the Ottoman Empire and Iran, and later between the
Ottoman and Russian empires -- with parts of Russian Armenia eventually
evolving into the first independent Armenian Republic (1918-1921), Soviet

Armenia (1921-1991), and the present independent Armenian Republic (since 1991). The Armenians in the Ottoman and Russian empires were in a unique situation. Although some of them lived on their own historic homeland, albeit under Ottoman or Russian rule, others lived in these empires' major cities, such as Tiflis, New Nakhichevan, Baku, Moscow, St. Petersburg, Smyrna, or Constantinople. Political and socioeconomic conditions in these urban centers had a major impact on the largely rural Armenian homeland.

The political divisions among the Armenians that followed the collapse of the first Armenian republic, as well as recent revisionist publications, have created some difficulties in writing the history of the Armenians in the last century. Controversies are inevitable. I have striven to examine all sources and to present an objective narrative of the modern history of a very resilient and enterprising people. The end of the Soviet Union has generated both optimism and pessimism among Armenians and "Armenia watchers." This second volume of *A History of the Armenian People* is presented with the hope that the region will be able to resolve its differences and that Armenia will finally gain the peace which has eluded its land and people for nearly three thousand years.

IRAN & OTTOMAN EMPIRE	WESTERN/CENTRAL EUROPE	RUSSIA & EASTERN EUROPE	SOUTH & EAST ASIA	AFRICA & THE AMERICAS
Bayazid I (1481-1512)	High Renaissance in Italy (ca. 1500-1530)	Basil II (1504-1533)	Ming Dynasty continues in China (to 1644)	Songhai Empire continues in the Sudan (to 1591)
Isma'il I (1501-1524)	Henry VIII (1509-1547)	Sigismund I (1506-1548)	Portuguese trade monopoly in East Asia (1500-1600)	Slave Trade (ca. 1500-1870)
est. Safavid Dynasty	Francis I (1515-1547)	Pskov conquered (1510)		Eleven million Africans brought to the New World
Shi'ism state religion in Iran (ca. 1510)	Concordat of Bologna (1516)	Smolensk conquered ((1514)	Portuguese in Goa (1510)	
Selim I (1512-1520)			Malacca falls to Portuguese (1511)	
Battle of Chaldiran (1514)	Charles V (1519-1556)	Battle of Mohacs (1526)		Portugal in East Africa (1500-1600)
Ottoman and Safavid wars in Armenia, deportation and scorched-earth policy (1514-1590)	Church of England (1534)	First siege of Vienna (1529)	Babur founds Mughal Dynasty (1526)	Balboa sights Pacific Ocean (1513)
	Luther's 95 Theses (1517)	Ivan IV (1533-1584)		
	Loyola est. Jesuits (1534)	Sigismund II (1548-1571)	Christian missionaries active in Japan and China (1550-1650)	Magellan rounds South America (1520)
	Council of Trent (1545-1563)	Fall of Kazan (1552)		Cortez ends Aztec Empire (1521)
Ottomans conquer Syria & Egypt (1516-1517)		North Cape Route discovered (1553)	Akbar (1556-1605)	
Suleiman I (1520-1566)	Schmalkaldic Wars (1546-1547)	Fall of Astrakhan (1556)	Portugal in Macao (1557)	Pizarro ends Inca Empire (1533)
Tahmasb I (1524-1576)	Peace of Augsburg (1555)	Oprichnina founded (1565)	Spain occupies the Philippines (1564)	Sa'idid Dynasty in Morocco (1554-1659)
Etchmiadzin sends mission to the West to liberate Armenia (1547-1562)	Philip II (1556-1598)	Union of Lublin (1569)	Toyotomi Hideyoshi (1585-1598)	
	Elizabeth I (1558-1603)	Russian expansion to Siberia (1581-1598)		St. Augustine colony in North America (1565)
Peak of Ottoman power (ca. 1550)	St. Bartholomew's Day Massacre (1572)	Livonian War ends (1582)	Plague in China (1586-1589)	Islamic state of Kanem-Bornu in Central Sudan (1575-1846)
Selim II (1566-1574)	Adoption of Gregorian Calendar (1582)	Moscow becomes a patriarchate (1589)	Unification of Japan (1590)	
Battle of Lepanto (1571)	Spanish Armada (1588)	Uniate Church est. in Ukraine (1595)	China and Japan fight in Korea (1592-1598)	
Murad III (1574-1595)	Henry IV (1589-1610)	Boris Godunov (1598-1605)	Hideyoshi bans Christianity in Japan (1597)	
'Abbas I (1587-1629)	est. Bourbon House	Times of Troubles (1598-1613)		
Iran relinquishes eastern Anatolia to the Ottomans (by 1590)	Gustavus Adolphus (1594-1632)			
	Edict of Nantes (1598)			

Table 1: 1500-1600

XII

Amiras and Sultans:
Armenians in the Ottoman Empire (ca. 1450-1876)

During the latter part of the fourteenth century and through the fifteenth, Western Europe experienced the Renaissance, succeeded in driving the Muslims out of Spain, and discovered the New World. For the next two centuries Europeans would be engulfed by the Age of Exploration, the Reformation and Counter-Reformation, the renewed struggle between Church and State, the decline of feudalism, the rise of urban classes, and the emergence of centralized nation-states and absolute monarchs. The Muslims and the Chinese were militarily equal or superior to the West. The former had repulsed the Crusaders from the Middle East, and would be free to rule over Orthodox and Slavic peoples in Asia Minor and Eastern Europe, Christians in the Caucasus, indigenous tribes in North Africa, and Hindus in India. The latter would hold sway over various peoples in Central and East Asia. Free trade between East and West would give way to more restricted trade through select channels and companies. While China became isolated and its Ming and Ch'ing dynasties could not pose a threat to the West, the Muslims, in the form of the Ottoman Turks, knocked at the door of Central Europe and hostile relations would exist between Europe and the Ottoman Empire for centuries to come.

In the late Middle Ages, the Muslim world itself witnessed major transformations. The Mamluks in Egypt, the Ottoman Turks in western Anatolia and the Balkans, the Black and White Sheep tribal confederations in eastern Anatolia and northwestern Iran, and the Timurids in northeastern Iran and Central Asia engaged in a power struggle which was to affect greatly the Muslim domains and which eventually resulted in the emergence of three powerful empires: the Ottoman, in Asia Minor, the Arab lands, and the

Balkans; the Safavid, in Iran, the Caucasus, and parts of Central Asia; and the Mughal, on the Indian subcontinent. In the sixteenth and the early part of the seventeenth centuries, the Ottomans and Safavids fought each other in eastern Anatolia, Transcaucasia, and Mesopotamia. Much of the conflict took place in the Armenian homeland and finally came to an end in 1639, when the two powers ceased their hundred-year hostilities and concluded the Treaty of Zuhab. The treaty once again partitioned Armenia, this time into eastern (also known as Persian Armenia) and western (sometimes referred to as Turkish Armenia) sections. The Plain of Shirak became a sort of boundary between the two. Lands west of and including the fortress of Kars fell into Ottoman hands, while territories east of Ani and the Arpachay River became part of Iran. Baghdad, another center of contention, ended in the possession of the Ottomans, who kept Mesopotamia. Destruction of property, famine, disease, forced conversions, and resettlement reduced the population and significantly diminished the region's economic viability. Apart from a few princes in Siunik and Lori, the hereditary landowning Armenian nobility virtually disappeared. The Armenian Church submitted to Muslim rule in order to assure its own survival as well as that of its flock. The Ottoman, Safavid, and Mughal rulers each dealt differently with their Armenian subjects. The Ottomans and Iranians granted the Church the political as well as the religious leadership of their Armenian subjects. The more tolerant Mughals did not have an established policy but generally left the Armenian secular leaders in charge of their communities. The next four chapters will examine life in these communities, which were scattered in historic Armenia as well as in the various cities of the Ottoman, Iranian, and Mughal empires.

The Armenians of western Asia Minor had emigrated there during the Byzantine era and by the early Middle Ages had established sizeable communities in a number of cities, particularly Constantinople, where they had achieved military and political importance.* By the eleventh century, however, their numbers had decreased in Constantinople and although the Seljuk Turkish invasions of Armenia brought new settlers to that city, the Armenian presence remained insignificant. Sources indicate that Sultan Muhammad II (1444-1446 and 1451-1481), shortly after conquering Constantinople, forcibly relocated a large number of Armenians from eastern Anatolia and the Crimea to that city. Such deportations continued through the sixteenth century and significantly increased the Armenian community of the Ottoman capital.

*See vol. I, pp. 112-113.

The Armenian Millet

By the late eighteenth century, the Ottomans had fully institutionalized what Arab conquerors had loosely established in the Middle East centuries earlier -- that is, organizing the various subject peoples in their empire not into political or racial groups, but into religious communities. The Greeks, the Jews, and the Armenians were thus grouped into distinct communities called *millets*, each under the supervision of its own religious leader. Each community eventually restricted itself to its own quarter of Constantinople and other urban centers. Recent scholarship has challenged the notion that the *millet* system emerged as a full-blown institution in the fifteenth century or soon after the fall of Constantinople. It now seems certain that the Ottomans had no consistent policy toward non-Muslims until much later and that the *millet* system evolved gradually. The Ottomans at first dealt with smaller groups of non-Muslims and rarely used the term *millet* until the nineteenth century, when they used it primarily for the Greek, Armenian, and Jewish communities.

New scholarship has also cast doubt on the role of Sultan Muhammad in the creation of the office of the Armenian patriarch of Constantinople. Tradition has it that in 1461, the sultan appointed Bishop Hovakim of Bursa as the first patriarch of the Armenians in the Ottoman Empire. In reality, however, the development of the Armenian patriarchate of Constantinople appears to have been a more protracted process. Until the first quarter of the sixteenth century, the Holy See of Etchmiadzin was outside the borders of the Ottoman Empire, in adjacent hostile territory; Sultan Muhammad, therefore, recognized the Armenian bishop of Constantinople as the leader of the Armenians of that city's and its environs. Later, since the Turkmen dynasties and, subsequently, the Iranians were tolerant and extremely generous toward the Armenian religious hierarchy, succeeding Ottoman sultans, fearing the influence of pro-Iranian Etchmiadzin, which prior to the seventeenth century had overall jurisdiction over western or Turkish Armenia, not only relocated many Armenians from the interior to Constantinople, but gave their bishop special authority, hoping to assure Armenian loyalty as well as to weaken Etchmiadzin. Other Armenian centers, such as Erzerum, had their own bishops with a similar status. The Armenian bishop of Constantinople, therefore, did not initially have authority over all the Armenians of the Ottoman Empire. The catholicosate of Sis had jurisdiction over the Armenians of Cilicia, that of Aghtamar over the Armenians of Van and its environs, and the patriarchate of Jerusalem over the Armenians of the Arab lands. By the nineteenth century, due to the rivalry of the catholicosates, the rise of an influential Armenian financial elite (the *amiras*), the establishing of schools by Armenian and non-Armenian Catholics, and the inclusion of Etchmiadzin within Russian territory, the Armenian bishopric of Constantinople was induced to and capable of assuming *de facto* authority over all the Apostolic Armenians of the Ottoman Empire and establishing itself as a separate patriarchate, with both political and religious prerogatives. The Ottomans, much to their relief, thus dealt with an Armenian ecclesiastical office that did not have to answer to the Armenian Holy See or any other authority within the Armenian Church. In reality, the catholicoses at Etchmiadzin, Sis, and Aghtamar, and the patriarch of Jerusalem exercised higher authority in religious matters; however, the political, financial, and geographical position of Constantinople made its Armenian patriarch a formidable personage indeed.

According to earlier interpretations, the Ottomans, after the fall of Constantinople, divided the Christians into two general groups: the dyophysites,* who were placed under the authority of the Greek patriarch, and the monophysites,* who were placed under that of the Armenian patriarch. Thus the various Orthodox Churches in the Balkans, such as the Serbian Church, while retaining some autonomy, fell under the jurisdiction of the Greek patriarch of Constantinople; and the autonomous Coptic, Ethiopian, and Syrian Jacobite Churches were technically subject to the Armenian patriarch. This notion has been challenged as well, and it now seems certain that although some attempts were made in that direction, they proved fruitless. In any case, by the late eighteenth century the various Orthodox and Eastern rite Churches had full control over their own religious institutions. In the first half of the nineteenth century, due to the activities of Christian missionaries and pressure from the missionaries' governments, two new *millets,* the Catholic and the Protestant, emerged as well.

Each *millet* was, in effect, self-governing. It was allowed to maintain its own institutions, such as schools, charities, and hospitals. It was responsible for law and order and for resolving disputes within the community. The Armenian patriarch was approved by the sultan and exercised full authority over his people. He had his own court and could dispense civil and ecclesiastical justice throughout his community. He maintained a small police force, as well as a jail. The Turks, who were a minority in parts of their empire, thus managed to keep order by permitting their various conquered ethnic groups to function semi-autonomously and by giving religious leaders greater administrative powers than they had under their own rulers. Armenians and other Christians were still conquered people, however, and were

*See vol. I, pp. 79-81.

treated as such. Their status, particularly in the hinterlands, was one of *reaya*, which can be best translated as "downtrodden." For example, the Ottomans, until the eighteenth century, subjected Christian villages, including the Armenian, to the *devshirme,* or collection of youths who were to be raised as Muslims and enlisted in either the janissary corps (foot-soldiers expert in the use of firearms) or the government administration. The Armenians, like other non-Muslims, were not permitted to bear arms and were, therefore, exempt from military service. They were usually required to pay a poll tax (*jizya* or *jizye*), and their testimony was seldom accepted in Muslim courts. Finally, Armenians in eastern Anatolia had to provide winter quarters for the flocks of the Kurds, nomadic people who were encouraged to move there from their traditional pastures by the Ottomans, or who simply settled in regions abandoned by the Armenians. At its best, during the Ottoman golden age, the *millet* system promised non-Muslims fairer treatment than conquered or non-Christian subjects enjoyed under the Europeans. At its worst, during the decline and fall of the empire, the Christian minorities were subjected to extortion and pogroms.

As the Ottoman sultans lost firm control of eastern Anatolia, and Kurdish raids and Shi`ite revolts created unstable conditions there, more and more Armenian artisans were attracted to Constantinople. A number of later sultans also encouraged Armenians to relocate there and as a result, by the late nineteenth century, the Armenian population in the Ottoman capital reached 250,000. The city had the largest Armenian community in the world and the Armenian patriarch, by some accounts, became the most important and powerful of all Armenian officials. But as the Ottoman Empire declined, so did the stability of the office of patriarch. Although only sixteen patriarchs occupied the seat from 1461 to 1600, fifty-four held office between 1600 and 1715. As bribery, corruption, and nepotism permeated all levels of Ottoman society, the patriarchate fell under the influence of groups with vested interests.

The Amiras

By the eighteenth century some stability returned to the office of patriarch. Not coincidentally, there emerged in this same period a powerful group of Armenian bankers and officials known as *amiras* (from the Arabic *amir,* meaning "chief" or "commander"). This unofficial oligarchy managed to gain power by loaning money to viziers, pashas, tax farmers, and others who needed to purchase an income-producing position. Some of the wealthiest *amiras* were money lenders to the sultan and, as such, had great influence at court. As a social elite they were permitted to wear clothes reserved only for Ottoman grandees and to ride horses, both privileges usually denied to non-Muslims. They supported charities and financed the education of many who would later become major Armenian leaders. Some 166 *amiras* belonging to 77 families have been identified by one historian. Members of the Duzian, Balian, and Dadian *amira* families held, respectively, the positions of director of the imperial mint, chief imperial architect, and superintendent of the gunpowder mill. The *amiras* by virtue of their wealth and status at Court had great influence over the affairs of the Armenian *millet* and the election of the patriarch. The *amiras* often consulted with Armenian merchants and intellectuals, but overall, until the latter part of the nineteenth century, they maintained a control over the Armenian *millet* equal to and often surpassing that of the patriarch himself.

The Mekhitarians

Although an Armenian printing press was functioning in the Ottoman Empire at the end of the sixteenth century, the two centuries of warfare and the treatment of the Armenians by local lords in eastern Anatolia had resulted in a backward society. Only a few books, all on religion, were published. The earliest concrete evidence of renewed Armenian cultural activity began in the late seventeenth century. The most important Armenian intellectual of the period was Yeremia Chelebi Kemurjian (1637-1695), who established a new printing press in 1677 to counter the preaching of Jesuit missionaries. The Armenian Church continued to resist change, however, which fostered dissatisfaction among progressive elements and which, indirectly, led the establishment of the Mekhitarian or Mkhitarist order.

This Catholic monastic order was founded by Abbot Mekhitar, who was born in Sebastia (Sivas) in 1676. After joining the Armenian Apostolic priesthood, he traveled in western Armenia and was convinced that Armenian education had reached a low ebb in his homeland. He sought to establish a religious order which would fulfill the spiritual and intellectual needs of his countrymen. He was rebuked by the Armenian clergy and, after meeting a number of Latin missionaries, felt that the Western Church possessed the necessary tools for his mission. After converting to Catholicism in Aleppo in 1695, Mekhitar founded a new order in Constantinople with ten members on September 8, 1701. Mekhitar maintained that it was possible to adhere to papal authority and to remain faithful to the Armenian nation. His activities

not only angered the Armenian patriarchate but were unfavorably viewed by
the Latin missionaries, none of whom could accept his dual loyalty. The
Mekhitarians were forced to leave for the Morea, in Greece, which at that
time was under the control of Venice.

In 1705 the Mekhitarians petitioned Pope Clement XI (1700-1721) to
recognize their order. The Vatican, concerned by the rumors circulated by
Catholic missionaries trained by the *Propaganda fide,* who accused Mekhitar
of tampering with the rites of the Catholic Church, delayed its recognition
until 1712. In 1715 the Ottomans took the Morea, destroyed the Mekhitarian
monastery, and forced the priests to leave for Venice. The Venetian senate
voted to grant the order the island of San Lazzaro, a former leper refuge, and
on September 8, 1717, sixteen years to the day after the founding of the
order, the Mekhitarians moved there. In 1718 Mekhitar traveled to Rome to
defend his order against continuing rumors. He was successful in convincing
the Vatican of his orthodoxy and devoted the rest of his life to religious and
intellectual activities. He died at San Lazzaro on April 27, 1749. In 1773 a
number of disaffected Mekhitarian fathers left Venice and eventually established a separate branch of the order in 1803 in Trieste. Following
Napoleon's invasion of Italy, they fled to Vienna, where they established a
new center in 1811. Both the Venetian and Viennese Mekhitarian congrega-
tions are active to this day.

The Mekhitarians were deeply concerned with preserving Armenian culture, as well as with the revival of the study of Armenian history and language. They were able to do more to achieve this end than any other Armenian institution. They translated European classics into Armenian and began
writing historical, linguistic, literary, and religious works using primary
sources in Latin, Greek, and other languages. The efforts of M. Chamchian
(1738-1823), G. Avetikian (1751-1827), A. Bagratuni (1790-1866), A.
Aytenian (1824-1902), P. Minasian (1799-1866) and Gh. Alishan (1820-
1901) produced grammars, dictionaries, histories, plays, and numerous
philological, geographical and theological works. With financial assistance
from Iranian-Armenian and especially Indian-Armenian merchants,* the
Mekhitarians established schools and produced two periodicals, *Bazmavep,*
printed in Venice from 1843 onward, and *Handes Amsorya,* printed in Vienna beginning in 1887. The Venetian congregation concentrated its efforts on
Armenian history and literature, while the priests in Vienna focused theirs on
Armenian language and philology. The Mekhitarians not only enabled
Europe to learn about the Armenian past, but their labors channeled Western

* See chapters XIII & XIV.

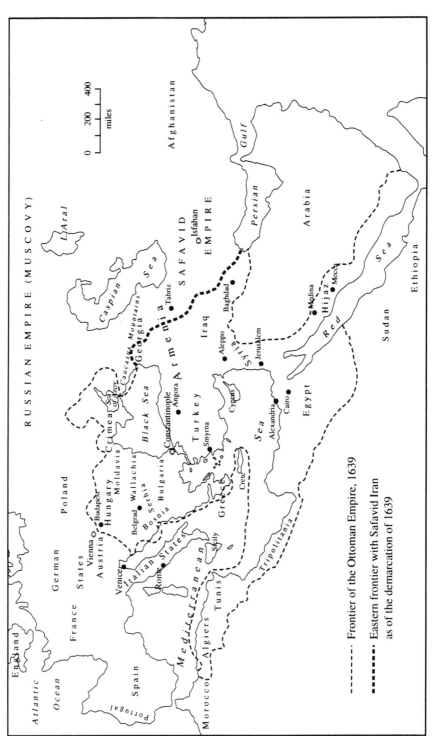

Map 1: The Ottoman Empire in 1639

------- Frontier of the Ottoman Empire, 1639

▬▬▬▬ Eastern frontier with Safavid Iran
as of the demarcation of 1639

thought to the Armenians in the Ottoman and Russian empires and played a major role in shaping the Armenian cultural revival of the nineteenth century.

The Eastern Question

From the fifteenth to the seventeenth centuries the Ottomans were the unquestioned masters of a large part of Eastern and Central Europe (see map 1). In the meantime, the Cossacks completed the long process of Slavic colonization of the pasture lands north of the Black Sea and transformed the Don region into a military base from which Russia would expand eastward into the Balkans. The Slavic and Orthodox peoples of Eastern Europe, encouraged by the actions of Russian rulers and statesmen, in time began to look to Russia as their liberator from Ottoman rule. In the seventeenth century the Ottoman Empire, which had begun its gradual decline following the death of Sultan Suleiman (1566), suffered a series of defeats by Austria, Poland, and Russia. Some Ottoman officials, especially viziers from the Köprülü family, tried to reverse the tide, but the failure to take Vienna after a two-month siege in 1683 ushered in the end of Ottoman supremacy. By the early eighteenth century the Treaties of Karlowitz (1699) and Passarowitz (1718) resulted in the first major Ottoman territorial losses in Europe. Austria received all of Hungary, Transylvania, Croatia, and Slovenia; Poland obtained Podolia; and Russia advanced to the Black Sea. The Ottomans were saved from further losses primarily by disagreements among the Europeans and by the support of France.

The eighteenth century witnessed a number of Russo-Turkish wars in which Peter the Great (1689-1725) and, especially, Catherine the Great (1762-1796) succeeded in expanding Russian influence into the Balkans and Transcaucasia. Austria's preoccupation with Prussia, the rising power of Central Europe, hindered its attempt to take advantage of the situation or to stop Russian expansion. The Austrians, despite their fear of Russia's expanding influence in the Balkans, had to cooperate with Catherine for fear that she would ally with Prussia against them. Catherine's first war with the Ottomans (1768-1774) resulted in major victories on land and sea. Maria Theresa (1740-1780) of Austria and Frederick the Great (1740-1786) of Prussia, concerned with Russia's gains, sought to halt its advance and, in 1772, agreed with Russia to partition Poland. Despite pressures from the Germans, Catherine refused to end the war with the Ottomans until 1774, when the Pugachev revolt in Russia (1772-4) forced her to conclude a treaty.

The Treaty of Küchük Kainarja (1774) gave Russia not only a number of forts in the Crimea, as well as free navigation for its trading vessels in the Black Sea, but it made the Crimean Tatars independent from Ottoman suzerainty. More important, however, was the Ottoman promise to grant a larger degree of self-government to people in Moldavia and Wallachia (present-day Romania), permitting Russia to intervene on their behalf. In addition, the Ottomans agreed to protect the Orthodox Christians and not only permitted Russia to build a church in Constantinople, but gave it extraterritorial privileges as well. The Treaty of Küchük Kainarja provided the pretext for all future Russian interventions in the Balkans. The Russian interpretation of this treaty gave them the right to champion the cause of Slavic and Orthodox minorities living in the Ottoman Empire. The Ottomans and the Western powers -- especially Britain -- disagreed. They felt that the treaty gave Russia only the right to a church in Constantinople and that the rest of the clauses dealing with the minorities were extremely vague.

The problem of how to address the rising tide of Balkan nationalism and the rivalry and expansionist designs of Russia and Austria in the region and how to gauge their possible effects on the Ottoman Empire became known as the "Eastern Question." If, as many believed, the "Sick Man of Europe" (as the Ottoman Empire came to be known in the nineteenth century) had to die, how was it to be dismembered without changing the balance of power in Europe and causing an all-out European war? For more than a hundred years, the Eastern Question was on the mind of every politician and was considered in every major conference or treaty. The failure to resolve it resulted in the assassination of Archduke Ferdinand of Austria in Sarajevo (1914), which ushered in the First World War and destroyed the Ottoman, Russian, German, and Austro-Hungarian empires. Although the Eastern Question primarily involved the Balkans, Britain's vital interests in India, Egypt, and the Persian Gulf forced it to support the Turks against Russian expansion into the Mediterranean. Furthermore, Britain harbored a fear of Russian moves toward Central Asia, which indirectly tied the Eastern Question to the "Great Game," as the Russo-British rivalry in the East was called. All of this political intrigue at times had major repercussions on the fate of the Armenians.

Following the Treaty of Küchük Kainarja, Austria, hoping to isolate Prussia, chose to delay or monitor Russian expansion by cooperation. In 1781 Catherine and Joseph II of Austria (1780-1790) discussed the "Greek Scheme," by which they hoped to drive the Ottomans out of Europe. According to this plan Austria would annex the western half of the Balkans, while Russia would gain the rest, restoring the Byzantine Empire with

Catherine's grandson, Constantine, as the new emperor at Constantinople. Catherine annexed the Crimea in 1783 and several years later began her second war with the Ottomans (1787-1792). Austria and Prussia, both preoccupied with the French Revolution, then sought to check Catherine's expansion into Eastern Europe. Prussia began to make moves into Poland, and Austria made a separate peace with the Ottomans. Russia was forced to sign the Treaty of Jassy (1792), by which it gained little territory. A year later, in 1793, Russia and Prussia concluded the second partition of Poland, and by 1795 they ended Polish independence with yet a third partition of that country.

The Reforms of Selim III and the Era of Tanzimat (1789-1876)

While the French Revolution shook Europe, some Ottoman leaders, aware of the external threats to their state, began to seriously consider reforming the structure of the once-great empire. Eastern Anatolia was controlled by local Muslim lords, or *derebeys,* and the Christian population of the Balkans, tired of extortion by Ottoman officials and encouraged by Russia, were in constant rebellion. The once-feared janissaries had become an inefficient force that conducted business rather than engaging in war. Together with conservative religious leaders, the janissaries resisted any modernization of the empire by deposing or killing sultans who favored such a course.

In the same year as the start of the French Revolution, Selim III (1789-1807) ascended the Ottoman throne. At first he, like some of his predecessors, felt that the empire could be saved if it reestablished its former discipline. With the exception of modern weapons, there was no need for modernization; the government had only to end abuses and inefficiencies. After the Treaty of Jassy, however, Selim realized that a more thorough reorganization was necessary. He established a small and effective military force, called the *Nizam-i Jedid* ("New Order" or "New Army"), modeled along European lines. He also revived the Ottoman navy and established several modern factories for the manufacture of weapons and gunpowder. His administrative, financial, and judicial reforms, although partially successful at best, opened the door to Western ideas and institutions and laid the groundwork for the modernization of Turkey.

By the nineteenth century, the sociopolitical changes advocated by the Enlightenment and the French Revolution had penetrated the Ottoman Empire through the introduction of the printing press and the arrival of European commercial and technical advisors. Ironically, the Christian minorities, especially those in the Balkans, were the first to benefit from these changes.

Their merchants imported the new ideas into Eastern Europe, while their diasporas encouraged and financed intellectual and revolutionary activities. The cultural nationalism of eighteenth-century European theorists like Herder and Fichte was embraced by most intellectuals in the Balkans. Vernaculars replaced the classical languages as the new literary vehicles of the region. The national consciousness of the ethnic minorities was thus expressed first through a literary revival and, after the spread of revolutionary ideas by Napoleon, through uprisings and demands for autonomy or independence. Some groups, such as the Serbs, the Greeks, the Romanians, and the Montenegrins, due to Russian political and religious influence, awakened quickly and won recognition in the first half of the nineteenth century, while others, like the Bulgarians, Armenians, and Arabs, began their political revivals later in that century. Yet others, such as the Macedonians, Albanians, and finally the Kurds, began their demands only in the early twentieth century.

Napoleon's campaigns in Europe, in the meantime, saved the Ottomans from further Russian or Austrian encroachments. Even Napoleon's defeat and the Congress of Vienna in 1815 also helped the Ottomans, for the European powers, in a conservative reaction to French revolutionary ideas, agreed to maintain their *status quo* and to quash future revolutions in Europe. As a result, the Austrian and English statesmen, Metternich and Castlereagh, convinced the Russian tsar, Alexander I (1801-1825) not to involve Russia in the Serb revolt (1815-1817) or the early phase of the Greek war of independence, which began in 1821. In the meantime, revolts by their Christian subjects in Serbia and Greece, as well as the independent actions of Muhammad `Ali Pasha, the Ottoman governor-general of Egypt, once and for all demonstrated to the sultans the urgent need for serious reforms in the Ottoman Empire. Although Selim III was killed by reactionary elements, Sultan Mahmud II (1808-1839) finally abolished the janissaries in 1826 and, with European help, began to form a completely modern army.

The new Russian tsar, Nicholas I (1825-1855), although a conservative autocrat was also a defender of Russian Orthodoxy and sympathized with the Balkan Christians. He took a harsher line against the Ottomans and in 1828 began a war against them. A year later, the Treaty of Adrianople (present-day Edirne) not only gave Russia most of western Georgia but created an autonomous Moldavia and Wallachia. A few months later, in 1830, Russian aid enabled Greece, which had attracted the sympathy of many European liberals, to also achieve its independence. Several years later, Russia increased its influence in the Balkans when it aided the Ottomans against Muhammad

`Ali's invasion of Syria and Asia Minor. By the Treaty of Unkiar Skelessi (1833), Russia became the protector of the sultan in exchange for closing the Straits (the Bosphorus, connecting the Black Sea to the Sea of Marmara, and, the Dardanelles, connecting the Sea of Marmara to the Aegean Sea) to all foreign warships except those of Russia.

Europe, led by Britain, could not accept Russian dominance of the region. In order to improve the image of the Turks and at the same time to weaken Russia's role as the protector of the oppressed Balkan Christians, the British convinced the Ottomans to enact reforms. In 1839 the young Sultan Abdul Mejid I (1839-1861), upon the advice of officials who favored Western reforms, issued the *Hatt-i Sherif-e Gülhane* ("Noble Rescript of the Rose Chamber"), which guaranteed the life, liberty, and property of all his subjects. It promised military and tax reforms, a centralized administration, an assembly of grandees, the establishment of provincial councils, mixed tribunals, and technical colleges. The *Hatt-i Sherif* actually initiated some reforms and ushered in the *tanzimat* ("reorganization" or "reform") period, which was to last until 1876. Although the decrees broke with tradition and were generally opposed by Muslim religious leaders, they were not enacted by legislation but were implemented by the sultan, who could rescind them at will. More importantly the promise of reforms enabled the Ottomans to counter Russian demands in the Balkans and by 1841, when the Unkiar Skelessi Treaty ran out, the Straits Convention, signed by all European powers, closed the Straits to all foreign warships. This effectively ended Russia's short-lived influence in the Ottoman Empire.

The reforms, overall, were not far-reaching and the Slavic minorities, awakened by cultural revivals and occasionally supported by Russia, continued to demand more concrete changes. The elusive peace was finally shattered by the Crimean War (1853-1856), which ostensibly began as a dispute between the Russians and the French over their protection of the Holy Places in Jerusalem but, in reality, was the united European challenge to continuing Russian claims arising from the treaty of Küchük Kainarja. Although Russia was victorious in Anatolia, its defeats in the Crimea prompted the new tsar, Alexander II (1855-1881), to sue for peace. In the Treaty of Paris (1856) the Ottomans were finally admitted to the "Concert of Europe," while Russia had to return regions captured in western Armenia and had to dismantle its fortifications in the Black Sea. In order to stop future Russian involvement in the affairs of the minorities of the Ottoman Empire, the British, French, and Austrian ambassadors forced Sultan Abdul-Mejid to issue another reform edict, the *Hatt-i Hümayun* ("Imperial Rescript"). The new decree guaranteed

Christian subjects security of life, honor, and property and abolished the poll tax. In addition it drastically curbed the civil power of the heads of the *millets*, an action which was to have a major impact on the Armenian community. Full freedom of conscience was also guaranteed and every civil office was open to all citizens. Christians became eligible for military service, but with the option of purchasing exemptions. Once again the reforms benefited the major urban centers and had little or no effect on the conditions in the provinces.

The Armenian Cultural Revival

By the nineteenth century, European historians, archeologists, and even artists had begun to develop a deep interest in Eastern cultures. Babylonian, Egyptian, Iranian, Greek, Chinese, and Armenian culture attracted French, German, and English followers. Orientalism became a vogue and travelers visited the Middle East producing many illustrated volumes on their experiences. The activities of the Mekhitarians facilitated the study of Armenian history and language in Europe. The English poet Lord Byron studied Armenian with them in Venice. Scholars such as Langlois, Brousset, and Hübschman not only wrote studies on Armenian history and language, but the latter determined that Armenian was a separate branch of the Indo-European language tree.

In the meantime, the Armenian intellectual class in Smyrna and the religious hierarchy in Constantinople, reacting to and influenced by Mekhitarian and Jesuit activities, the writings of the Madras circle,* and the reforms initiated by Selim III, had established half a dozen schools, two hospitals, and ten new presses that published numerous religious and secular works. Many of these projects were financed by the *amiras*. In addition, the Armenians founded the Mesropian College in Smyrna, which attracted teachers like Stepan Voskanian, who imbued a whole generation of intellectuals with French literary thought. A graduate of the college was the translator, novelist, and journalist Matevos Mamurian who, after studying in Paris, opened a school in Smyrna in 1851, and, in 1871, became the editor of an Armenian literary periodical. Armenian novelists such as Mamurian, Dzerents, and Diusap were influenced by Scott, Goethe and Dumas and their work emulated the romantic nationalism of their European counterparts. The result of all this activity was the *zartonk*, a renaissance or cultural awakening, of the Armenians in Ottoman Turkey.

*See chapter XIV.

The reforms of 1839 enabled the appearance in 1840 of the first vernacular periodical, *Dawn of Ararat,* which appeared in Smyrna. By the second half of the nineteenth century, many Armenian writers, ignoring the admonitions of the Church and the conservative hierarchy, adopted the spoken vernacular of Constantinople and developed the modern western Armenian language spoken today in most of the Middle East, Europe, and the Americas. A kind of rivalry emerged between Smyrna, where the Armenian literary revival had started, and Constantinople, whose more cosmopolitan atmosphere attracted Smyrna's intellectuals. In 1852 the Dedeyan family established a new press in Smyrna, which within three decades had published some 200 Armenian translations of French, English, and German romantic writers who, in turn, influenced modern Armenian authors such as Petros Turian (1852-1872). Classical tragedies were translated into Armenian, as well, and performed in the first theater in Constantinople under the direction of the poet Mkrtich Beshiktashlian (1828-1868).

The press played a crucial role in the Armenian cultural revival. The first newspaper published in Ottoman Turkey was founded by Armenians in 1812. Between 1840 and 1866, fourteen Armenian periodicals were established in Constantinople. Most noted among these were *Masis,* edited by Garabed Utudjian; *The Bee,* edited by Harutiun Svajian; and *Fatherland,* edited by Arpiar Arpiarian. The most influential journals in western Armenia were *The Eagle of Vaspurakan* and *The Eagle of Taron,* published by the future catholicos, Khrimian, in Van and Mush respectively. In the second half of the nineteenth century these periodicals, some of which had become dailies, played a major role in the political awakening of the Armenian masses living in Anatolia.

Other forces served to awaken the Armenian spirit as well. Although early Catholic missionary activity had faced stiff resistance from the Armenian Church, by the nineteenth century reforms had weakened the *millet* chiefs. European states had gained major influence in the Ottoman Empire, and French and Italian missionaries, as well as English and American evangelists, opened missions and schools, including institutions of higher learning, in Ottoman Turkey. Having little success in converting the Muslims, they concentrated their efforts on Armenians and other Christians. Although most Armenians remained with the mother Church and simply took advantage of the education offered by the missionaries, they were nevertheless influenced by the progressive ideas. The number of Armenian Catholics grew, especially after the establishment of the Mekhitarian order, and French influence established a separate Armenian Catholic *millet* in 1831. American

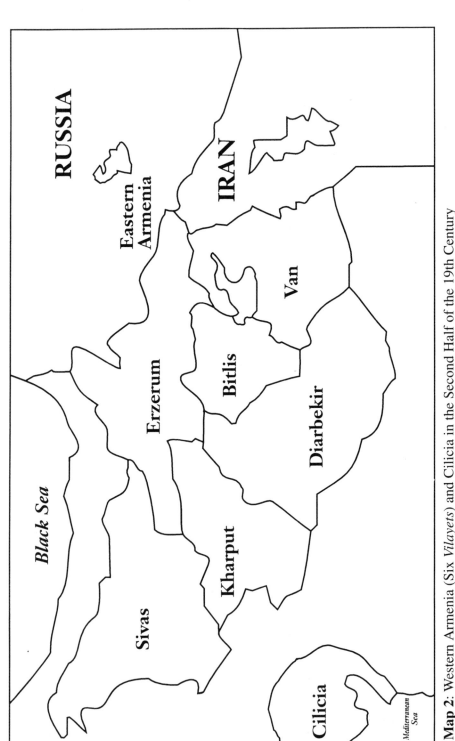

Map 2: Western Armenia (Six *Vilayets*) and Cilicia in the Second Half of the 19th Century

Evangelical missionaries arrived in the early nineteenth century. They began by printing the Bible in the vernacular and in Turkish, written with Armenian characters. They sent over able and committed individuals such as Eli Smith, one of the first two Americans ever to visit Armenia (1830-1831), and William Goodell; opened schools in every major city of Anatolia and Cilicia; and by mid-century had made over 8000 Armenian converts. American and British pressures established a separate Armenian Evangelical *millet* in 1847. The establishment of these *millets* gave Catholic and Evangelical Armenians (some two percent of the Armenian population) opportunities not only to pursue their higher education at home or abroad, or to emigrate to Europe and the United States, but, at times, to enjoy the diplomatic protection of their European co-religionists.

Armenian schools played a key role in the Armenian awakening, as well. The reforms of Selim III removed the restrictions placed on public education. A small number of elementary parochial schools opened in Constantinople between 1790-1800, and girls' schools opened after 1820. Challenges from the Catholic and Evangelical missionaries forced the Armenian Church to open many more schools, including an upper-level academy (*Jemaran*) in Constantinople in 1839. By mid-century, thanks to the *tanzimat,* Constantinople alone had close to 5000 students attending some forty schools and two colleges. Levies on the community, particularly on the wealthy, supported these schools, which were practically free, and made it possible for some two dozen students to receive scholarships to study in France annually. On their return these students spread European ideas by teaching, writing, or publishing newspapers. By the end of the *tanzimat* era (1876), elementary and secondary schools had spread to the six western Armenian *vilayets* or provinces of Van, Bitlis, Erzerum, Diarbekir, Kharput, and Sivas (see map 2). Five centuries after the fall of the last Armenian kingdom in 1375, the Armenians finally had the tools to begin a political revival. Political movements in Russia and the last Russo-Turkish war of the nineteenth century were to present a unique opportunity in that direction.

The Armenian National Constitution

Unlike the Christians in the Balkans, the Armenians did not rebel or agitate against the Sublime Porte (the official residence of the grand vizier and the seat of government was called *Bab Ali*, Sublime Porte, or Porte) and were favored by the Ottomans, who viewed them as the "loyal" *millet*. By the mid-nineteenth century, the Armenian community in Constantinople and

Smyrna was socially and economically stratified. After Greek independence in 1830, all Greeks in the empire were suspect and the Armenians replaced them in many positions, further enhancing the power of the *amiras*. Armenian merchants, as well as the *amiras*, had also amassed a good deal of wealth and many had become agents for European firms, trading spices, jewels, carpets, fabrics, glassware, amber, weapons, dried fruit, and fur with Italy, the Netherlands, France, Iran, India, and Russia. The Armenian middle class consisted of artisans and craftsmen who were grouped into *esnaf* or guilds. Some one hundred Armenian guilds, with approximately 40,000 members, were recorded by the mid-nineteenth century. Not all the Armenians of Constantinople and Smyrna were well-to-do, however. The resettlement of tens of thousands of Muslim refugees from the Balkans and the Caucasus had led to deteriorating living conditions in the eastern provinces of Anatolia. By 1860 some 20,000 Armenian migrant workers, or *pandukht* in Armenian, had flocked to the two cities, where they lived in crowded dwellings, performed menial jobs, and died from disease and neglect. Many more arrived by the end of the century.

Since the *tanzimat* guaranteed individual rights and equality before the law for everyone, the authority of the patriarch and the *amiras* was finally challenged by Armenian liberals who demanded changes. Less influential merchants, intellectuals (some of whose education the *amiras* themselves had financed) craftsmen, and even some of the common workers began to demand an end to their oligarchic rule. In 1838 some of the active guild members rebelled against the *amiras* and demanded a voice in affairs of the community. The division became so serious that the patriarchate and the Ottoman government had to intervene, and in 1841 the guilds achieved a major victory when a committee of twenty-four merchants and craftsmen was established to assist the *amiras* in administering the Armenian Apostolic *millet's* finances. By 1847 two more bodies, a religious council of fourteen clerics and a civil council of twenty laymen, began to supervise the affairs of the community. Councils for education, economic, and judicial affairs soon emerged as well. In 1848 the *amiras* tried to reassert their control by forcing the resignation of a popular patriarch. Armenians of Constantinople rose in protest and elected another popular cleric. The Ottomans provided the final stimulus for change. In 1856 the *Hatt-i Hümayun,* as stated, officially decreed that the subject communities could have a representative government chosen from among their lay and religious members. The power of the Armenian patriarch, as the sole spokesman for the Armenian Apostolic *millet,* was waning.

Each religious community was to prepare a self-governing document and submit it to the Sublime Porte. The Armenians were the first minority group to submit a draft in 1857 and a revised document in 1859. Both were rejected by the *amiras* and the conservative clerics. Finally a compromise was achieved and on May 24, 1860, a constitutional assembly of religious and lay members of the Armenian *millet* approved the Armenian National Constitution, or *azgayin sahmanadrutiun,* to be implemented by an elected council. Although the council argued with the patriarchate of Jerusalem over the latter's authority and jurisdiction and had some problem getting the document ratified by the Porte, by March 1863 a slightly revised document became a part of Ottoman law as it related to the Armenian *millet.*

The constitution was the work of a new type of Armenian: young men who had visited Europe or who had been trained in European institutions and who had been affected by the liberal and constitutional ideas of the late eighteenth and the early nineteenth centuries. The document laid out six principles outlining the individual's and the community's rights and obligations towards each other. If the individual was to pay his share of taxes, perform services, and obey the administrative council, for example, he should expect, in return, an education for his children, preservation of his traditions and his Church, and security for his community. The constitution had ninety-nine articles, which covered the religious and civil affairs of the community at all levels. The national council was to have one hundred and forty representatives from Armenians throughout the empire: twenty clerics and eighty laymen from Constantinople and forty from other major urban centers. Most of the Armenians from the six provinces, that is, western Armenia, were neither involved in nor affected by this undertaking. The council participated in the election of the patriarchs of Constantinople and Jerusalem -- although their role in the election of the latter was questioned. They also participated in the election of the catholicos at Etchmiadzin. The catholicosates of Sis and Aghtamar, contrary to earlier assumptions of the council, were not answerable to it. It should be noted that the Porte continued to reserve the right to confirm the patriarch and refused to officially guarantee the individual or collective rights of the Armenians, an issue which was to come up some two decades later.

By 1865, the activities of the Christians and the ease of censorship initiated by the *tanzimat* had also resulted in the emergence of a group of Turkish intellectuals known as the "Young Ottomans." Most of them had studied in France, had been influenced by European liberalism, and sought a constitutional government. This circle, like their Russian counterparts,* were the children of the elite, who had remained in Europe and conducted anti-gov-

*See chapter XVI.

ernment activities in exile. In time they would evolve into an ultra-national-
ist group which not only changed the course of the empire but resulted in
near-extermination of the Armenians in Turkey.

IRAN & OTTOMAN EMPIRE	WESTERN/CENTRAL EUROPE	RUSSIA & EASTERN EUROPE	SOUTH & EAST ASIA	AFRICA & THE AMERICAS
Ottoman power challenged (ca. 1600-1700)	Thirty Years' War (1618-48)	Romanov Dynasty est. (1613)	Battle of Sekigahara (1600)	British est. Jamestown (1607)
'Abbas' deportations of Armenians to Iran (1603-4)	Richelieu (1624-42)	Alexis (1645-76)	Dutch East India Co. (1602)	Champlain est. Quebec (1608)
New Julfa est. (1605)	Frederick William of Prussia (1640-88)	Revolt of Stenka Razin (1670-71)	Tokugawa Shogunate (1603-1867)	Mayflower lands at Plymouth (1620)
Murad IV (1623-49)	English Civil War (1642-49)	Armenians granted trade privileges in Russia (1667)	Jahangir (1605-27)	Dutch found New Amsterdam (1624)
Safi I (1629-42)	Louis XIV (1643-1715)	Church reforms by Nikon, Schism and the rise of Old Believers (1667)	East India Co. (1609)	Portuguese in West Africa (ca. 1630)
Zuhab Treaty (1639)	Mazarin (1643-61)	Andrusovo Treaty (1667)	Shah Jahan (1627-58)	Montreal est. (1642)
'Abbas II (1642-66)	Peace of Westphalia (1648)	Jan Sobieski (1674-96)	Korea under China (1627)	New England Confed. (1643)
Catholicos Hakob (1655-80)	Cromwell (1653-58)	2nd Battle of Mohacs (1687)	Dutch take Java (1628)	Dutch settle in Cape Town (1651)
Köprülü viziers (1656-91)	Colbert (1661-83)	Peter the Great (1689-1725)	Japan expels Europeans (1637)	Portuguese take Brazil (1654)
Decline and fall of Safavid Dynasty (1666-1732)	Second siege of Vienna (1683)	Treaty of Nerchinsk (1689)	Dutch in Indonesia (1641)	British take Jamaica (1655)
Safi II (1666-94)	Edict of Nantes revoked (1685)	Azov and Kamchatka taken (1696)	Manchus est. Ch'ing Dynasty (1644-1911)	Peter Stuyvesant surrenders New Amsterdam (New York) to Britain (1664)
Russo-Turkish War (1677-81)	War of the League of Augsburg (1688-97)	Battle of Zenta (1697)	Aurengzeb (1658-1707)	Westminster Treaty (1674)
Ahmad II (1691-95)	Glorious Revolution (1688)	Peter's first trip to Europe (1697-98)	Britain gets Bombay (1661)	La Salle claims Louisiana for France (1682)
Hosein I (1694-1722)	Bill of Rights (1689)	Streltsy revolt (1698)	Aurengzeb bans Hinduism (1669)	
Russo-Turkish War (1695-6)	Charles XII (1697-1718)		Maratha state (1674-1750)	
Mustafa II (1695-1703)	Treaty of Ryswick (1697)		Dutch in Canton (1683)	
Karlowitz Treaty (1699)			British est. Calcutta (1690)	

Table 2: 1600-1700

XIII

Khojas, Meliks and Shahs:
Armenians in Iran (ca. 1500-1896)

Prior to the third century A.D., Iran had more influence on Armenia's culture than any of its other neighbors. Intermarriage among the Iranian and Armenian nobility was common. The two peoples shared many religious, political, and linguistic elements and traditions and, at one time, even shared the same dynasty.* Sasanian policies and the Armenian conversion to Christianity, in the fourth century, however, alienated the Armenians from Zoroastrian Iran and oriented them toward the West.* The Arab conquests which ended the Iranian Empire and the conversion of Iran to Islam in the seventh century culturally separated the Armenians even further from their neighbor. In the eleventh century, the Seljuk Turks drove thousands of Armenians to Iranian Azerbaijan, where some were sold as slaves, while others worked as artisans and merchants. The Mongol conquest of Iran in the thirteenth century enabled the Armenians, who were treated favorably by the victors, to play a major role in the international trade among the Caspian, Black, and Mediterranean seas.* Armenian merchants and artisans settled in the Iranian cities bordering historic Armenia. Sultanieh, Marand, Khoi, Salmas, Maku, Maraghe, Urmia, and especially Tabriz, the Mongol center in Iranian Azerbaijan, all had, according to Marco Polo, large Armenian populations.

Ottoman-Safavid Rivalry and the Depopulation of Armenia

Tamerlane's invasion at the end of the fourteenth century and the wars between the Black and White Sheep Turkmen dynasties in the fifteenth century had a devastating effect on the population of historic Armenia. The latter part of the fifteenth century witnessed the weakening of the White Sheep

* See vol. I, pp. 54-69, 138-139.

and the attempts of the Ottoman sultan, Bayazid II (1481-1512), to take advantage of the situation and to extend his domains eastward into Armenia and northwestern Iran. At the dawn of the sixteenth century, however, Iran was unified under a new dynasty, the Safavids (1501-1732) and after some nine centuries once again acquired the sense of nationhood which has continued into the present.

The Safavids assumed importance during the early fourteenth century when Sheikh Safi ad-Din established his Sufi order in Iranian Azerbaijan. A century later, the order, now known as the Safavi, had assumed a wholly Shi`i nature and began gathering support among the Turkmen tribes of northwestern Iran and eastern Anatolia. The order obtained the support of a number of major Turkic tribes, who called themselves the *kizil-bash,* or "red heads" (from the red caps that they wore). By 1501 the Safavid leader Isma`il seized Transaraxia from the White Sheep and declared himself shah. Ten years later he managed to gain control over Iran, historic Armenia, and much of eastern Transcaucasia, and he founded a theocratic dynasty that not only claimed to be descended from `Ali, the son-in-law of the prophet Muhammad, but that also portrayed the shahs as reincarnations of the Shi`i imams or saints. Shi`ism thus became and remains the state religion of Iran.

The emergence of the Safavids and the rise of Shi`ism in eastern Anatolia were major threats to the Ottomans, whose claim to the caliphate and the leadership of the Muslim world was challenged by the new Iranian dynasty. In 1514 Sultan Selim I (1512-1520) crossed the Euphrates River and for the first time entered historic Armenia. Shah Isma`il was not ready to fight the Ottomans and withdrew his forces, burning many villages en route to forestall the advancing Ottoman army. Thousands of Armenians were forced to leave their land. The Ottomans pushed deep into Armenia and on August 23, 1514, at the Battle of Chaldiran, destroyed the Iranian army through their superior numbers and artillery. Although Selim captured Tabriz, the administrative center of the Safavids, he had to withdraw a week later, as Ottoman military leaders refused to winter in Tabriz or to pursue the enemy into the Iranian highlands. This pattern was to be repeated a number of times, particularly during the reign of Shah Tahmasb I (1524-1576), who also pursued a scorched-earth policy when he had to face the mighty Sultan Suleiman the Magnificent (1520-1566). The harsh Armenian climate and difficulties in transportation and in communications with Constantinople made it possible for the Safavids to repeatedly survive such defeats. Although the Safavids managed to recover Tabriz, Iran relinquished most of eastern Anatolia. The first peace agreement between the two powers in 1555 left the western parts of historic Armenia in Ottoman hands, while the eastern parts ended up under Iranian control. Realizing the vulnerability of Tabriz, Tahmasb moved the capital south to Qazvin. The uncertain situation over Tahmasb's succession encouraged the Ottomans to invade Armenia again in 1578 and to continue their campaign until 1590, taking most of Transcaucasia and once again occupying Tabriz.

Caught in the middle of these warring powers, some Armenians were deported by the Ottomans to Constantinople from Tabriz, Karabagh, and Nakhichevan and others, by the Iranians, to Iranian Azerbaijan from Van. To replace them, Sultan Selim and his successors settled Kurdish tribes in Armenia, a policy which continued into the seventeenth century. Indo-European speakers like the Armenians, the Kurds were Muslims who were divided into Sunni, Shi`i, and Yezidi sects. They were a nomadic people who were exempt from cash taxation, but had to present a quota of their herds and guard the border regions. Their settlement in historic Armenia was to create a major problem later for the Armenians when the state was powerless to control the Kurds or, conversely, when it actually used them against the Armenians. The protracted Ottoman-Safavid war and the resulting forced migrations depopulated parts of historic Armenia, and the Kurdish settlement changed its social and ethnic balance.

The Great Migration

It was Shah `Abbas the Great (1587-1629) who left the greatest imprint on modern Iran and the Iranian Armenian community. Recognizing the comparative weakness of the Iranian army, he quickly concluded a treaty with the Ottomans in 1590, ceding eastern Armenia and parts of Iranian Azerbaijan. He then began the formation of a new force, recruiting Georgian and Armenian mercenaries and converts as sharpshooters, and, with European help, fashioned an artillery and the basis of a modern army. He moved his capital from Qazvin to Isfahan, a safer location. Isfahan was also closer to Baghdad, the soft underbelly of the Ottoman Empire.

By the start of the seventeenth century `Abbas felt strong enough to break the peace he had made with the Ottomans in 1590. In the autumn of 1603 the shah advanced to retake Iranian Azerbaijan and to force the Ottomans out of Transcaucasia as well. He succeeded in taking the cities of Tabriz, Marand, Ordubad, Akulis, and the province of Nakhichevan, which included the town of Julfa. The shah was greeted as a liberator by the Armenians, who could no longer endure heavy Ottoman taxes, and the Shi`i Muslims, who were tired of religious persecutions. The Armenian merchants of Julfa, who had been engaged in international trade for some time, were especially happy with the Iranian capture of Julfa. According to one primary source, the Sunnis of Nakhichevan province were killed and their villages were razed by the Safavid army. The same source adds that `Abbas deported the Armenian merchants of Julfa to Iran at this time in order to prevent the region from regaining its economic viability. All other contemporary sources, however, indicate that only the main fortress of Nakhichevan was destroyed in 1603 and that the Armenian population was not moved until 1604.

In November 1603, `Abbas laid siege to the fortress of Yerevan, a formidable bastion constructed by the Ottomans. The siege lasted over seven months and resulted in the conscription of over 10,000 local Armenians and Muslims, which, in turn, spelled an economic and demographic decline of that province. In the summer of 1604, at the news of an Ottoman counteroffensive, `Abbas laid waste much of the territory between Kars and Ani and deported its Armenians and Muslims into Iranian Azerbaijan. `Abbas was sure that the Ottomans would not launch an attack so close to winter and according to some sources, demobilized most of his army in the fall. The Ottomans, however, did advance, catching the shah unprepared. Orders went out from `Abbas to forcibly remove the entire population residing in the regions of Bayazid, Van, and Nakhichevan and to carry out a scorched-earth policy.

Primary sources estimate that between 1604 and 1605 some 250,000 to 300,000 Armenians were removed from the area. Thousands died crossing the Arax River. Most of the Armenians were eventually settled in Iranian Azerbaijan, where other Armenians had settled earlier. Some ended up in the Mazandaran region and in the cities of Sultanieh, Qazvin, Mashhad, Hamadan, Arak, and Shiraz. The wealthy Armenians of Julfa were brought to the Safavid capital of Isfahan. The Julfa community was accorded special care and seems to have suffered less in their migration. They were settled across the banks of the Zayandeh Rud and in 1605 a town, called New Julfa (*Nor Jugha*), was constructed especially for them.

Persian masons, together with Armenian craftsmen, built the new settlement. Many churches were constructed, thirteen of which survive today. Armenians had rights which were denied other minorities. They elected their own mayor, or *kalantar*, rang church bells, had public religious processions, established their own courts, and had no restrictions on clothing or the production of wine. No Muslims could reside in New Julfa. The Armenian mayor was given one of the shah's royal seals in order to bypass bureaucratic tangles and had jurisdiction over the two dozen Armenian villages around Isfahan. He collected and paid to the throne a poll tax in gold, which was gathered from each adult male. In time, the Armenian population of New Julfa and the surrounding villages grew to some 50,000. Here they were granted trading privileges and a monopoly on the silk trade, which transformed the community into a rich and influential one and New Julfa into a main center of trade between Iran and Europe. Interest-free loans were granted to the Armenians to start businesses and light industries. Soon a major part of Iran's trade with Europe, Russia, and India was handled by the Armenians, who enjoyed the shah's protection and who had outbid the British on the silk monopoly. The New Julfa merchants formed trading companies which competed with the Levant, East India, and Muscovy companies, and established businesses in Kabul, Herat, Qandahar, Marseilles, Venice, Genoa, Moscow, and Amsterdam, and in cities of Sweden, Poland, Germany, India, China, Indonesia, and the Philippines. `Abbas would spend time in New Julfa at the houses of the most successful merchants, known as *khojas* or notables, whom the silk monopoly had made extremely prosperous. Sources describe their fabulous houses, decorated with Oriental and Western artwork, with tables set with gold utensils.

The Armenians paid a set fee for each bale of silk and most of their profits remained in Iran. Ottoman profits from overseas trade fell and the Persian Gulf became a center of trade with Western ports. The military decline of the Ottoman Empire encouraged the West to establish new contacts in the East. Western diplomats, visitors, and merchants were dispatched to Iran and most were housed in New Julfa. The Armenian merchants' contacts with the West made them a conduit through which the shah was able to secure diplomatic and commercial alliances against the Ottomans.

The Armenians of New Julfa became a unique part of the diaspora in other ways as well. They formed a separate ecclesiastical unit under their own bishop, appointed by Etchmiadzin, which had jurisdiction over all Armenians of Iran and Iraq. New Julfa soon became a cultural center. A school was opened for the sons of the *khojas* as well as for some of the talented boys from less prominent Armenian families. The future catholicos, Hakob Jughaetsi (1655-1680), was among its graduates, as were a number of historians and translators. One graduate, a priest, was sent to Italy to learn the art of printing and brought back the first printing press in Iran. The first book printed in Iran, in any language, was an Armenian translation of the Book of Psalms, produced in 1638. Manuscript illuminators developed a distinct New Julfa style, beginning in the first half of the seventeenth century,

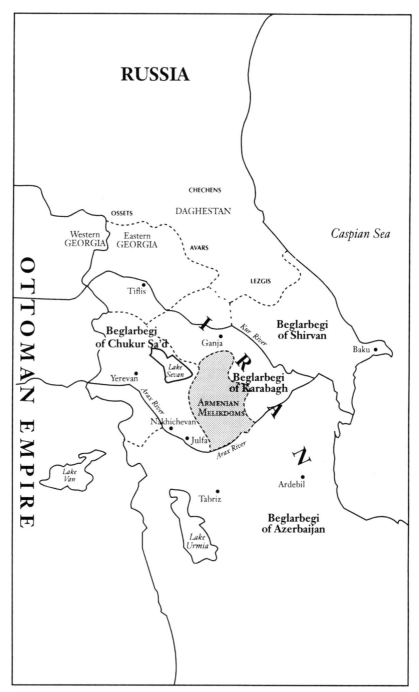

Map 3: Eastern Armenia, the Rest of Transcaucasia, and Iranian Azerbaijan in the Late 17th and Early 18th Centuries

with the work of Mesrop of Khizan, originally from Armenia. A few artists even began to copy European works brought to New Julfa by the *khojas*. Prior to 1600, Armenian merchants had for some five hundred years conveyed Eastern technology to Europe. From the seventeenth century onwards, beginning with the New Julfa merchants, the Armenians were one of primary channels for the introduction of Western technology and culture to Asia.

European sources of the seventeenth century portray `Abbas as a great benefactor of the Armenians, who secured them from the Turks and who made them wealthy in New Julfa. Armenian historians of the time, however, such as Arakel of Tabriz, view Shah `Abbas' deportations and the Turko-Iranian conflict in Armenia as a major catastrophe, during which the land and the people suffered terribly, with the resulting depopulation making the Armenians a minority in most of their historic land. `Abbas' policies did indeed have varying short-term effects, in the long term, however, the forced deportations established the basis for the Armenian diaspora in Iran and India, communities which, as we will see, were to play an important role in the Armenian cultural and political revival of the nineteenth century.

One of the intangible benefits of Armenian economic power in Iran was the transformation of the Armenian self-image. After centuries of conquest by Muslim invaders, Armenians were granted equal and at times even greater privileges than Muslims. This increased prestige extended to the Church as well, and enabled the leaders at Etchmiadzin to regain some control over outlying dioceses and communities and to establish ties with the patriarchs of Constantinople and Jerusalem. This new status also allowed a number of Armenian secular leaders to achieve recognition and to rally support. This was particularly true of the lords, or *meliks,* of Karabagh and Zangezur who, under the patronage of the shahs, the Church, and the Armenian merchants, retained and expanded their ancestral fiefdoms in Karabagh. The *meliks* were the last scions of Armenian nobility in eastern Armenia. They lived in mountainous regions and usually paid tribute directly to the shah. Unlike the Church leaders, they lacked unity and had to contend with Muslim rulers, who viewed any landed and armed Christian nobility as a threat. Their autonomy and occasional defiance, however, attracted some popular support, and, as will be seen, they initiated, together with some Armenian merchants and clerics, the Armenian emancipation movement.

Eastern Armenia (1639-1804)

The Treaty of Zuhab partitioned historic Armenia in 1639 between the

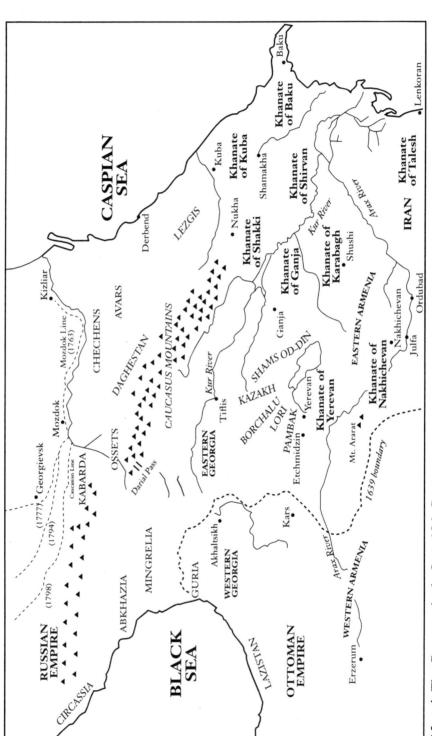

Map 4: The Caucasus in the Late 18th Century

Ottomans, who took western Armenia, and the Safavids, who took eastern Armenia. Eastern Armenia was itself divided into the *beglarbegi* of Chukhur Sa'd (the regions of Yerevan and Nakhichevan), and the *beglarbegi* of Karabagh (the regions of Karabagh-Zangezur and Ganja). The first was thus composed of sections from the historic Armenian provinces of Ayrarat, Gugark, and Vaspurakan; the second from Artsakh, Siunik, and Utik (see map 3). Administered by khans, mostly from the Qajar clan, the regions were under the supervision of a governor-general stationed in the city of Tabriz, in Iranian Azerbaijan. The *beglarbegi* of Chukhur Sa`d was especially important, for its main city, Yerevan, was a center of Iranian defense against the Ottomans.

Although `Abbas protected the Armenians of New Julfa and prevented the Catholic missionaries from making major inroads in the community, his death and the eventual decline of the Safavids in the second half of the seventeenth century forced some of the *khojas* to emigrate to India and Italy, where they established branches of their trading houses. The absence of an Iranian merchant marine meant that the Armenian merchants of New Julfa, over time, could not keep up with the large English or Dutch joint-stock venture companies such as the East India Company, which, by the mid-eighteenth century had taken over much of the trade of the region. By the beginning of the eighteenth century, growing Shi`i intolerance and new laws unfavorable to the Armenians also created a difficult situation for the *khojas,* and more of them emigrated to Russia, India, the Middle East, and Western Europe. Insecurity at home also meant that Armenians would look to Catholic Europe and especially Orthodox Russia for protection or even deliverance. The fall of the Safavids and the Afghan occupation of Isfahan and New Julfa in 1722 marked the end of the influence of the *khojas*, but did not end the Armenian presence in Iran. Large Armenian communities remained in Isfahan, New Julfa, and a number of Iranian cities.

The fall of the Safavids encouraged Peter the Great to invade the Caspian coastal regions, while the Ottomans broke the peace of Zuhab and invaded eastern Armenia and eastern Georgia in 1723. In two years' time the Ottomans were in control of the entire region, save for Karabagh and Siunik, where Armenian *meliks* under the leadership of David Beg, Avan Yuzbashi, and Mekhitar Sparapet held them off for nearly a decade. The Ottomans installed garrisons in Tiflis (present-day Tbilisi), Nakhichevan, Ganja, and Yerevan. The fortress of Yerevan was repaired and served as the administrative headquarters of the Ottoman military-governor of eastern Armenia.

By 1736 a new ruler, Nader Shah (1736-1747) and a new dynasty, the

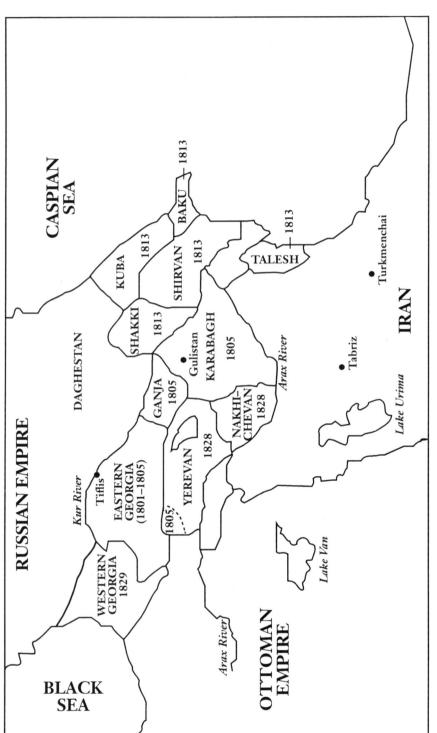

Map 5: The Russian conquest of Transcaucasia (1801-1829)

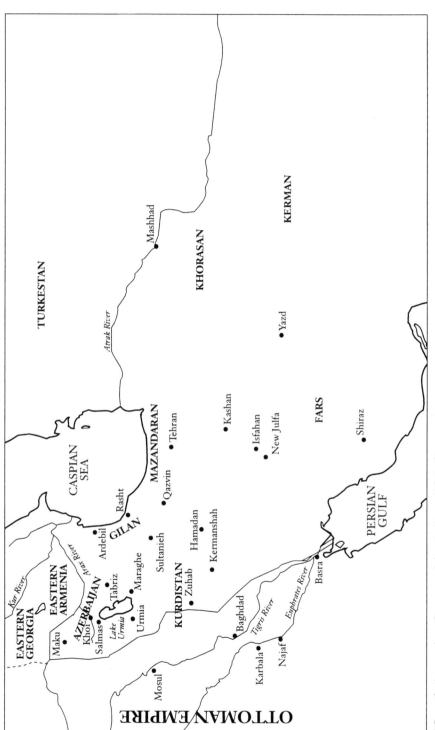

Map 6: Armenian Communities in Iran (19th Century)

Afshars, had restored order in Iran, had convinced the Russians to withdraw, and had pushed the Ottomans back to the boundaries of 1639. Rewarding the Armenian *meliks* for their stand against the Ottomans, the shah exempted them from tribute and recognized their autonomy. Catholicos Abraham Kretatsi (1734-1737), who had befriended the shah, was a guest of honor at Nader's coronation. The new shah not only visited Etchmiadzin but reconfirmed its tax-exempt status. Nader removed a number of Turkic tribes from eastern Armenia, especially Karabagh, and divided the region into four khanates: Yerevan, Nakhichevan, Ganja, and Karabagh (see map 4).

Nader's assassination in 1747 unleashed a fifteen-year period of chaos in eastern Armenia. The exiled Turkic tribes returned and, led by the Javanshir clan, established a strong presence in the plains of Karabagh. The highlands of Karabagh, composed of the five districts of Gulistan, Khachen, Jraberd, Varanda, and Dizak, as well as a number of districts in Siunik, as noted, had been controlled by Armenian *meliks* and became known as *Mountainous Karabagh* and *Zangezur*, respectively. The region had its own See in Gandzasar. The lowlands, stretching to the Kur River, were populated by Turkic and Kurdish confederations. By allying themselves with Melik Shahnazarian of Varanda, Panah Khan Javanshir and his son Ibrahim Khan managed to gain a foothold in a part of the exclusively Armenian stronghold of Mountainous Karabagh. By 1762 another ruler and dynasty, Karim Khan Zand (1750-1779), took control of most of Iran and was recognized as their suzerain by the khans of eastern Armenia. His seat of power was in southern Iran, however, and Transcaucasia was left to Ibrahim Khan of Karabagh and King Erekle II (1762-1798) of eastern Georgia, both of who divided parts of eastern Armenia into two zones of influence. The death of Karim Khan in 1779 started another fifteen-year conflict among Ibrahim, Erekle, the khans of Yerevan and Ganja, and the Armenian *meliks*. More Armenians emigrated from the khanates of Yerevan and Karabagh to Russia and Georgia. Tiflis, the main city of eastern Georgia, became a major Armenian center.

Russia's annexation of the Crimea and its 1783 Treaty of Georgievsk with Erekle once again involved Russia in Transcaucasian affairs.* The khans of the region rushed to make their own separate peace agreements with each other, and with Georgia, Russia, or Iran. Iran, in the meantime, was in the throes of another dynastic struggle. By 1794, Aqa Mohammad Khan, the leader of the Qajar clan, had subdued all other pretenders to the throne and now swore to restore the territory of the former Safavids. Most of the khans of eastern Armenia soon submitted, but Erekle of Georgia, relying

*See chapter XVI.

on Russian protection, refused. Aqa Mohammad invaded Georgia, sacked Tiflis in 1795, and on his return was crowned shah (1796). To restore Russian prestige, Catherine the Great declared war on Iran and sent an army to Transcaucasia. Her death, shortly after, put an end to that campaign, however. Aqa Mohammad soon contemplated the removal of the Christian population from eastern Georgia and eastern Armenia. His new campaign began in Karabagh, where he was assassinated in 1797. Aqa Mohammad Khan, who had been castrated by his enemies as a youth, was succeeded by his nephew, Fath `Ali Shah Qajar. At the dawn of the nineteenth century, the new shah had to face a third and final Russian challenge.

Socioeconomic Conditions in Eastern Armenia (17th-early 19th centuries)

During the seventeenth century the Safavids transformed Iran's economy. A number of towns in eastern Armenia, located on the trade routes between Asia and Europe, served as depots for goods from India, China, and Iran, which, in turn, found their way to the markets of Russia, the Ottoman Empire, and Western Europe. Well-maintained, safe roads, uniform tariffs, and comfortable caravansaries aided in the transfer of merchandise. Eastern Armenia itself exported wheat and silk from Karabagh and dried fruit, salt, hides, and copper from Yerevan. The large nomadic population supplied wool and Caucasian carpets and rugs woven by Armenians and Turkic craftsmen, which were valued for their colors and design.

The population of eastern Armenia prior to the Russian conquest consisted of a Muslim majority and an Armenian minority. The Muslims were divided into Persians, who formed much of the administration and part of the army; the settled and semisettled Turkic tribal groups, who were either engaged in farming or formed the balance of the army; and the Kurds, who led a traditional nomadic existence and who formed a part of the Iranian cavalry. Although the Armenians were engaged in trade and formed the majority of the craftsmen, most of them were farmers.

The khans were responsible for the defense and the collection of taxes and were usually the sole authority in their khanates. They themselves were exempt from taxes and received lands from the crown in recognition of service. When the central government was weak or had collapsed, the khans tended to become the hereditary owners of their domains. Tax collectors, accountants, scribes, police officers, judges, and other officials managed the administration. Various property and personal taxes and a rigid land tenure system supplied the revenues and compensated the administrative officials. Corvée, or forced labor, was performed by most peasants. The Armenian villages were supervised by their elders or belonged to the Church as endowed and charitable tax-exempt property, or *waqf*. The Muslim villages were supervised by their own elders *(begs)*. Since eastern Armenia was a dry region, irrigation played a crucial part in the life of the inhabitants. Canals, some stretching twenty miles, were common, and officials in charge of irrigation followed a rigid set of rules to supply all farmers with water.

Large villages farmed communally, while small settlements were generally farmed by large clans. Agricultural lands followed a primitive two-field rotation system; half the plot planted, half left fallow. Oxen and wooden plows were used, and manure was used both as a fertilizer and as a fuel. Honey, nuts, millet, barley, and various oil seeds were the major crops. Cochineal insects, the source of the famed Armenian red dye, were highly prized. Gardens and orchards were especially abundant and produced a large variety of fruit, especially grapes, and vegetables. Since the peasants surrendered much of their harvest as taxes to the state or the lord, life was frugal. Rice, meat and high-quality wheat were reserved for holidays. Yogurt, cheese, and bread baked in clay ovens, accompanied by greens and vegetables, were the main diet. Few people had beds, most slept on mats and used wooden utensils.

Family life was patriarchal. Men worked in the fields or pastures, while women, supervised by the oldest female *(tantikin)*, threshed the grain, spun wool, and made carpets. The oldest male *(aqa, tanmetz,* or *tanuter)* headed the clan and had the final word on most matters. Sons inherited, while daughters generally received a dowry. Just like their Muslim counterparts, Armenian women rarely spoke in the presence of men or strangers, covered their faces, and were secluded. Apart from religion and customs concerning marriage and divorce, there were few differences between Muslims and Armenians. Age-old habits, prejudices, and superstitions were shared equally by both groups.

Armenians in Nineteenth-Century Iran

In 1801, Russia annexed eastern Georgia and began its final penetration of Transcaucasia.* In 1804 Russia started the First Russo-Iranian war (1804-1813) and a year later, with the assistance of the Armenians of Karabagh, had captured half of eastern Armenia. The chaotic political and socioeco-

* See Chapter XVI.

nomic conditions of the previous century and the departure of many Armenians to Georgia hurt the economy of Yerevan, the center of the Iranian defense of Transcaucasia. Iranians, in order to save the rest of eastern Armenia, heavily subsidized the region and appointed a capable governor, Hosein Qoli Khan, to administer it. The khan, together with the Iranian crown prince, `Abbas Mirza, initiated a number of administrative and military reforms and, aided by Napoleon's campaigns in Europe, managed for two decades to thwart Russian designs on the remaining territories in eastern Armenia. In the end, superior Russian forces conquered all the lands north of the Arax River during the Second Russo-Iranian war (1826-1828). Transcaucasia became part of the Russian Empire, and the fate of eastern Armenia, henceforth known as Russian Armenia, was inextricably tied to that of Russia (see map 5). Some 30,000 Armenians left northern Iran and settled in Russia. The Armenian community in Iran revived in the second half of the nineteenth century, thanks to commercial ties with Armenian merchants in Russia and to the benevolence of the Qajar shahs. New Julfa re-emerged as well and its cathedral-monastery complex of the Holy Savior organized an excellent library. The first Armenian periodical, and a history of the Armenians of New Julfa were published in 1880. The Armenian school in New Julfa received a state subsidy, Armenian clergy and churches were exempted from taxes, and confiscated Church property was returned. Armenian merchants opened new trading houses in the Caspian and Persian Gulf regions and traded with Russia, India, and Europe. Dried fruit, leather, and carpets were exported, and machinery, glassware, and cloth were imported. Royal sponsorship brought Armenians to Tehran, where, taking advantage of their linguistic abilities and foreign contacts, Nasr al-Din Shah (1848-1896) used them as envoys to Europe. Some of them, like Mirza Malkum Khan, David Khan Melik Shahnazar, and Hovhannes Khan Masehian were responsible for the introduction of Freemasonry, Western political thought, and technological innovations into Iran. Armenian tailors and jewelers introduced European fashions, and Armenian photographers were among the first in that profession. Armenians were also among the first Western-style painters and musicians. By the end of the nineteenth century there were some 100,000 Armenians living in a dozen cities in Iran (see map 6). The Armenians in Iranian Azerbaijan were soon exposed to the national and political ideas of the Armenians in Transcaucasia and, as will be seen, were to play a significant role in the history of twentieth-century Iran.*

* See Chapter XXII.

IRAN & OTTOMAN EMPIRE	WESTERN & CENTRAL EUROPE	RUSSIA & EASTERN EUROPE	SOUTH & EAST ASIA	AFRICA & THE AMERICAS
Decline of Ottoman Empire (ca. 1700-1800)	War of the Spanish Succession (1701-13)	Battle of Narva (1700)	Decline of Mughals (ca. 1700-1800)	Rise of Ashanti Empire on Gold Coast (ca. 1700-50)
Russo-Turkish War (1710-11)	British take Gibraltar (1704)	St. Petersburg founded (1703)	Mohammad Shah (1719-48)	Benjamin Franklin (1706-90)
Passarowitz Treaty (1718)	England & Scot. Union to form Great Britain (1707)	Great Northern War (1709-21)	China controls Tibet (1720)	German immigration to North America begins (1709)
Fall of Isfahan (1722)	Peace of Utrecht (1713)	Battle of Poltava (1709)	Treaty of Kyakhta (1727)	John Paul Jones (1747-92)
Russo-Iranian War (1722-23)	Rise of Prussia under King Frederick William I (1713-40)	Death of Ori (1711)	Ch'ien Lung (1736-96)	French-Indian War (1756-63)
Armenians of Karabagh led by David Beg resist Ottoman attacks (1724-34)	Louis XV (1715-74)	St. Petersburg capital of Russia (1713)	Sack of Delhi by Nader Shah (1739)	British take Quebec (1759)
Turko-Iranian War (1734-35)	Walpole P. M. of Britain (1720-43)	Peter's second trip to Europe (1716)	Ahmad Shah Durrani of Afghanistan (1747-73)	End of Funj Sultanate in eastern Sudan (1762)
Treaty of Rasht (1732)	War of the Austrian Succession (1740-48)	Peace of Nystad (1721)	Battle of Plassey (1757)	Stamp Act (1765)
Catholicos Abraham Kretatsi (1734-37)	Frederick the Great (1740-86)	Holy Synod est. (1721)	Clive gov. of Bengal (1758)	Mason-Dixon Line drawn (1766)
Treaty of Ganja (1735)	Maria Theresa (1740-80)	Russo-Turkish accord (1724)	China occupies eastern Turkestan (1758)	Boston Tea Party (1773)
Nader Shah Afshar (1736-47)	Maria Theresa accepts crown of Hungary (1741)	Anna (1730-40)	English oust French from India (1761)	American War of Indep. (1775-83)
Russo-Turkish War (1736-9)	Seven Years' War (1756-63)	War of the Polish Succession (1733-35)	British take Madras (1766)	Declaration of Independence (1776)
Belgrade Treaty (1739)	George III (1760-1820)	Bering Straits discov. (1741)	First Mysore War (1767-69)	
Turko-Iranian treaty (1747)	Peace of Paris (1763)	Elizabeth (1741-62)	W. Hastings in India (1772-85)	
Karim Khan Zand (1750-79)	Louis XVI (1774-92)		Ram Mohan Roy (1772-1833)	
Catholicos Simeon (1763-80)	Joseph II (1780-90)	Russo-Austrian accord (1746)	Maratha War (1779-82)	
Russo-Turkish War (1768-74)	Pitt the Younger, P. M. of Britain (1783-1801)	Catherine the Great (1762-96)	Second Mysore War (1780-84)	
Küchük Kainarja Treaty (1774)	French Revolution (1789-91)	First partition of Poland (1772)	Cornwallis Gov.-Gen. of India (1786-93)	
Aqa Mohammad Qajar (1779-97)	France a republic (1792)	Pugachev revolt (1772-74)	White Lotus Rebellion (1789)	US Constitution (1789)
Catholicos Ghukas (1780-99)	Reign of Terror (1793-94)	Cossacks submit (1775)	Third Mysore War (1790-92)	Washington president (1789-97)
Russo-Turkish War (1787-92)	The Directorate (1795-99)	Crimea annexed (1783)	Hyderabad Treaty (1798)	Canada Constitution (1791)
Treaty of Jassy (1792)		Russo-Swedish War (1787-90)	Wellesley Gov.-Gen. of India (1798-1805)	Bill of Rights (1791)
Selim III (1789-1807)		Second partition of Poland (1793)	Kingdom of Mysore loses its sovereignty (1799)	San Lorenzo Treaty (1795)
Sack of Tiflis (1795)		Third partition of Poland (1795)		Adams president (1797-1801)
Fath `Ali Shah (1797-1834)		Paul (1796-1801)		
French in Egypt (1798)	Napoleon's Consulate (1799)			

Table 3: 1700-1800

XIV

From the Mughals to the Raj:
Armenians in the Indian Subcontinent (ca. 1550-1858)

The Armenian community of India has a special place in the history of the Armenian diaspora. Although not large, the community's wealth and national aspirations had a significant impact on the Armenian cultural awakening. At the same time, the rise and decline of the community is a perfect example of the effects of internal and external, political and economic forces on the survival of a diaspora community.

Although some Armenian merchants had conducted trade with India prior to the sixteenth century, it was the benevolent policies of the Mughal emperor Akbar (1556-1602) that encouraged Armenian traders to settle there and to invest capital, trading primarily in jewels and spices. Akbar trusted and favored the Armenians and appointed them to a number of high administrative positions, including the post of chief justice. One of Akbar's wives, Maryam Begum, was Armenian. The first Armenian church in India was built in 1562 in Agra, the center of the Mughal dynasty. An Armenian by the name of Mirza Zol-Qarnain was adopted by Akbar and grew up in the royal household. He attained the position of *amir*, or commander, and later served both the son and grandson of Akbar.

The largest Armenian influx arrived in the seventeenth century when New Julfa merchants opened commercial branches in various Indian cities. Several of these merchants attained prominence and served as agents of the Iranian court. The Mughal shahs, Jahangir (1602-1627) and Jahan (1627-1658), continued the benevolent policies of their predecessor, attracting more Armenians to India. The Armenians imported woolen cloth, amber, Venetian glassware, mirrors, guns, swords, and clocks. They exported spices, pearls and precious stones, and cotton. The jute trade was almost totally in

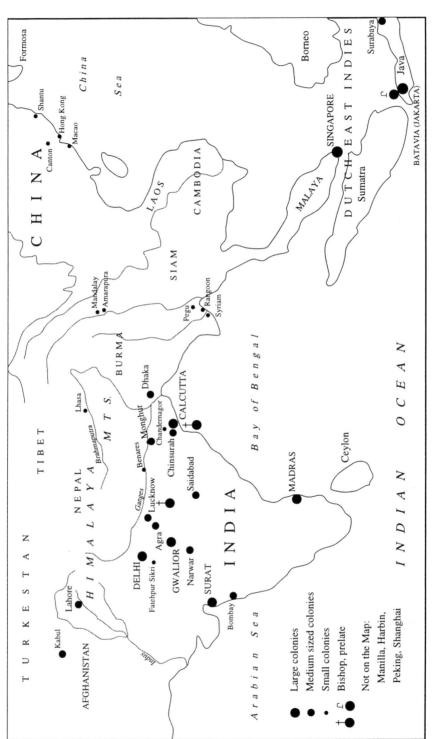

Map 7: Armenians in South and Southeast Asia (19th Century)

the hands of the Armenians of Bengal who concentrated in the Armenian sector of Dhaka (the capital of present-day Bangladesh), where they built a very large church. Indian Armenians became an important link in the trade among South Asia, Iran, and Europe, and like their New Julfa counterparts, were granted privileges and religious freedom by their Muslim overlords.

Armenians had their own quarter in Agra, where they operated a caravansary and had their own cemetery. As Christians, Armenians were requested to act as hosts or interpreters for various European envoys who arrived in India. A number of Europeans who settled in India married Armenian women. The community increased in size, wealth, and importance throughout the seventeenth century. Armenian trade centers were eventually established in some two dozen cities of the empire including Surat, Delhi, Kabul (the present-day capital of Afghanistan), Chinsurah, Lucknow, Dhaka, Saidabad, Heydarabad, Benares, Lahore (in present-day Pakistan), Calcutta, Madras, and Bombay (see map 7). Armenian churches were eventually constructed in Saidabad, Surat, Chinsurah, Dhaka, Calcutta, Madras, Bombay, and other centers; some of these churches survive to this day. The Armenian churches of India maintained regular contact with the Holy See at Etchmiadzin. Armenians carved out their own neighborhoods and a number of streets in these cities still bear the name "Armenian Way."

Armenians do not seem to have faced any major problems during the reign of Aurengzeb, also known as Alamgir (1658-1707), who, unlike his traditionally tolerant predecessors, adopted extreme anti-Hindu and a number of anti-Christian measures. Iran's anti-Christian policies at the start of the eighteenth century were far worse and drove a number of Armenian merchant houses to their branches or associates in India. The intolerance of the late Mughals had a long-term consequence for Indian Armenian merchants, however, for it encouraged the Hindus to cooperate with the British and hastened the subsequent British colonization of India and full control of its trading activities.

The British established their presence in Surat at the start of the seventeenth century. The Armenians, who had utilized British shipping in their trade activities and had contacts with various British companies, became intermediaries between them and a number of Indian rulers. In 1661 the British gained Bombay as part of the dowry of the Infanta (crown princess) of Portugal, who had married the English king, Charles II. Realizing the importance of Armenians in Indian trade, the British invited them to settle there. In 1688, the British East India Company and Khoja Panos Kalantar, representing the Armenian merchants in India, signed a formal agreement which diverted trade from the traditional routes to the new British-dominated sea lanes of the Persian Gulf and the Cape of Good Hope. In 1715, Armenians helped the British to establish themselves in Bengal, and to make Calcutta the new commercial center of that region. The British aided in the construction of Armenian churches, and, like the Mughals, employed Armenians in their civil administration, and permitted Armenians to trade throughout their territories in South Asia. Armenians became active in the legal, medical, and military services and even became expert gunsmiths. By the eighteenth century Bombay, Calcutta, and Madras became the new centers of Armenian activities, with large churches and a school.

Armenians not only served the Mughals but a number of independent rajas in India, as well as various grandees in Burma and Malaysia. Armenian traders constructed a number of churches In Burma and Malaysia in the seventeenth century. Armenian merchants in Java and Sumatra (present-day Indonesia) engaged in the spice trade and became quite wealthy. A community of some 2,000 Armenians in Indonesia is recorded in Java and Sumatra by the seventeenth century. They built schools and churches in Batavia (present-day Jakarta) and Surabaya. The Surabaya church survives to this day. The arrival of the Dutch in the area in the first half of the seventeenth century, altered the economic prominence of the Armenians there, and they were reduced to functionaries and shopkeepers under Dutch colonial rule. Armenian merchants also settled in the Philippines and were the only foreigners allowed to continue trading after the Spaniards conquered the region in the sixteenth century. By the nineteenth century a large number of them had relocated to Indonesia.

Although the arrival of the British in South Asia adversely affected Armenian trade monopolies, it brought the Armenians into contact with British education and political systems, and imbued them with the ideas of parliamentary rule and other tenets of English political tradition. Influenced by English liberalism, Armenian leaders of Calcutta and Madras initiated an Armenian national revival in the second half of the eighteenth century. Joseph Emin, an Indian Armenian whose family had migrated from New Julfa, became convinced that superior strategy and weapons had enabled the Europeans, especially the British, to take control of large parts of Asia. He studied in England, joined the British army, and was befriended by English liberals such as Edmund Burke. He visited Armenia in 1760 and was amazed by the passivity of the Armenians and their religious leaders, who seemed to accept their subjugation as the will of God.

Emin returned to England and, realizing that the British were not interested in helping the Armenians, went to Russia in late 1761. He visited Moscow and St. Petersburg, traveled to eastern Armenia and Georgia, and remained in the region throughout the 1760s, trying to convince the Russians that a united Armeno-Georgian army financed by Indian Armenian merchants and under the leadership of Russia could free the Caucasus from Muslim control. Emin also advocated the establishment in the Caucasus of modern schools and administrative reforms to further this goal. Emin met with Russian officials, with the Georgian king Erekle II, and with the Armenian catholicos Simeon (1763-1780). Emin's ideas were poorly received. The Russians were not ready for liberal reform and were too busy fighting the Ottomans to consider military assistance. Armenian and Georgian leaders insisted on more concrete assurances before embarking on a rebellion against their Muslim overlords. Emin left the region at the end of 1768 and returned to Calcutta in early 1770. He did not abandon his dream, however, and a few years later, when Catherine had inflicted severe defeats on the Ottomans, he traveled to Madras, where he convinced the Armenian merchants to pledge a huge sum in gold for the creation of an Armenian army. He then went to New Julfa to gather funds from the *khojas*, who, facing an uncertain future in war-torn Iran, might be willing to contribute to his plan of liberating Armenia. Once again, his efforts were fruitless and in 1783 he returned to India, where he died in 1809.

Indian Armenian merchants financed the establishment of the first printing press in Etchmiadzin in the latter half of the eighteenth century and, as we have seen, sponsored the educational and printing efforts of the Mekhitarians in Venice. At the same time, a group of Armenians from Iran established a political union in Madras and were responsible for printing the first Armenian political pamphlets. These works codified the agenda initiated by Joseph Emin to liberate the Armenians from Muslim rule and to establish a democratic and independent state based on the principles of the Enlightenment. The leaders of this group, Shahamir Shahamirian (1723-1797), his two sons Hakob and Eghiazar, and their teacher, Movses Baghramian, the latter of whom had worked with Emin in Russia, were not freedom fighters, but liberals, who wished to promote and spread their ideas through the power of the printing press. In 1771, Hakob Shahamirian established a printing press in Madras. Between 1772 and 1789 he published three political documents written by his father and teacher, *The New Pamphlet of Exhortations*, *The Snare of Glory* and *A Booklet of Counsel*. These works are significant for, although the authors had deep religious beliefs, these were very secular works and differed considerably from previous Armenian political writings.

For the first time Armenians expressed a wish for individual and collective equality and freedom for both physical and intellectual endeavors. *The Snare of Glory* was a particularly important document. It detailed 521 tenets for the constitution of an independent Armenian republic. The new state would have mandatory education for girls as well as boys, an elected parliament, a tax-collection and judicial system, and, most importantly, would be governed not by kings, but by natural and divine laws; laws which were to be formulated by the rational spirit and promulgated by the elected representatives of the citizens. Citing the Roman republic, Shahamirian advocated a social contract between the government and the governed. Although this document predates both the American and French revolutions and their constitutions, it took many of its ideas from the late seventeenth-century English revolution, known as the Glorious Revolution, and from the fervor of the Enlightenment, particularly Jean Jacques Rousseau's *Social Contract* of 1762. By the end of the eighteenth century the first Armenian periodical, *Monitor* (*Azdarar*), appeared in Madras, where it was published for two years (1794-1796) under the efforts of an Armenian priest from Iran, Harutiun Shmavonian. The concept of the rights of man and the notion of self-determination were thus introduced to a segment of the Armenian public. During the early nineteenth century, these ideas found their way to the Armenian communities in Europe, Russia, and the Ottoman Empire. The Mekhitarian order in Venice, the Armenian *meliks* of Karabagh, as well as Hovsep Arghutian* (Iosif Argutinskii), prelate of the Armenians in Russia, and the Lazarian (Lazarev) merchant family of Moscow* all had contacts with the Madras group and were, to a degree, influenced by their ideas.

The nineteenth century brought a new attitude from the British. Although England had secured its predominance in India following the 1763 Treaty of Paris, the French had retained their economic and cultural centers in India. Napoleon's invasion of Egypt, however, created a general Francophobia and the desire to rid India of all French influences. At the same time, the British governor-general, Lord Richard Wellesley, whose older brother was to become Duke of Wellington, was determined to rid India of its native rulers and to make the entire subcontinent subject to the British Empire. During his tenure (1798-1805) he began the process which continued through the first half of the nineteenth century and eventually subordinated the various southern and central provinces of India. In the meantime the British expanded their influence into Burma, Punjab, and Afghanistan. The prominence of the Armenian community of Madras was soon eclipsed by the Cal-

* See Chapter XVI.

cutta community which established their own printing press in 1797 and opened another school in 1798. By 1818 an Armenian weekly, the *Mirror of Calcutta,* was being printed. New presses in Calcutta published European authors in Armenian translations, and by 1821 an Armenian college was established in Calcutta. However, despite the efforts of newcomers from Iran, especially Mesrop Taghiatian, who started a journal called *Patriot,* the Armenians had soon to accept the Anglicization of Indian Armenian culture.

By the mid-nineteenth century the introduction of railroad and telegraph -- as well as challenges to Indian traditions and encroachments against a number of independent principalities by the new governor-general, the Marquess of Dalhousie -- had angered many natives. In 1857 the British introduced a new rifle that used cartridges smeared with pig and cow fat. The British ignored the fact that eating any part of a pig was prohibited by Islam and that cows were sacred to the Hindus. Before inserting the ammunition into the guns, the native troops (sepoys) were required to bite the tip off the cartridges. A rebellion known as the Sepoy Mutiny erupted all over India; a number of British soldiers and their families were killed. Armenian merchants, who were viewed as associates of the British, lost property in the looting of European businesses, especially in Calcutta.

In 1858 the British government took complete control of India and made it a crown colony. Their rule called the Raj, continued until 1947 and brought with it a new order. British businessmen and administrators flooded India. Indians were trained to work under British supervision and Armenians lost their economic edge. The Armenian community in Calcutta was the only one to remain viable, thanks mainly to a cooperative formed by a number of merchants that competed with the British. The Armenian college, church, clubs, and philanthropic organizations managed to keep 1,000 Armenians in Calcutta by the end of the nineteenth century. Armenians from other parts of India, however, lost their economic advantages and began to emigrate in the second half of the nineteenth century. Some joined their families and associates in Burma, Malaysia, or Indonesia. In Burma, Armenians obtained the monopoly of a number of oilfields and opened shipbuilding and shipping enterprises. An Armenian called Captain Manouk became a well-known seafarer and was decorated by the Burmese government. Armenians eventually purchased the famed Strand Hotel in Rangoon and opened businesses and hotels in Malaysia, as well. Singapore became a major Armenian center when the British made it one of the focal points of their colonial administration. By the mid-nineteenth century Armenians from India had built the first Christian church, an Armenian center, and were publishing a periodical in

Singapore.

Some Indian Armenians emigrated to China, where Armenian merchants had settled earlier. In Canton, in fact, an Armenian church had been built in 1307. Armenian merchants and artisans also settled in Shanghai, and some, like Hovhannes Ghazarian, studied Chinese culture. His translation of the Bible from Armenian into Chinese is well respected by scholars. A number of Armenian merchants settled in Hong Kong and Macao. Paul Chater, an Armenian, took part in the planning of the Hong Kong harbor and another Armenian, Khachik Asvadzadarian, was one of the founders of Hong Kong University.

By the end of the nineteenth century, European colonial governments in South and East Asia had sent their own officials, bureaucrats, and merchants to manage those regions. Armenians, who had earlier played a key role, became secondary and their numbers dwindled there. Worse was yet come.

XV

Protected Minorities:
Armenian Communities in the Arab World
(From the Middle Ages Through the Nineteenth Century)

Armenians have been part of the Middle East from the very beginning of their history. They came into the region as citizens of the Persian Empire, traded and settled there during the Hellenistic and Roman periods, and were, at times, forcibly moved within the area during the Byzantine era. The rise of Islam and the Muslim conquests introduced a new order, for in a Muslim state, the individual's place in society is determined primarily by his religion. All non-Muslims, including the Armenians, were included among the *dhimmis*, the protected and tolerated minorities, who had a subordinate status and who had to pay a special poll tax, but who were exempt from military service.* When the Ottomans conquered the Arab lands in the sixteenth century, a separate Armenian *millet* was eventually created. The Ottoman rule over the Arab lands was at times tenuous and the Armenian communities there developed somewhat differently from those in Ottoman-controlled Eastern Europe or Anatolia. In addition, the arrival of the French and the British, in the nineteenth century, had a significant impact on the Armenians in the Arab lands.

The Armenian Communities of Egypt and Ethiopia

Armenians had trade relations with Egypt from ancient times; some Armenians had settled in Alexandria during the Hellenistic period. Armenians were welcomed by the Egyptian Copts, who preferred the anti-Chalcedonian** Armenians to the Byzantines. There is little information about Armenians in

* See vol. I., p. 79-81.   ** *Ibid.*, p. 93.

Egypt just after the Arab conquest, apart from a seventh-century description of a unit of five hundred Armenian troops under the command of an Armenian officer. A certain Vartan Rumi is credited with building a covered bazaar (*Souk el-Vartan*) in Fustat, or old Cairo. By the ninth century there is mention of an Armenian governor, `Ali ibn Yahya Abul-Hasan al-Armani. The Armenian community grew and gained prominence under the Fatimid dynasty (969-1117), a period during which the Arabs maintained generally peaceful relations with Byzantium and cooperated with them against the Turkish threat in Syria and Anatolia. In fact, except for the early part of the reign of Caliph al-Hakim (996-1021), Christians and Jews were comparatively well-treated in Egypt. The Fatimids controlled Greater Syria, thus approaching the lands ruled by the Armenian Bagratids. Armenian merchants and soldiers made their way to Cairo, and a number of Armenian viziers, the most famous of whom was Badr al-Jamali (1070-1094), are mentioned by Arab sources. Some of these Armenian viziers were slaves who had converted to Islam and who had risen in the ranks of the Egyptian hierarchy. Badr al-Jamali's son, Avdal, succeeded him (1094-1121). The two supported the arts and sciences by building libraries and observatories. Another Armenian, Bahram al-Armani (Vahram Pahlavuni), who was related to the great churchman, Nerses Shnorhali of Cilicia,* held the post of commander of the army, as well as vizier. Armenian architects built several gates along the ramparts of Cairo. Cilicia and the Fatimid state had commercial and political ties to each other, and Armenian soldiers from Cilicia were recruited by the Fatimids. Cilician Armenian merchants and artisans settled in Cairo and Alexandria. Estimates place some 30,000 Armenians in Egypt during the height of Fatimid rule.

Ayyubid rule in Egypt (1169-1250) was not favorable to the Armenians, who were viewed as allies of the deposed Fatimids and friends of the Crusaders. The founder of the Ayyubids and the champion of Islam against the Crusaders, Saladin (1169-1193), despite having a number of Armenians in his service, was nevertheless especially harsh to the Armenians, causing many of them to leave for Cilicia and Ethiopia. The condition of the Egyptian Armenians worsened during Mamluk times (1250-1517).* The Mamluks treated all Christians unfavorably, attacking Cilicia and the remaining Crusader states which had survived Ayyubid assaults. Armenian slaves were brought from Cilicia and Syria as prisoners of war. Christian children were brought from Russia and Armenia as slaves and enlisted in the Mamluk army. In one attack on Hromklay, some 30,000 Armenians were taken as

*See vol. I, pp. 128, 130.

prisoners and slaves, as were Armenians from Cyprus.

Following the Ottoman conquest of Egypt in 1517, the condition of the Armenian community deteriorated further at first. By the seventeenth century, though, Ottoman military successes and stability in the region increased trade and brought a few Armenian merchants and artisans from Aleppo and Constantinople. It was a brief period of expansion. By the end of the eighteenth century most Armenian churches in Egypt were in ruins, and the few Armenian families remaining there had to use Coptic churches for their services. Not all Egyptian Armenians were prosperous. There is evidence of Armenians engaged in menial jobs and living in the poorer sections of Cairo. Then, during the viceroyalty of Muhammad `Ali Pasha and his son Ibrahim Pasha, in the first half of the nineteenth century, Armenian fortunes improved. Merchants and craftsmen from the Morea, Asia Minor, and Greater Syria gravitated to Cairo and Alexandria, where Western ideas were gaining influence and where educational, economic, and military reforms were carried out by the progressive viceroys. Armenian goldsmiths, tailors, and shoemakers were sought after, and Armenians were among the new merchant classes who increased their fortunes in this period.

The Nubarian family -- who were originally from Karabagh and who had settled in Smyrna and Cairo -- and the Yusufian and Tcherakian families became the most prominent. The most noted member of the Nubarian family was Nubar. He had studied in Europe and, in 1842, at the age of sixteen, was invited to Egypt by his maternal uncle Boghos Bey, who was a government official in charge of commerce and foreign affairs. Nubar became secretary to his uncle and, after the latter's death in 1844, was given the title *bey* and became a secretary of Muhammad `Ali. After the death of Ibrahim Pasha, Nubar served `Abbas and Sa`id Pashas in their negotiations with France and England. Nubar met with the British statesman, George Canning, and was sent to London by the viceroy to discuss Anglo-Egyptian relations with Lord Palmerston in 1851. It was during the reign of Isma`il (1863-1879) that Nubar's fortunes and those of the Egyptian Armenians rose to new heights. Recognizing Nubar's talents, Isma`il elevated him to the rank of *pasha*, granted him diplomatic status, and dispatched him on a number of missions. In 1867 Isma`il secured from the Ottoman sultan the title of *khedive* and hereditary succession for his descendants. Egypt, although technically under Ottoman rule, became virtually independent, and began to expand into Ethiopia and the Sudan. Such ventures, as well as the building of the Suez Canal, soon put Egyptian finances under the control of European creditors and by the end of the century resulted in the British protectorate of the country.

Nubar Pasha served the two khedives who succeeded Isma`il; he was thrice prime minister of Egypt and carried out a number of important social, agricultural, and judicial reforms. Disliked by some Egyptians as pro-Western, Nubar was in fact pro-Egyptian. He not only established mixed tribunals, but opposed the sale of Suez Canal shares to the British and clashed with foreign officials when they began to interfere in the administration of Egypt. Intrigues by the British Foreign Office forced his dismissal in 1888. In 1894 he returned as prime minister and served the government for another year.

Armenian bankers, merchants, artisans, and agriculturalists, such as Hovhannes Yusufian, prospered in Egypt during the second half of the nineteenth century and Armenian churches, schools, and community centers were built in Cairo and Alexandria, where close to 50,000 Armenians lived. Although favored by the Europeans, Armenians by and large remained loyal to the ruling family of Egypt and were a major force in the country's modernization.

Armenians had traded with Ethiopia from the first century A.D. Armenians began to settle there, however, during the Arab invasions of the Middle East in the seventh century. The Armenian community of Ethiopia continued to be connected to the Arab world, both economically and culturally. The Armenians were welcomed by the Ethiopian Church for their anti-Chalcedonian stand, as they had been by the Copts in Egypt. They established good relations with the Ethiopian royal family and some were raised to high posts. The Ethiopian Church, in particular, was grateful to the Armenian Church for permitting them to hold services in the Armenian-controlled churches in Jerusalem. By the sixteenth century an Ethiopian Armenian named Matevos was an envoy to Portugal and another named Murad negotiated agreements in the Netherlands on behalf of the Ethiopians. In 1875 additional immigrants arrived from the Middle East. A number of them served as regional governors and worked as officials in a number of Western embassies. Most Ethiopian Armenians were engaged in trade, importing metals and exporting hides and coffee. An Armenian church and school were built in Addis Ababa, the Ethiopian capital. In time there was some intermarriage between Armenians and Ethiopians and a number of black Armenians resulted from those unions.

The Armenian Communities of Greater Syria and Mesopotamia

The Armenian communities of Greater Syria and Mesopotamia date back to the pre-Christian era. Armenian lands bordered the region and Armenian merchants frequented Syria during Achaemenid times and continued to do so in the Hellenistic period, especially during the Seleucid era, when many Armenians settled in Antioch. During the reign of Tigran II, part of Syria was under Armenian rule; Armenian administrators, artisans, and merchants settled in Greater Syria, where they continued to live after Rome reconquered the area. Armenians resided in the cities of Antioch, Edessa (present-day Urfa), and Amida (present-day Diarbekir) and attended a number of institutions of higher learning. Armenian sources state that Mesrop Mashtots and several of his students went to Edessa and Amida in search of a model for the Armenian alphabet.*

The beginnings of the Armenian diaspora in Greater Syria can be traced with more certainty, however, to the sixth century. In 539/540, and again in 544, the Iranian king, Khosrow, having defeated the Byzantines, settled some Armenians -- along with the Nestorians of Iran -- in Edessa and Antioch as a buffer against the Byzantines. A number of Byzantine Armenians, unhappy with that state's policy towards them, emigrated to Greater Syria. Others were forced there by the Byzantines, who wanted to weaken the Armenian nobility.

The Arab conquests and the establishment of the caliphate in Damascus brought the Armenians in Syria under the rule of the Umayyads.** In general, the relations of the Arab rulers with princes and nobles in Armenia, determined the living conditions of the Armenians of Greater Syria. Armenians fared better overall under the Umayyads than they did later under the `Abbasids.** At the same time, the Byzantines began to resettle their rebellious Armenian subjects on their borders with Syria. This policy was facilitated when the northern part of Syria was recaptured by the Byzantines in the ninth century. Beginning in the tenth century, Byzantium settled more Armenians in the region as a buffer against the Arabs. The fall of the Bagratids brought more Armenians there and resulted in the formation of Cilician Armenia.

During the Crusades, Syria was divided under successive Fatimid, Crusader, and Ayyubid rule, with the Armenians living under these various Christian and Muslim rulers. They settled in various cities, built a number of churches, and were engaged as small merchants and artisans. In the thirteenth century, the Armenians of Cilicia, hoping for a more powerful state, joined the Mongols and attacked the Mamluk forces in Syria. Although initially successful, the Armeno-Mongol armies were defeated by the Mamluks in 1260, and Syria was united with Egypt. By the fourteenth century the

*See vol. I, pp. 69-72. ** *Ibid.*, pp. 92-98.

decline of the Ilkhanids, or the Mongol rulers in the Middle East, and their conversion to Islam enabled the Mamluks to capture Cilicia and the remaining Crusader states.*

Those Armenians who remained in the region settled primarily in the northwest, particularly in Alexandretta and Aleppo. There were small Armenian enclaves in Antioch, Damascus, Latakia, Beirut, and Musa Dagh (Jabal Musa or Musa Ler). The establishment of the regional catholicosate of Cilicia at Sis in 1446 added prestige to the community. Aleppo, located on the trade routes between east and west, became the main Armenian center in Syria. The remaining Armenian communities of Syria suffered under Mamluk rule. Prisoners and slaves were taken to Cairo and many Armenians were forced to emigrate to Western Europe or Constantinople.

The Ottoman conquest brought stability and growth of trade, which was evident most of all in Aleppo. From the sixteenth to the nineteenth centuries Armenian immigrants arrived in Aleppo from Marash, Zeitun, Sasun, Erzerum, and Erzinjan. A number of churches were constructed in Aleppo during this period. The Franco-Ottoman treaty of 1535 and other agreements with various European states opened the region to trade and missionary activity. The Europeans gained extra-territorial rights and traded under the protection of their consuls through native Christian and Jewish middlemen. The merchants of Julfa played a prominent role in Aleppo and controlled most of the silk trade. After their move to New Julfa, they continued a part of their trade via Aleppo. The Ottomans established a mint in Aleppo and, in the seventeenth century, a number of Armenians served as its superintendent. Armenians and Jews were the primary money-changers in that city, as well.

The decline of New Julfa, the Napoleonic wars, the campaigns of Muhammad `Ali Pasha and Ibrahim Pasha in Syria, and the opening of the Suez Canal all affected the Armenians of Greater Syria. Although the economy of Aleppo declined, Armenian merchants there retained some of their economic power. By the end of the nineteenth century the city once again revived, thanks to the commercial and banking activities of the Armenians of Constantinople. Armenian schools and cultural centers opened in Aleppo and the city gained new Armenian residents.

The Armenians of Damascus, in contrast, did not form an important commercial base, but were primarily shopkeepers and artisans. The Armenians of Antioch, Alexandretta, Homs, Latakia, Kessab, and Musa Dagh included few merchants; rather they were primarily engaged in agriculture and crafts. A number of villages in the region were populated solely by

*See vol. I, pp. 126-128.

Armenians, who planted tobacco and produced oil from laurel leaves.

There were also small Armenian communities in Mesopotamia, the area later known as Iraq. Armenians concentrated in Baghdad, Mosul, and Basra, and built several churches. These communities, as will be seen, gained new immigrants in the first half of the twentieth century.

The Armenian community of Lebanon was formed after the fall of Cilicia, when Armenians settled in Tripoli and Sidon. Lebanon was unique in that it was controlled by Druze and Maronite lords, who at times sought to free themselves from direct Ottoman rule. In 1736 the Maronite Church united with Rome and opened its territories to Greek, Armenian, and Syrian refugees, particularly those who had themselves converted to Catholicism. Catholic Armenians, who were persecuted by the Armenian Church in the Ottoman Empire, began to settle in Lebanon. In 1742, the Vatican established an Armenian Catholic patriarchate there. The religious strife between Druzes and Maronites ended in massacres of the Christians which, in turn, prompted the French to send forces to Lebanon in 1861. The European powers forced the Ottomans to accept a special status for Lebanon as an autonomous region under a Christian governor-general. This agreement provided some stability to the region, which benefited the Armenians. Two Armenians, both Catholics, served as governors general. By the end of the nineteenth century Beirut was attracting Armenians belonging to the Armenian Apostolic Church, who were fleeing religious and political persecutions in Anatolia.

The history of the Armenian community of Jerusalem up to the Middle Ages has been discussed earlier.* The community fell under Mamluk rule and suffered to the same extent as all of the other Armenian centers in this region. Ottoman rule began in 1517 and continued until the end of World War I. The Armenians were drawn into arguments between the Catholic Church (supported by France) and the Orthodox Church (supported by Russia) regarding their rights to the Holy Places. The Ottomans exploited this situation, and although, at times, the Ottomans supported the Armenian patriarchate, in the long run, the Armenians lost some of their historic prerogatives to Catholic and Orthodox incursions. The Armenians had both lay and clerical residents in the city and the monastery of St. James served as educational and cultural center for all. The Armenian population of Jerusalem was never large, however, and seems to have decreased after the Ottoman conquest. The community revived somewhat in the nineteenth century, when a seminary was established in 1843. The economic gains of

*See vol. I, p. 129.

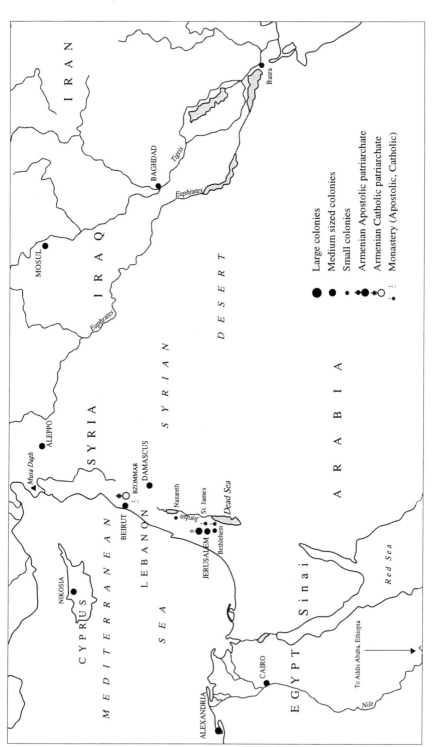

Map 8: The Armenian Diaspora in the Arab World (19th Century)

Armenians in Egypt and Syria, and the rise of the Armenian *amiras* in Constantinople in the nineteenth century enabled the wealthy bankers to support the patriarchate in Jerusalem and to help it maintain its historical custodianship of the houses of Annas and Caiaphas and its shared custodianship of the Church of the Holy Sepulcher, the tomb of Mary at Gethsemane, the Church of the Ascension, and the Church of the Nativity. After the Greek Orthodox and Roman Catholic Churches, Armenians rank third in their jurisdiction over the Holy Places of Jerusalem. Beginning in 1866, donations from Armenian *amiras* also sponsored the publication in Jerusalem of a monthly periodical, *Sion*.

The majority of the Armenian communities in the Arab lands (see map 8) were in a state of decline by the end of the nineteenth century. Few realized that historic Armenia and the Armenians who remained there would have to endure yet another catastrophe. The events of the closing years of that century and the early decades of the next century made the death and destruction caused by Iranian, Arab, and Turko-Mongol invasions of Armenia pale by comparison and brought thousands of new immigrants to the Middle East.

XVI

Promises of Deliverance:
Armenians in the Russian Empire (ca. 1400-1828)

Armenians had contacts with Kievan Russia as early as the tenth century, but their presence in Moscow is recorded only at the close of the fourteenth century. From the fifteenth century onward there is evidence of the activities of Armenian merchants and artisans. Armenians were one of several ethnic groups that the Mongols of the Golden Horde used as traders, emissaries, and tax collectors. They thus began traveling in the Caucasus, the Crimea, and especially along the Volga River, where they settled in various cities of that region.

When Ivan the Terrible defeated the Mongols and took Kazan, in 1552, and Astrakhan, in 1556, there was already a sizable group of Armenians in both cities. By the end of the century, the Russians had reached the Caucasus and had established colonies along the Terek River. During the seventeenth century, Armenians and Georgians petitioned the Christian Russians to expand their presence into Transcaucasia. The Muslim tribesmen of Daghestan, however, routed the Russian armies and the Russians soon retired beyond the Terek.

This military defeat did not adversely affect trade or the part that the Armenians played in it. Russian control of the area's waterways -- the Caspian and North seas and the Volga River -- created stable overland routes between Europe and Asia, which were less costly than the sea lanes controlled by European ships. Armenian traders made good use of these cheaper routes. The favorable situation of the Armenian community in Iran encouraged and fostered the exporting of eastern goods to Russia and the rest of Europe and the importing of Western goods to Russia, Iran, India, and the Ottoman Empire. Armenians set up trading stations -- not communities in the true sense -- in Kazan, Novgorod, Astrakhan, Smolensk, Nizhni-Novgorod, Archangelsk, and Moscow. Astrakhan became the focal point of this trade and by 1639, an Armenian community began to take shape with the building of a church.

The genesis of the large Armenian community in modern Russia began in 1660 when Armenian merchants from New Julfa, representing Armenian traders in Iran and India, sought to increase their trading activities with Russia. They presented Tsar Alexei Mikhailovich (1645-1676) with the famous Almazi or Diamond Throne (currently on display in the Kremlin's Armory Museum) and other rare gifts. A treaty between the Armenian merchants and the Russian ruler was eventually concluded in 1667. The agreement granted the Armenians a monopoly on selling specific Iranian merchandise, primarily silk, in Russia. By the late seventeenth century, the Armenians had built a church and a tanning factory in Moscow.

Opportunities for Armenians in Russia soon expanded beyond trade. Armenians found employment in the Russian diplomatic service and a number of Armenian artisans were employed by the Russian court. Such security and support from the state created several Armenian centers by the eighteenth century. In 1716 the Armenian Church in Russia, due partly to Russian political goals, was granted formal recognition and a prelacy with its center in Astrakhan was established. Armenians were exempt from military service, were permitted to construct their own churches and to practice their religion, build schools and establish printing presses. These opportunities would eventually foster the building of a new leadership and a new spirit which, after centuries of conquest and degradation, would lead to hopes and plans for political emancipation.

Peter the Great and the Armenians

By the mid-sixteenth century, a number of catholicoses at Etchmiadzin had initiated missions to Europe to urge Western rulers to free Armenia from the warring Safavids and Ottomans, going so far as to consider a union with Rome. Although Shah `Abbas and his immediate successors considerably improved the conditions of the Armenians, by the late seventeenth century, as we have seen, the economic and political privileges of Armenians in Iran had begun to deteriorate. In 1678 Catholicos Hakob Jughaetsi called a secret meeting of the Karabagh *meliks* and the leading clerics of eastern Armenia. He proposed to head a delegation to Europe to seek aid in freeing Armenia from Muslim rule. The death of the catholicos en route ended the project, but one of the delegates, Israel Ori, the son of a Zangezur *melik*, continued on to Europe on his own. He proceeded to Venice and then France, where he remained for several years as a merchant and sometime mercenary. He eventually married and entered the service of Prince Johann Wilhelm of the Palatinate. Ori took the initiative of offering the crown of a restored Armenian kingdom to the prince. In return, the prince gave Ori letters addressed to the king of Georgia and the Armenian *meliks* of Karabagh. Ori returned to Karabagh in 1699.

Although he was met with skepticism and received no encouragement from the new catholicos, Ori was nevertheless backed by a number of *meliks*. He returned to Europe, where Johann Wilhelm dispatched him to his overlord, the Holy Roman Emperor Leopold, in Vienna. The emperor showed some interest in Ori's project but pointed out that little could be accomplished without the cooperation of Russia, whose territory had to be crossed in order to reach Armenia.

The ever-persistent Ori continued on to Russia and in 1701 managed to receive an audience with Peter the Great (1682-1725). Peter, who had his own plans for the Caucasus, promised that Russia would be willing to aid in the proposed plan, once it had concluded its war against Sweden. In the meantime, Ori entered Peter's service and was appointed his envoy to the court of Iran. Ori was dispatched to Isfahan to assess the chaotic conditions in Iran and possibly to gain the cooperation of Iranian Armenians in his plans. Ori spent two years in Iran (1709-1711) without any major success in this effort. In 1711, he was on his way back to St. Petersburg when he died in Astrakhan and was buried in the Armenian church there. Ori was the first, but certainly not the last, advocate for the liberation of Armenia from Muslim rule. Other strong-willed and self-appointed individuals, both secular and religious, would play roles in rallying the Armenians and in drawing the attention of outside powers to the plight of their people.

. Meanwhile, the collapse of the Safavids and the murder of a number of Russian merchants in the Caucasus gave Peter, who had just concluded his war with Sweden, the pretext for invading Transcaucasia. Russian troops once again crossed the Terek in 1722, conquering the Caspian littoral. The Ottomans, fearful of a Russian presence along their eastern borders, protested, and, after realizing that Russia concentrated its expansion efforts along the Caspian, broke the 1639 treaty with Iran and invaded eastern Armenia and Georgia in 1723. Armenian and Georgian pleas to Peter went unanswered, for Peter did not want to risk a war with the Turks and came to an agreement with them in 1724. Ironically, according to its terms Russia would

Map 9: Armenian Communities in Russia (19th Century)

take over predominantly Muslim-populated eastern Transcaucasia, while the Ottomans would take control over predominantly Christian-populated western Transcaucasia, or eastern Armenia and Georgia. The Armenians were thus left without Russia's promised support and were forced to rely upon themselves. Peter's death in 1725 ended Russian interest in the region and his successors pulled back across the Terek River.

The Turks had little trouble taking over fortresses in Yerevan, Nakhichevan, Ganja, and Georgia, as well as most of Iranian Azerbaijan. But the Armenian *meliks* of Karabagh and Zangezur, as we have seen, managed to set up formidable defenses from their mountain-top forts and maintained their autonomy until Nader Shah forced the Turks out of the region in 1735. Although Empresses Anna and Elizabeth of Russia continued their nation's policy of encouraging Armenians to settle in their realm, practice their religion, and enjoy royal protection, Russia kept out of Transcaucasia itself for the next fifty years.

Catherine the Great and the Armenians

The reign of Catherine the Great (1762-1796) witnessed a major revival in Armeno-Russian relations and the growth of the Armenian communities (see map 9). After her war with the Ottomans (1768-1774), Catherine relocated the Armenian community of the Crimea to a new settlement along the Don River in 1779. The settlement, known as Nor, or New Nakhichevan (now within present-day Rostov-on-Don), became a major Armenian center.* It had its own church, subordinate to the Armenian bishop of Astrakhan, whom Catherine had earlier, in 1763, recognized as the prelate of all Armenians in Russia. Her benevolent policies towards the Russian Armenians enabled a number of them to achieve high positions. One of the families who prospered were the wealthy Lazarevs (Lazarians), who founded the Lazarev Institute of Oriental Languages in Moscow (currently the Armenian Embassy in Russia). Catherine built a church for the Armenians in St. Petersburg and made possible their later rise to high diplomatic, military, and administrative positions in the nineteenth century.

Catherine's interest in the Caucasus and her victories against the Ottomans encouraged Georgians and Armenian leaders, such as Joseph Emin**, once again to place their hopes in Russia and to promise financial and military cooperation in exchange for autonomy under Russian protection. Meanwhile, difficult conditions in Iran and Transcaucasia brought

*Also see chapter XVII.   **See Chapter XIV.

Armenian refugees into Georgia and Russia. By 1783, the weakness of the Ottomans, new civil unrest in Iran, renewed petitions from Armenian and Georgian leaders, and the prompting of Catherine's advisor, Potemkin, and of Iosif Argutinskii, the prelate of the Armenians in Russia, convinced Catherine to act. In that year, as noted, she annexed the Crimea and concluded the Treaty of Georgievsk, placing eastern Georgia under the protection of Russia. The treaty frightened the Muslim khans of the Caucasus and they scrambled to make their own agreements with Russia or Georgia. Aqa Mohammad Qajar, who was in the process of consolidating his power in Iran, reminded the Georgians of their vassalage to Iran. Catherine ignored Aqa Mohammad Khan's threats and Georgian fears of Iranian attack, as she was convinced that the "eunuch" was merely boasting.

In 1795, Aqa Mohammad Khan attacked Georgia and sacked Tiflis taking some 15,000 Georgian and Armenian prisoners as slaves. A large number of Christians, including priests, were killed by the khan. Among the casualties was the famous Armenian bard, Sayat Nova, whose grave is in one of the Armenian churches in Tbilisi. Shocked by the sacking of the capital of a Russian protectorate, Catherine ordered the Russian army to cross the Terek once again. Russian troops were well advanced into Transcaucasia when Catherine died and her son Paul, disagreeing with the policy of his mother and disliking her favorite generals, recalled the Russian forces.

Russo-Iranian Wars and the Conquest of Eastern Armenia

At the start of the nineteenth century, Russia, for the third and last time since the reign of Peter the Great, began to move beyond the Caucasus Mountains. In 1801 it annexed Georgia, which had been under Russian protection since 1783 but which was technically under the suzerainty of Iran. In 1804, under the pretext that Ganja belonged to the Georgians, Russia invaded that khanate and sparked the First Russo-Iranian war (1804-1813). General Tsitsianov, the Russian commander, received help from the Armenians of Ganja and Karabagh, who had been waiting for years for the Russian arrival. By 1805 half of eastern Armenia was in Russian hands. Tsitsianov was not successful in taking Yerevan, however, and Napoleon's adventures in Europe soon diverted Russia from the Caucasian front. Iran signed the short-lived treaty of Finkenstein (1807) with France, which brought French officers to Iran to train a new army. The Russians tried and failed to take Yerevan again in 1808. A stalemate then ensued until 1812. In the meantime, more Armenians from Yerevan left for Tiflis, and the Armenians there, whose numbers had gradually increased during the latter part of the eighteenth and the early part of the nineteenth century, achieved a plurality in that city. With the exception of the Tiflis community, the influential Armenian leadership within the Russian Empire was all outside the Caucasus, in Astrakhan, New Nakhichevan, Moscow, and St. Petersburg, as well as the now-Russian regions of the Crimea, Ukraine, and Poland.

Having concluded the peace of Bucharest (1812) with the Ottomans and having repelled Napoleon, the Russians concentrated in earnest on the Caucasus, and, in 1813, defeated the Iranian armies in several battles. The Treaty of Gulistan in that year awarded the khanates of Karabagh, Ganja, Shirvan, Shakki, Kuba, Baku, and Talesh (see map 5) to Russia. By controlling Karabagh and Ganja, Russia became master of half of eastern Armenia. The Armenian leaders, however, did not take advantage of their position and this favorable situation to press St. Petersburg to create a separate administrative unit out of Ganja and Karabagh. Rather, in the wake of Russia's wresting of one half of eastern Armenia, the Russian Armenian leadership's main concern was liberating most of the other half, that is, the khanates of Nakhichevan and Yerevan, which included Etchmiadzin, the religious focal point for many Russian Armenians. No one could predict that by the time the remainder of eastern Armenia would be annexed to Russia, earlier administrative configurations would have already incorporated Ganja into Georgia, and Karabagh, with its sizable Armenian population, within the Caspian, or Muslim, Province.

The new khan of Yerevan, Hosein Khan Qajar, as we have seen, had tried to reverse past abuses and succeeded in gaining the support of some of the Armenian population. However, by the second decade of the nineteenth century Armeno-Iranian relations in Yerevan had deteriorated and the catholicos had left Etchmiadzin for Georgia. Moreover, neither Iran nor Russia were content with the Gulistan treaty. The Russians planned to expand further, the Iranians hoped to regain their losses, and some Armenian leaders, led by archbishop Nerses of Ashtarak, who had left Etchmiadzin for Tiflis in 1814, actively campaigned for the resumption of hostilities and the liberation of the rest of eastern Armenia. Taking advantage of the death of Alexander I and the Decembrist uprising in Russia (1825), the Iranians invaded Karabagh in the beginning of 1826 and began the Second Russo-Iranian war (1826-1828). Having caught the Russians off-guard, the Iranian army scored a number of initial victories. The local Muslims rose against the Russians, while the Armenian population stood fast by the outnumbered Russian garrisons. Armenian volunteer brigades were formed in Georgia and

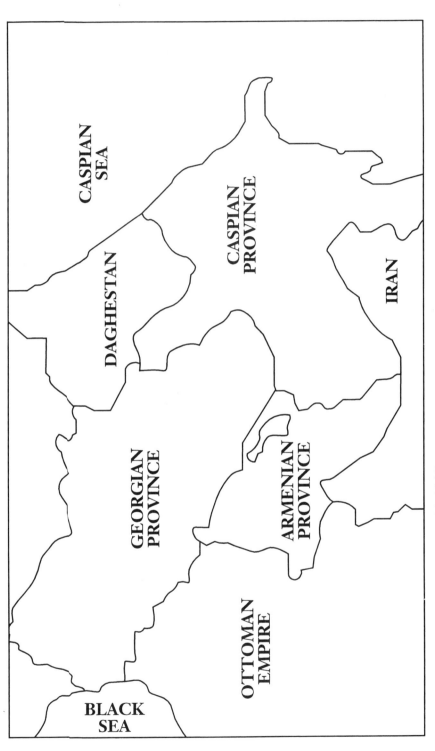

Map 10: The Armenian Province (1828-1840)

Karabagh and, under a newly-designed Armenian flag, joined the Russian forces. The new Russian tsar, Nicholas I, appointed a new commander, Ivan Paskevich, who arrived with reinforcements and artillery. Within a year the Russians had captured `Abbasabad, Ordubad, Sardarabad, Nakhichevan, and Yerevan. When the Russians crossed the Arax and approached Tabriz, the capital of Iranian Azerbaijan, the shah sued for peace and agreed to the treaty of Turkmenchai (1828). The khanates of Yerevan and Nakhichevan, or much of the rest of eastern Armenia, now became part of Russia and the Arax River became the border between Iran and Armenia (see map 5). The treaty, in addition, awarded Russia an indemnity of twenty million rubles, exclusive naval rights in the Caspian Sea, and other economic and political prerogatives in Iran which bound the Qajar dynasty to Russian whims.

The Formation of a Russian Armenian Province

At the conclusion of the war a number of influential Armenians and Russians, such as Archbishop Nerses of Ashtarak, the wealthy Russian-Armenian merchant Christopher Lazarev, Count Argutinskii-Dolgoruki, and the writer and statesman Alexander Griboedov, advocated the establishment of an "Armenian Province." They felt that the role of the Armenian volunteers during the war had been significant and that Armeno-Russian historical ties proved that the Armenians were one group upon whom the Russians could truly rely. They began an immediate campaign for the restoration of an Armenian homeland under the supervision of the Church and the protection of Russia. The major problem, however, was the fact that a large part of the Armenian population had, in the last three centuries, left eastern Armenia and the Armenians had become a minority of twenty percent in the Yerevan region. To resolve this, the Armenian leaders, and their Russian supporters, set about to convince the Russian commanders and diplomats to include as a condition in their negotiations with Iran the repatriation of those Armenians who had been forcibly taken to Iran at the time of Shah `Abbas.

This idea was formally incorporated into article 15 of the Treaty of Turkmenchai, which allowed for a specific period of population transfers across the Arax River. Eventually over 30,000 Armenians returned to eastern Armenia, the majority settling in the Russian Armenian Province, which was officially formed in 1828 from the combined territories of the khanates of Yerevan and Nakhichevan (see map 10). A year later the Russians concluded the Russo-Turkish War of 1828-1829. The Treaty of Adrianople (1829) awarded Russia the territories of Akhalkalak and Akhaltsikh in western

Georgia, both of which had sizeable Armenian populations. Although the Russians had occupied a large part of western Armenia, the treaty forced the return of almost all of it. Some 20,000 Armenians from western Armenia left Kars, Ardahan, Bayazid, and Erzerum, and arrived in Yerevan, Nakhichevan, and Tiflis. In the meantime nearly 50,000 Persians, Kurds, and Turks left eastern Armenia for Iran, and the Ottoman Empire. A small number of Armenians also returned to Yerevan, Ganja, and Karabagh from their temporary exile in Georgia, and thus, after two centuries, the Armenian population of the Armenian Province slightly surpassed that of the Muslims. The city of Yerevan, however, retained its Muslim majority until the early twentieth century. These migrations began a trend which resumed after the Crimean War as well as after the final Russo-Ottoman conflict in the last quarter of that century, and finally created a solid Armenian majority in a part of the Armenian homeland, a situation which was later to have great political significance.

XVII

Between Orthodoxy and Catholicism:
Armenian Dispersion in Eastern and Western Europe
(From the Late Middle Ages Through the Nineteenth Century)

Most of the European diaspora communities were formed when deteriorating conditions in historic Armenia and the fall of the Cilician kingdom forced the Armenians to leave their homelands in large numbers. Those European Armenian communities with earlier origins became even larger and assumed new importance. The several centuries following the fall of the last Armenian kingdom were not, contrary to popular belief, a "dark age" -- certainly not for Armenian arts and sciences. As in the Middle East, unique works of art and scholarship were produced in the European diaspora. Moreover, some European-Armenians also played a role in the later political and intellectual resurgence of the Armenian people and their eventual road to independence.

ARMENIAN COMMUNITIES IN EASTERN EUROPE

The Eastern European communities were formed when the Armenians in the Byzantine Empire, who had formed the first major diaspora, began to leave that area in the medieval period. They were joined by immigrants from historic Armenia and formed half a dozen major communities, some of which have survived into the present.

The Armenian Community of Cyprus

Armenian merchants from Byzantium had established a minor presence in

Cyprus in the fifth century. In 578, however, the Byzantine general Maurice, who later became emperor, forcibly relocated many Armenians to Cyprus during his pacification of Byzantine Armenia. This created the core of the Armenian community on that island. Cyprus came under the rule of the Arab caliphate from 648-958 (except for the short-lived Byzantine control of 868-874). In 958 the Byzantines recaptured Cyprus and replaced most of its Muslim population with Greeks and Armenians. In fact, a number of Byzantine Armenians became military governors of the island.

The Cilician kingdom of Armenia opened commercial contacts with the Armenians of Cyprus, whose numbers grew. By the twelfth century, the Armenian population there was large enough to require the creation of a separate *theme,* under its own administrator. The importance of the community is demonstrated by the fact that its bishop attended the Church Council of 1179 in Hromklay, Cilicia. During the Crusades, the sack of Cyprus by Richard the Lionhearted does not seem to have affected the Armenian community, which continued its commercial activities with both Cilicia and Europe. Armenian merchants and artisans concentrated in the cities of Limassol, Famagusta, Nicosia, and Paphos. Closer ties between Cilicia and Cyprus were established during the reign of the Lusignans, a Crusader family of French origins, who had earlier intermarried into Cilician nobility and gained the throne of Cilicia in the mid-fourteenth century. Dissatisfaction with Roman Catholic influence in Cilicia, Mamluk attacks, the fall of Cilicia, and subsequent repressive Mamluk policies brought many Armenians to Cyprus. By the first quarter of the fifteenth century some 50,000 are estimated to have resided there.

In 1426 the Mamluks captured Cyprus, causing terrible damage to the Armenian community and taking some 5,000 prisoners to Cairo as slaves. Better days arrived when the Venetians conquered the island in 1489 and the Venetian senate recognized the rights of the Armenians to administer their own separate community. In 1570 the Ottomans captured Cyprus, and although conditions did not change drastically at the beginning, they began to deteriorate in the seventeenth and especially the eighteenth century. Armenians began to emigrate from the island to more secure places, particularly Italy.

The Armenian Community of the Crimea

One of the largest and longest-lived Armenian communities of the diaspora was that settled by the Byzantines in the Crimea. The Crimean community was composed at first of Armenian soldiers and their families, who, starting in the eighth century, were stationed there in the service of the Byzantine state. By the eleventh century, following the Seljuk Turkish invasions of Armenia, the community was enlarged by Armenian immigrants from Armenia proper and from Constantinople, the latter group facing persecution from the Greek Orthodox Church of Byzantium. Greek and Italian commercial activities had made the Crimea a major trading center with Europe, thus particularly appealing to Armenian merchants. Kaffa, also known as Theodosiopolis (modern Feodosiya or Teodosia), became the major Armenian commercial and cultural center in the Crimea.

The Mongol invasion of the region in 1239 had little effect on these merchants; they simply paid their taxes to the Golden Horde, or the Mongols, who had settled in Russia, and continued their commercial enterprises. During the second half of the thirteenth century, the Genoese concluded a number of agreements with the Mongols and Byzantines and gained trading monopolies which gave them virtual control over parts of the Black Sea. Armenian merchants found the Crimean trade lucrative and more Armenians, including those uprooted from Ani by the Mongols, settled in that region. By the fourteenth century, a number of Armenian churches, including a Catholic one, were already functioning there. As a result of the fall of Cilicia, the invasions of Armenia by the last major Turkic conqueror, Timur (Tamerlane), and the Ottoman-Safavid conflict, even more Armenians settled in the region. It is estimated that over 300,000 Armenian peasants, merchants, artisans, soldiers, and several nobles made their way to the Crimean peninsula, establishing new centers in Karasubazar (present-day Belogorsk), Kazarat, Akmechit (present-day Simferopol), Bakhchesarai, and Odabazar (present-day Armiansk) among others. Kaffa alone had over forty Armenian churches, the foremost being the monastery of St. Sargis. So strong was the Armenian presence in the Crimea that by the first half of the fifteenth century, the area was sometimes referred to by Europeans as "Maritime Armenia."

In Kaffa and Kazarat the Armenians had their own quarters, chose their own officials, and managed to maintain their culture. Crimea became a major center of Armenian art. The artist Nikoghos, who continued the tradition of the great Cilician illuminator Toros Roslin, produced unique illuminated manuscripts. Although the Armenians spoke their own language, they conducted business in Italian, Greek, and most often, Kipchak Turkish, the language of the Turko-Mongols (Tatars). Armeno-Kipchak, written in Armenian script, remained one of the primary languages of Armenian merchants in parts of Eastern Europe until the seventeenth century.

Neither the Catholic Genoese nor the Muslim Tatars forced or actively encouraged Armenians to convert. The Armenian community of the Crimea was given its own prelacy and the town of Surkhat, with its Holy Cross monastery, became a bishopric. One of the most significant legacies of the Crimean community was the voice gained by artisans and farmers in the late fifteenth century in the election of their prelates. This development later contributed to the nineteenth-century political climate in Constantinople, where the descendants of Crimean Armenians would demand the participation of the artisans and workers in the election of that city's Armenian patriarch.

In 1475 the Ottomans attacked the Crimea, putting an end to Genoese control. A Tatar khanate, subordinate to the Ottoman sultan, emerged in 1478, and Armenian dominance diminished thereafter. Some Armenian churches were converted to mosques; executions and forced conversions occurred as well. Many Armenians fled to other parts of Eastern Europe, primarily to Ukraine and Poland, where they bolstered the small Armenian communities which were already there; others were taken captive by the Ottomans and joined the growing Armenian community in Constantinople. A revival of the community did occur, however, in the seventeenth century when new immigrants, fleeing the resumption of Ottoman-Safavid wars in eastern Anatolia, settled in the Crimea.

In 1778, some 12,000 Crimean Armenians migrated to Russia as a result of the treaty of Küchük Kainarja (1774), which forced the Ottomans to accept the independence of the Tatar khanate of the Crimea. After 1774 the region fell under Russian influence and in order to cripple the Crimean economy, Catherine the Great encouraged its Greek and Armenian merchants to migrate to Russia before she annexed the Crimea in 1783. The Armenians were permitted to establish their own center of New Nakhichevan, in memory of the community in historic Armenia that many of their ancestors had fled a century earlier. The Armenians of New Nakhichevan later played a significant role in the intellectual development of the Armenians of Transcaucasia.

The Armenian Communities of Poland

The Armenian communities of Poland were primarily located in the eastern part of that kingdom, that is, in regions which are, at present, part of Ukraine. The ancestors of some of the Armenian merchants and mercenaries who eventually settled in Poland first arrived in what historians refer to as Kievan Russia in the tenth century. Following the Seljuk invasions of Armenia in the eleventh century, more immigrants arrived in Kiev. In that same century the first important Polish colony was established in the city of Kamenets-Podolsk. During the same period, Armenians from Ani emigrated to Ruthenia, which later became part of Poland. The Mongol invasions in the thirteenth century brought even more Armenians into Kiev, but the Mongol sacking of the city in 1240 soon forced many in the community to relocate to Poland, where they settled in the regions of Galicia, Podolia, Volhynia, and in the city of Lvov or Lemberg, which became the second most important Polish-Armenian center. An Armenian church was constructed in Kamenets-Podolsk in the mid-thirteenth century and a hundred years later, Armenians from the lower Volga region increased the size of the community there.

In 1340, the king of Poland, Kasimir the Great, occupied Galicia and Volhynia and, recognizing the Armenians' contribution to commerce, granted them the right to observe their own laws and traditions. A cathedral, still standing, was built in Lvov in 1363. By the fifteenth century more Armenians arrived in eastern Poland from Cilicia and from the Crimea and, during the Iranian-Ottoman wars of the sixteenth and seventeenth centuries, others joined them from historic Armenia.

Armenians had their own guilds in Poland and were considered by the Poles to be excellent artisans. Armenian jewelers, painters, and weavers were especially well regarded. Their merchants played a major role in the trade with Russia, Iran, and the Ottoman Empire. Many Armenian trading houses in Lvov had branches in Moscow, Isfahan, and Constantinople. Although there have been estimates of over 300,000 Armenians in Poland at the height of the community, the actual numbers were probably less. Armenians had their own elected officials and judges and established their own courts in Lvov and Kamenets-Podolsk which utilized the late thirteenth-century law code of Mekhitar Gosh. The documents of the Armenian courts were written in Kipchak Turkish, which continued to remain the language of business, and Polish, both transcribed in the Armenian script. An Armenian printing press was established in Lvov in 1616 and the first play written in Armenian was performed there in 1668. Polish Armenians even joined the army and an Armenian battalion participated in the lifting of the siege of Vienna in 1683. Polish Armenian intellectuals such as Stepanos Lehatsi and Stepanos Roshka, wrote historical, theological, and grammatical works. Lvov attracted Armenian priests from the homeland who, in the seventeenth century, came to study at its seminary and copy manuscripts at its scriptorium and upon their return, transferred Western ideas to lay and religious leaders in historic Armenia.

By the third decade of the seventeenth century, the Polish Armenians began to feel the effects of the Catholic Counter-Reformation. The Catholic Church established a seminary in Lvov to prepare young Armenian Catholic priests, who, with the approval of the Polish crown, soon replaced the older priests of the Armenian Apostolic Church. Armenian lay leaders began to convert to Catholicism as well. Since the lay members controlled all Church property, their conversion meant the gradual assimilation of the Armenians and their Church into Polish society. By 1629 the Polish prelacy, under the leadership of Archbishop Nicholas Torosowicz, accepted the supremacy of Rome but maintained its ties and, according to some historians, allegiance, to Etchmiadzin. The ordination of young Armenian Catholic priests, however, eventually resulted in a complete union with Rome. In 1689 Archbishop Vardan Hunanian broke with Etchmiadzin. The community declined thereafter for other reasons. The Turkish takeover of Podolia in 1672 led to a general economic decline which, in turn, resulted in an Armenian emigration to Constantinople and a number of cities in present-day Romania and Bulgaria. The final blow was Catherine the Great's occupation of eastern Poland during the first partition of Poland in 1784 and her occupation of Podolia in 1793. This act cut off the Armenians of Poland from Lvov, which had been given to Austria and was renamed Lemberg. These events resulted in the decline and the eventual demise of the community.

The Armenian Communities of Bulgaria, Romania, and Hungary

The Armenian community of Bulgaria began when Byzantine emperors such as Justinian (527-565) and Maurice (582-602) relocated a number of Armenian lords and their followers to Thrace and Macedonia in order to weaken Armenian power in western Armenia and to create a buffer zone against the nomadic invaders in the Balkans.* This initial group of Armenians were joined by Armenian Paulician heretics and other immigrants and by the eleventh century a significant Armenian element emerged in Bulgaria, especially in Burgas, Sofia, and Philippopolis (present-day Plovdiv), where a prelacy was established. The Armenians were mainly engaged in trade and eventually formed communities in Burgas, Varna, and Sofia. Between 1363 and 1393 the Ottomans conquered Bulgaria and the Armenians there were later included in the Armenian *millet*. New arrivals from historic Armenia came during the Irano-Turkish wars of the sixteenth century. Following the Counter-Reformation, Armenians from Poland who had refused to convert to

*See vol. I, pp. 83-86.

Catholicism came to Bulgaria where, ironically the Ottoman *millet* system permitted them to practice their own form of Christianity. After 1878, deteriorating political and socioeconomic conditions in Turkey and Bulgaria's recent autonomy attracted many Armenians there.

The community of Romania was formed as a result of immigrations from the lower Volga into Moldavia, Wallachia, and Bukovina in the fourteenth century. Here, too, churches were built and a prelacy was established in Moldavia. The fall of Constantinople (1453) and Kaffa (1475) brought more Armenians to Romanian lands. The Armenians in Bukovina and Moldavia had to endure invasions by Poland and the Ottoman, Russian, and Austro-Hungarian empires. In 1654 religious persecutions and economic difficulties forced some to Transylvania. The Armenians in Wallachia fared better. They concentrated on the trade between the Ottomans and northern Europe and by the early seventeenth century had built a church in Bucharest. The Armenians retained their language and religion and participated in the political and cultural life of Romania. Unlike Bulgaria, Romania, backed by Russia, gained its autonomy in the first half of the nineteenth century. The treaty of Adrianople (1829) had also awarded Bessarabia to Russia. Armenians in Bessarabia made contacts with the influential Armenian community in Russia and gained their own prelate soon after. Armenians in the rest of Romania benefited from the various reforms carried out by the governors of these Danubian principalities. Armenian churches and monasteries flourished, and Armenian schools, newspapers, and journals were published in large numbers. The Armenians in Romania became more affluent than their counterparts in Bulgaria and participated in the political and cultural life of their adopted land.

Although there is evidence of Armenians in Hungary as early as the tenth century, the main influx arrived in Transylvania, then part of Hungary, in the sixteenth century, following religious intolerance in Moldavia. A second wave arrived following tax increases in Moldavia in the seventeenth century. The Armenians joined the Hungarians against the Ottomans and, after the unification of Hungary, were given internal autonomy and the right to conduct commercial activities. They were also allowed to elect their own judges and to have their own courts. The Transylvanian cities of Gherla, also called Armenopolis, and Elizabethopolis (present-day Dumbraveni) were the main Armenian centers where some 20,000 Armenians engaged in leather works, candle making, and trade.

The Armenians of Hungary were forced to convert to Catholicism when the Hapsburgs took over Transylvania at the start of the eighteenth century.

The Armenian Catholic bishops of Lvov, now under Austrian rule, took control of the Armenian churches in Transylvania. The Apostolic Armenians in Hungary were thus cut off both from Russia and from the rest of the Balkans and, lacking the religious protection of the *millet* system, converted to Catholicism. The Hungarian Armenians, however, managed to establish a separate bishopric and, with the help of the Mekhitarian order of Venice, operated a school and maintained some autonomy for themselves as Armenian Catholics.

The Hungarian Armenians involved themselves in the political life of Hungary and participated in the 1848 revolution against the Hapsburgs. After crushing the rebellion, the Hapsburgs punished the Armenian leadership by executing two Armenian generals, abolishing the bishopric, and demanding considerable war reparations. The Armenians of Hungary lost the right to have schools and soon forgot their own language, which, in turn, discouraged new immigrants and resulted in the total assimilation of the Armenians of Hungary.

ARMENIAN COMMUNITIES IN WESTERN EUROPE

The Armenian communities in Western Europe have their earliest origins in the sixth century. The main influx of Armenians, however, came there during the Crusades and the Cilician period, from the eleventh to the fourteenth centuries, and once again during the seventeenth century when, as we have seen, Armenian merchants from Iran established trading houses in various cities of Western Europe.

The Armenian Communities of Italy

Armenians arrived in Italy as part of the army of the Byzantine Empire during the sixth century. Armenian generals, together with Armenian contingents, fought in Sicily during the seventh century under the leadership of Emperor Constance. Two Armenian bishops from Italy even attended the Lateran Council of 649. The main Armenian communities of Italy, however, were formed in the thirteenth century, primarily as a result of the trade treaty negotiated by King Leo I of Cilicia with the Italian city states of Genoa and Venice in 1201 and with Pisa in 1216. The Armenian and Italian merchants, who were acquainted through the Black Sea trade, now engaged in large-scale trade in the Mediterranean. Soon small Armenian communities grew in

Rome, Venice, Genoa, Ancona, Lugano, Mantua, and Pisa. The Mamluk incursions into Cilicia and the decline of that kingdom, combined with Turkish advances in Asia Minor, brought more Armenians to Western Europe, especially Italy. The significant inroads made by the Latin Church among the Armenian nobility and merchants of Cilicia, plus these two groups' knowledge of French and Italian, made Western Europe in general, and Italy in particular, a logical choice for emigration and eased their transition to a Western society.

The fall of Cilicia in 1375 brought a large flood of Armenian refugees to Italy via Cyprus. According to the historian Ghevond Alishan, some 30,000 Armenians were living in Italy by the first quarter of the fifteenth century. Venice, where a street and bridge were named after the Armenians, became their main center. "Armenian houses" (*case degli Armeni*), hostels where Armenian merchants and artisans congregated, were established in various Italian cities. A number of Armenian churches, among them the Church of the Holy Cross in Venice, were also constructed. Since Italy was not a united state and each Italian city-state operated independently, the Armenian communities in these various cities followed suit -- they functioned as individual units and did not develop a collective Italian Armenian identity.

The Armenians of Venice can take credit for the printing of the first books in Armenian. The two volumes, a prayer book and a ceremonial calendar *(Urbatagirk* and *Parzatumar),* were printed by Hakob Meghapart in 1512. Soon various scientific books were printed as well and, by the second half of the eighteenth century, Italy became a center for the publication of Armenian secular books. The art of Armenian printing moved from Italy in the second half of the sixteenth century, when Abkar Tokhatetsi left Rome due to the harsh policies of Pope Pius V (1566-1572) against non-Catholic Armenians, and set up his press in Constantinople, the first in any language in the Ottoman Empire.

During the sixteenth century, the Italian communities were augmented by silk merchants from Julfa in Nakhichevan. They were really enlarged in the seventeenth century, however, when Shah `Abbas, who had transferred Armenian merchants from Julfa to New Julfa, sent an official delegation to Venice in 1607 to purchase various goods. In 1610 the shah sent the Armenian merchant Khoja Safar as his envoy to conclude trade and alliance treaties against the Turks. Khoja Safar visited Venice, Rome, and Florence and returned with commercial and military agreements. Armenians soon controlled the silk trade between Iran and Italy, and were given tax-exempt status in a number of Italian cities. Iranian Armenians in Venice were concentrated around the Church of St. Mary of Formosa located on a street which became known as Julfa Street. Armenian merchants soon left their traditional hostels and began to purchase individual houses.

By the seventeenth century a large stone church was constructed in Venice, where by then some 2,000 Armenians resided. Perugia, Ancona, Siena, Milan, and Ferrara also gained Armenian residents. Several Armenian churches, named after St. Gregory, were built in Naples, Nardo, and Livorno. Catholicism was a strong force in Italy and most Armenians converted to the Roman Church. By the late seventeenth and early eighteenth centuries, when Armenian fortunes in Iran declined, a number of prominent *khojas* moved to Venice. Most important of these were the Shahumians (1650-1757), the Martirosians (1690-1737), the Sharimanians (1697-1800), and Noratunkians (1717-1757). Armenian merchants from Poland, France, and Russia also set up trading houses in Venice. A number of Armenian sailors and artisans settled in Italian ports as well.

The most significant event in the history of the Armenians of Italy was the relocation of the Mekhitarian order to Venice, described earlier. Thanks to the generosity of wealthy Armenian merchants from India, the Mekhitarians established two colleges, one in Venice (Murad-Raphaelian) and the other in Padua (later transferred to Paris and then to Sèvres). The activity of the Mekhitarians assured a continued Armenian presence in Italy.

The Armenian Communities of France

Armenian trade contacts with France began as early as the seventh century and increased during the tenth century. A number of Armenians were reportedly among the envoys sent by the `Abbasid Caliph Harun al-Rashid to the court of Charlemagne in 807. The Byzantines also sent Armenian envoys to France. In the ninth century a number of Armenian Paulicians arrived via Dalmatia and Italy to France where they may possibly have had some influence on the rise of the later Albigensian movement in the south. After the fall of Ani in the eleventh century many Armenians fled to Europe and established a community in France as well. Armeno-French contacts were sporadic, however, until the Crusades. The Crusades and subsequent trade between France and Cilicia brought not only commercial but military agreements, as well as inter-marriages between Armenian and French merchants and nobles, from the twelfth to the fourteenth centuries. French merchants received special privileges from King Oshin of Cilicia in 1314 by which they paid a custom duty of only two percent. French ships and merchants made stops at Ayas, Tarsus, Mersin, and Sis, and Armenians visited French ports. The French brought mirrors, soap, and beeswax, while Armenians brought silk and other oriental luxury items to Marseilles, Narbonne, and Nîmes.

After the fall of Cilicia numerous Armenian merchants relocated to French cities including the city of Avignon. In 1389 the last Armenian king of Cilicia, Leo V, after being ransomed from Egypt, came to France and tried to mediate between the French and the English and to encourage them to abandon their own conflict (the Hundred Years' War) and to start a new crusade to liberate the Christians in the Middle East. Nothing came out of that and he died on November 29, 1393. Of French descent and related to French kings, Leo was buried in St. Denis in Paris, the resting place of French monarchs.

Armenian artisans and builders also came to France. An Armenian architect built the early ninth century Church of Germigny des Près in Orleans, the oldest Carolingian church in France. The church evinces both Armenian and Visigothic architectural styles. In 1453, after the fall of Constantinople, a number of Armenians arrived in Paris and Marseilles. By the seventeenth century Armenian *khojas* from Iran initiated new trade with France. The great ministers of France, Richelieu, Mazarin, and Colbert, recognized the importance of Armenian merchants and encouraged them to settle in Marseilles. By 1622 Armenian merchants were competing so well that their French counterparts complained and forced the government to restrict Armenian goods, forbidding French ships to carry them. Silk was restricted, and taking French gold and silver coins out of the country was forbidden. Armenian merchants complained to Shah `Abbas, who send a letter with Antoine Armeni, a commercial agent appointed by France, to Louis XIII in 1629, resulting in the revocation of some of these restrictions. By the 1660s, Colbert, despite objections from the French merchants of Marseilles, revoked most of the restrictions. A street called rue Armeni still exists in Marseilles.

Armenians opened businesses inland, in Paris and Lyon, as well as in the ports of Nice (then part of Savoy) and Toulouse. An Armenian from Nakhichevan, Hovhannes Altoun (Jean Altin) introduced madder, a plant from whose roots a red dye (alizarin) is produced, to the cloth dyers of Avignon in the mid-eighteenth century. Until the introduction of synthetic alizarin, the Rhone valley was a major center of the production of this dye. As in Italy, the Armenian community set up a printing press in France, producing an Armenian-Latin dictionary in the 1630's. The famous Armenian printer, Voskan Vardapet, who had already relocated from Amsterdam to

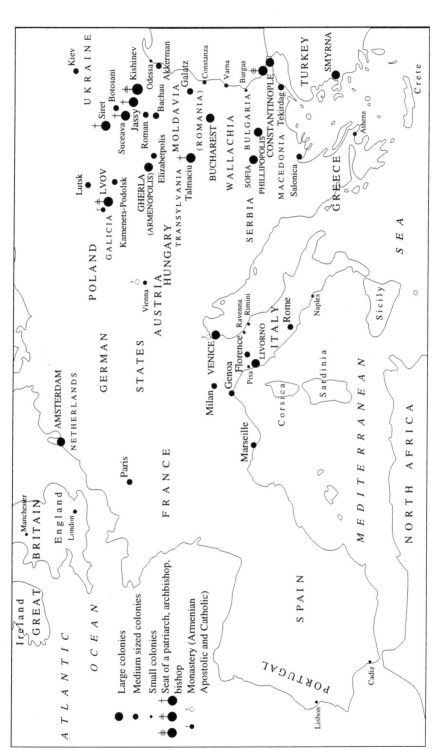

Map 11: The Armenian Diaspora in Eastern and Western Europe (19th Century).

Livorno, came to Marseilles and, beginning in 1673, printed some thirty books in Armenian. Armenians continued immigrating to France during the eighteenth and especially in the nineteenth century, when some Armenians from the Ottoman Empire and the Arab lands settled there. Catholic influence upon the Armenians was strong in France, and in time most of these Armenians converted.

The Armenian Community of the Netherlands

There is evidence of Armenians in the Low Countries, that is Belgium, Holland, and Luxembourg, beginning in the eleventh century. Trade became active, however, in the thirteenth and fourteenth centuries, when Dutch and Flemish merchants arrived in Cilicia and Armenian trading houses opened in the Low Countries. Armenians brought in carpets, dyes, cotton, and spices, concentrating their trade in the city of Bruges, specifically St. Donat's Church square, where they traded their goods for woolen cloth, Russian furs, Spanish oil, and other items brought from the four corners of Europe.

After the fall of Cilicia, Armenian refugees arrived in Bruges where they were supported by a number of Flemish Christian charities. In 1478 Armenians built a large hostel in Bruges which became the "Armenian Hospice." By the end of that century Armenians began to move to Amsterdam, the new center of commerce in the region. Dutch sources record Armenian merchants selling pearls and diamonds there in the second half of the sixteenth century. Armenian commerce in Amsterdam received a major boost when Armenian merchants from Iran began trading in Western Europe in the first half of the seventeenth century. Dutch merchants went to Isfahan and some even settled in New Julfa, while Armenians opened trading houses in Amsterdam. The first Armenian Bible was printed in 1666 in that city, by Voskan Vardapet. Armenians from Amsterdam also introduced the first printing press to Iran. Soon after the conclusion of a trade treaty between the Turks and the Dutch in 1612, Armenian merchants from the Ottoman Empire arrived in Amsterdam. Silk was the primary item traded by the Armenians there, as in the rest of Europe, and they continued to control the Dutch silk trade until the mid-eighteenth century. According to Dutch sources there were some 500 Armenians living in Amsterdam, concentrated in the Monnikenstraat, Dykstraat, and Keiserstraat streets and selling their wares in the Qoster ("Eastern") Market.

In 1713 the Armenians constructed an Armenian Church in Amsterdam and received permission from Etchmiadzin to have their own priest. A number of Armenian merchants were wealthy enough to have their own ships flying the Dutch colors and to be escorted by armed frigates on their journeys to Smyrna. A hundred years later, however, due to various European conflicts, particularly the blockade enforced during the Napoleonic wars, as well as the rise of English trading companies, the Armenian community had lost its economic power in the Netherlands. By the mid-nineteenth century, the Armenian church of Amsterdam was closed down and eventually sold.

By the end of the nineteenth century most of the Armenian communities in Europe (see map 11) had reached the low ebb of their social and economic influence in their adopted lands. No one could predict that cataclysmic events at the end of that century and the first two decades of the twentieth would bring new, and very different, Armenian immigrants to the shores of Eastern and Western Europe.

XVIII

The Armenian Question and Its Solution:
Armenians in Ottoman Turkey (1876-1918)

The reforms initiated by Selim III which culminated in the "Imperial Rescript" of 1856 had not resolved the socioeconomic and political troubles of Ottoman Turkey. Although the urban population in Constantinople had benefited from the new safeguards, the majority of the inhabitants, that is the peasants, were not affected. Yet, the Armenians were the only large Christian group who, despite a cultural revival, had not sought autonomy or separation from the Ottomans. In the Balkans, with the exception of the Bulgarians, most of the other major national groups had already gained autonomy or independence. The Armenians, however, only longed for a stable and fair government. There were a number of reasons for the behavior of the *loyal millet*. More than a thousand years of invasions, Armenian emigrations, and the settlement of Turkish and Kurdish tribes in Armenia, had resulted in the fact that Armenians had but a plurality in some places and a majority in only a handful of districts of western Armenia. Thus, unlike the Arabs or the Christians of the Balkans, Armenians did not constitute a majority in their homeland. More importantly, the Armenian leadership consisted of urban merchants, who did not live in Armenia, among the still-dissatisfied peasants. By the mid-nineteenth century, almost all of these leaders lived in Constantinople, Smyrna, Cairo, Alexandria, Aleppo, Tiflis, Baku, New Nakhichevan, Moscow, St. Petersburg, or other urban centers of Europe and Asia. They not only were far removed geographically from the Armenian workers and peasants, but had little in common with them. With the exception of a few mountainous enclaves, Armenians in the interior, had no military leaders or noblemen to rally the population. The Armenian urban elite was generally respected by the states in which they lived and, in fact, found working with the ruling power advantageous to their socioeconomic well-being. With the exception of Etchmiadzin and Aghtamar, the Church hierarchy was also removed from Armenia and the majority of Armenians. It, too, advocated conservatism and advised its flock to accept their condition. The Armenian political awakening began in the diaspora and found its way to the agrarian homeland only in the second half of the nineteenth century.

Socioeconomic Conditions in Western Armenia

The Armenian population of western Armenia, unlike that of eastern Armenia, was dispersed on a much larger territory and was separated by numerous Kurdish and Turkish settlements or pasturelands. Certain common features dominated village life in eastern and western Armenia. Like most peasants of that period, the Armenians of eastern Turkey were, until the last quarter of the nineteenth century, generally illiterate. They spoke local dialects of Armenian, Kurdish, or Turkish. Family structure was patriarchal and patrilineal, with property divided equally among the sons. Local traditions and regional customs were strictly observed and except for articles of personal use, such as weapons, tools, and jewelry, most property was shared among the extended family. Houses were small and mud-brick and centered around the *tonir*, or clay-oven which was dug in the ground. The wealthiest and most experienced man was usually elected the village elder. He mediated disputes, administered justice, and distributed the tax load of each extended household. His compensation for this work was in the form of free labor and gifts. Prior to the second half of the nineteenth century, few families, except those claiming noble ancestry, had surnames. After that time individuals took the root of their surname from either the Christian name of the clan's founder, his profession (if he was a craftsman or tradesman), or his birthplace. To this root was added the ending *ian, iants, ints, units,* or *ents.*

Aside from speaking a different dialect of Armenian than their eastern countrymen, the residents of western Armenian villages differed most greatly in the configuration of their houses. Ever on guard against Kurdish raids, extended Armenian families lived in close proximity, with houses connected by covered passageways and contiguous roofs. As the photograph of Zeitun illustrates, the western Armenian village could appear to be one unending maze of houses. This sense of physical insecurity also resulted in western Armenian women marrying at a younger age -- usually from thirteen to fifteen -- and in both men and women seeking to blend in with their Muslim neighbors by wearing clothing similar to theirs. Western Armenian women thus appear to have worn more embroidery, jewelry, and in some regions, even veils.

The decades of reforms not only did not improve the lot of western Armenians, but actually worsened it. The local Turkish or Kurdish chiefs resented any interference by the capital and felt that the reforms threatened their control over their Muslim and Armenian peasants. Armenian village heads and provincial churchmen, encouraged by the reforms, would seek redress by writing petitions. The central government's inevitable inaction, however, would embolden the local *agha*, *beg*, or *pasha* to retaliate against the Armenians by driving them away from their land. The number of land-less Armenians who migrated to the cities increased dramatically after 1856. Many of those who remained were reduced to what can only be described as serfdom or slavery.

The Zeitun Rebellion

Arab, Byzantine, Turkish, Mongol, and Turkmen invasions had decimated the ranks of Armenian feudal lords and military leaders. The fall of the Armenian kingdoms in Armenia and Cilicia nearly obliterated the remaining power of the princes and nobles. Some emigrated, others converted or entered the service of the new rulers of the land. Some nobles, however, managed to escape to the mountainous valleys of Armenia, notably Karabagh and Zeitun, where they remained autonomous. Zeitun, northeast of Cilicia, had been attacked, but its 25,000 inhabitants, ruled by these autonomous princes, defended themselves against Turkish incursions and had never been conquered. In the first half of the seventeenth century, Sultan Murad IV (1623-1640) agreed to leave the Zeituntsis in peace, in exchange for its tribute for oil for the lamps of the Hagia Sophia Mosque. No Turkish officials were sent there and the population, some of them armed, maintained their autonomy.

By the mid-nineteenth century, the national awakening in the Balkans and the Russian encroachment into the Black Sea region and Transcaucasia, brought close to half a million displaced Muslims into Anatolia. Having been driven from their homes by Christians, they demanded that the central government find them a place to live. Those coming into western Anatolia were settled around Cilicia, while those arriving in eastern Anatolia found a new home in western Armenia. The central government, which had once more tried to take Zeitun by force but had failed, hoped that the arrival of these groups would aid in curbing Zeitun's growing independence. By settling Circassian and other immigrants in western Anatolia, they hoped that they would accomplish what the Kurds and Turkmen had in eastern Anatolia. When that proved unsuccessful, the Turks in 1862, alarmed by the French intervention in Lebanon a year earlier, decided to take control of Zeitun. Claiming that the people of Zeitun had not paid their taxes, a large Turkish army attacked the region. On August 2, 1862 the Armenians defeated the Turkish army inflicting heavy losses, and capturing cannons and ammunition. The Turks then laid siege to Zeitun, hoping to starve it. The Armenians, as the Maronites had done in Lebanon, asked the help of Napoleon III. The French forced the Turks to lift the blockade, but the Turks were permitted to build a fort in Zeitun and station troops there. The Zeitun rebellion had left its mark, however. Uprisings in Van (1862), Erzerum (1863), and Mush (1864) followed and according to some historians, may have been the first signs of the political awakening of the Armenians in Ottoman Turkey. Between 1862 and 1878 a number of small self-protection unions, lodges and societies were formed in Cilicia and Van. The Union of Salvation (1872) and the Black Cross Society (1878), both established in Van, set the stage for the first Armenian political party.

The Armenian Question

The Armenian Question, according to at least one historian, had its origins in 1071 when the Seljuk Turks defeated the Byzantines in the Battle of Manzikert and became the first foreign group to systematically settle in Armenia. The question was not placed on the international agenda, however, until 1878. Until then the problems of Armenians in eastern Anatolia were unknown in the West and were not included in any discussions concerning the conditions of the Christians living under Turkish rule.

Three years earlier, in 1875-76, Bosnian and Bulgarian peasants rebelled against Turkish misrule and the entire population of several of their villages was massacred in retaliation. Europe and its press demanded an immediate solution for the century-long complaints of the Balkan Christians. The British government was in the hands of the conservatives, led by Benjamin Disraeli, who believed that as the only bulwark against Russian penetration into the Mediterranean, the Turks had to be supported at all costs. Pressures from the liberal opposition led by William Gladstone, as well as mounting world opinion, however, forced Disraeli to call a conference.

In December 1876, the major European powers all gathered in Constantinople to resolve the Eastern Question once again. To their surprise, they were presented with a constitution that had been drafted by the Young Ottomans -- Armenians, represented by Grigor Odian, were also involved in creating the document -- and had been signed by the new young sultan, Abdul-Hamid II (1876-1909). Based on the Belgian constitution of 1830, with some changes to assure the sultan's power, the Ottoman constitution guaranteed civil rights, religious freedom, and security of life and property for all. It contained articles for the separation of the legislative, judicial, and executive branches and provided equality for all citizens before the law.

The diplomats, especially the British, felt that such a liberal constitution made any discussion relating to the Balkan Christians superfluous and the conference adjourned. The Bulgarians and other Orthodox or Slavic minorities in the Balkans felt betrayed and the Eastern Question, now labeled the *Eastern Crisis*, continued to smolder. Pan-Slavic feelings in Russia were extremely high and encouraged the tsarist government to resolve the issue by war. The Russians calculated that this was the best time to totally nullify the Paris Treaty of 1856. They had already begun to break the terms of that treaty in 1870 when, taking advantage of the Franco-Prussian War, they abrogated the clauses relating to the Black Sea and once again fortified their Black Sea ports. The defeat of France and the emergence of Germany as a new power in 1871, freed Russia to act and in 1872 resulted in the Three Emperors' League, by which Prussia, Austria, and Russia loosely agreed to support each other against outside attacks.

The refusal of the Turks to discuss the situation in Bulgaria gave Russia the excuse to enter Moldavia in 1877 and the last Russo-Turkish war of that century began. Once again the war was fought on two fronts, in Eastern Europe and western Armenia. The Armenian hierarchy in Constantinople, which did not trust Russian pan-Slavism or the Russian Orthodox Church, publicly supported the Ottomans. The Armenian population in western Armenia, however, was weary of its intolerable conditions, and when Kurds, taking advantage of war, once again attacked Armenian villages, the Russian army, led by Armenian generals and accompanied by Russian Armenian volunteers, was welcomed. By 1878 almost all of western Armenia was liberated and the Russian army in Europe was within reach of Constantinople. The Turks agreed to a cease-fire and negotiations began. The Armenian intellectuals of Constantinople, after receiving news of the atrocities committed in western Armenia by Kurds, Circassians, and Turkish irregulars, demanded that their leaders end their caution and ask the former Russian ambassador to Constantinople and other Russian officials to include the future of the western Armenians in the peace talks.

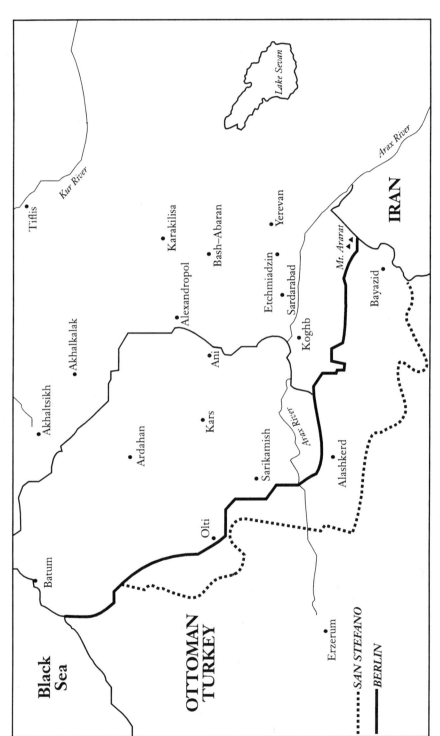

Map 12: The Russo-Turkish Border after the San Stefano and Berlin Treaties (1878)

The Treaty of San Stefano (March 3, 1878) formed a totally independent Romania, Serbia, and Montenegro, the latter two receiving additional territory from Bosnia and Herzegovina and Macedonia. A large autonomous Bulgaria, which included most of Macedonia and had access to the Aegean was also created. As for western Armenia, the Russians annexed Kars, Ardahan, Alashkert, and Bayazid (see map 12). Although the rest of western Armenia was to be returned to the sultan, article 16 of the treaty provided for Russian troops to remain in the Armenian provinces until the Turkish government carried out the reforms requested by the Armenian inhabitants, and to secure them against Kurdish and Circassian raids.

The British, headed by Disraeli and Foreign Secretary Robert Salisbury, and the Austrians headed by Count Andrassy, denounced the treaty and threatened war. Tsar Alexander II, troubled by revolutionaries,* and urged by the German chancellor, Otto von Bismarck who promised to act as the "honest broker," agreed to a European gathering in Berlin within two months. An Armenian delegation, led by the former patriarch of Constantinople and later Catholicos, Khrimian, visited the various capitals of Europe to convince the European diplomats to grant western Armenia the same status as Lebanon -- that is, a Christian governor, local self-administration, use of revenues for local projects, civil courts, and a mixed Armenian and Muslim police force. The great powers, however, spent the time prior to the conference in secret meetings in which the British, Austrians, Russians, and Turks made their own separate agreements. By the time the delegates arrived for the Berlin Congress (June 13-July 13, 1878), the fate of the Balkans and the Armenians was, for all intents and purposes, already decided.

The Treaty of Berlin created a smaller autonomous Bulgaria with no outlet to the Aegean, with most of Macedonia remaining under Turkish rule. Serbia and Montenegro became independent but did not gain much territory. The Serbs were especially stung when Austria was handed a mandate to administer Bosnia and Herzegovina, which remained under the authority of the sultan, and to garrison the sanjak of Novi Bazar, a strip of land lying between Serbia and Montenegro. The British were granted Cyprus, an important base in the Mediterranean from where they could keep an eye on the Suez Canal. In exchange, they promised that if the Turks carried out new reforms, they would defend them against any further Russian aggression in Anatolia, that is western Armenia. French ambitions were satisfied by granting France the right to occupy Tunis. Romania became independent, but gave up southern Bessarabia to Russia. In Anatolia, the Russians annexed Kars,

*See chapter XIX.

Ardahan, and Batum, but gave back to the Turks Bayazid and Alashkert, through which the main overland trade route from Iran to the Black Sea port of Trebizond passed (see map 12). Armenian self-rule was not discussed; instead article 61 removed Russian troops and substituted them with a collective European responsibility -- without direct supervision -- for the implementation of reforms in western Armenia. Khrimian's disappointment was expressed in a speech in which he advocated armed struggle.

Armenian Political and Revolutionary Movements

For the next two years the great powers carried out their responsibility and would occasionally remind the Porte of its promises towards the Armenians. Gladstone, a supporter of the Christians in the Ottoman Empire, became prime minister in 1880 and may have pressured the Ottomans to carry out new reforms, but a year later global events diverted Europe into other directions. Pan-Slavic activities in Austria-Hungary and concerns over a possible Franco-Russian alliance resulted in Germany and Austria coming to terms and favoring the Turks. Tsar Alexander II was assassinated and his son and successor, Alexander III (1881-1894) was not a friend of the Armenians or other minorities.* Moreover, colonial expansion in Africa, Southeast Asia, and China distracted the great powers from the Armenian Question.

In the meantime, the Congress of Berlin had not only disappointed the Armenians, but had left them in a precarious position. The *loyal millet* was now suspect. A number of Armenian villages were raided by Kurds and Circassians. The patriarch tried to ease the situation by declaring his loyalty and stating that unlike the Balkan Christians, the Armenians had never wished to separate from the Ottoman Empire. He hoped that the promised reforms would resolve the Armenian Question. Sultan Abdul-Hamid did not accept the patriarch's assurances. Realizing that the European powers would not now intervene, he encouraged local officials to use a free hand in western Armenia. The petitions of Armenian leaders in the provinces regarding extortion, abductions by the Kurds and Circassians, and the breakdown of law and order were completely ignored by the government. Most Armenians had lost the courage to defend themselves or speak out against injustice. Like the Jews of Russia, they accepted their fate. In addition, Sultan Abdul-Hamid recruited some of the Kurds into irregular cavalry units (known as the *Hamidiye*) to carry out pogroms against the Armenians similar to those against the Jews perpetuated by the Cossacks in Russia. Although the estab-

*See chapters XIX.

lished Armenian leadership did not support the activists, whose anti-clerical and socialistic slogans disturbed the Church and merchant elite, Abdul-Hamid viewed all the Armenians as a threat. He distorted the ideas of the Islamic reformer Jamal ad-Din al-Afghani (1838-1897) to his own ends. Whereas al-Afghani, who had visited Constantinople and who had communicated with the sultan, preached the union of Islamic peoples and values to resist and overthrow Western imperialism, Abdul-Hamid used his position as caliph to unite all Muslims in the empire against Christian revolutionaries in the Balkans and Anatolia.

The disappointment following the Congress of Berlin affected Armenian writers as well. The romantic period was at an end. The romantic novelists were replaced by realists. Hakob Baronian (1841-1892) wrote satirical plays, Grigor Zohrab (1861-1915) wrote vivid short stories, and Ruben Zartarian (1874-1915) gathered country legends and folk tales. Others from this generation include Siamanto, Varoujan, Medsarents, and Odian. The press followed the movement and in 1884 Arpiar Arpiarian (1852-1908), started *The Orient* as a forum for the realists.

By 1881, realizing that European assurances concerning western Armenia meant little, a number of Armenian intellectuals ignored the advice of their elders, and, following the resistance movements of the Balkans and the armed struggle of the Armenians in Zeitun, began to organize defense groups in a number of locations. The most famous of these was the Defense of the Fatherland Society of Garin (Erzerum) where armed youth vowed to protect their people. By 1885, the first Armenian political party (the only one formed in Armenia), the Armenakan, was formed by the students of Mkrtich Portugalian, a teacher in Van. Organized by Mkrtich Terlemezian and influence by the nationalism of Khrimian, the Armenakan platform advocated general education, armed resistance, and the preparation for eventual self-government. Portugalian, who had been expelled from Turkey a few months earlier, founded the newspaper, *Armenia*, in Marseilles that same year. His activities in Europe influenced a number of Russian Armenians studying abroad, who, as will be seen, soon started their own revolutionary organization, the Social Democrat Hnchakian Party in Geneva. The Armenakans continued their activities in Van and recruited members among the Armenians in Iranian Azerbaijan, Caucasus, and Bulgaria. Neither Portugalian nor the Armenakans advocated independence. They organized armed bands and for the next decade defended the region of Van from Kurdish raids. By the end of the century a small number of Armenakans were absorbed into the larger and more organized Armenian political parties, such as the aforementioned

Hnchaks and the later Federation of Armenian Revolutionaries, or the Dash-naktsutiun, which had emerged in Tiflis.* The majority eventually joined the Sahmanadir Ramkavar and the later Ramkavar party.**

The Armenian revolutionaries disagreed on their course of action. The Hnchaks felt that anti-government demonstrations would send a message to the European powers that article 61 of Berlin was not forgotten by the Armenians. The Young Ottomans, who soon established themselves in Geneva as the "Young Turks," did not agree with much of the Hnchak platform, but decided to join with the Armenians in the hope of overthrowing the sultan and achieving a constitutional government. In 1890 the Hnchaks, challenging their own clerical leaders, organized demonstrations in Erzerum and in the Armenian cathedral of Constantinople in Kum Kapu. Such protests attracted new members, but also resulted in repression and the death of numerous demonstrators and party officials. Armenians in Russia reacted as well, and in the same year a small expeditionary force, apparently sanctioned by the Dashnaktsutiun, under the leadership of Sarkis Gougounian planned a raid on Turkey. Although it failed, the message was clear: Armenians in Russia had not forgotten the Armenian Question either. In 1894, the Armenian mountaineers of Sasun, frustrated by unfair taxes and services required by Kurdish and Turkish khans and pashas, and encouraged by the Hnchaks, rose in armed rebellion. Although they managed to hold out for a month, promises of amnesty and submission of an official petition to the sultan, induced them to surrender. The agreement was merely a ruse, however, and some 3000 Sasuntsis were killed. Europe protested but did not act and killings occurred in other regions. In September 1895, the Hnchaks, in order to force the Europeans to act, conducted a huge demonstration in front of the Sublime Porte (known as the Bab Ali demonstration) which ended in terrible bloodshed, with hundreds of Armenians losing their lives. The action, however, forced the British to demand some changes, to which Abdul-Hamid, after some procrastination, agreed.

The Massacres of 1895-1896

The sultan, however, had no intention of changing his policy toward the Armenians. For the time being Russia, under the new tsar, Nicholas II (1894-1917), had abandoned its active role in the Balkans and Anatolia, while the remaining European powers had other issues to attend to. Their interest in the Balkans and Anatolia could resurface at anytime, however. Faced with

*See chapters XIX. ** See below and chapter XXII.

the disintegration of his empire in the Balkans, Middle East, and Africa, Abdul-Hamid considered an Armenian national and political awakening in eastern Anatolia especially dangerous, for, if the Armenians succeeded in gaining autonomy or independence, as had the Balkan Christians, the Turks would lose a large part of what, by then, they had come to view as their homeland. Relatively few Turks, after all, had settled in the Arab lands or in the Balkans; the majority had settled in Anatolia. In addition, Anatolia was the Turks' main agricultural and mineral base, and included their principal trade routes. As long as the Armenians accepted an inferior position they could continue to be of service to the empire. Otherwise they would have to be taught to submit.

In October 1895 Turkish and Kurdish forces, with orders from Constantinople, began a systematic attack on Armenian villages and on the Armenian quarters of towns in the six Armenian provinces. Massacres, forced conversions, and looting continued until the summer of 1896. Sources estimate between 100,000 to 200,000 Armenians were killed and over half a million were left in poverty. Hundreds of monasteries and churches were desecrated, destroyed, or converted into mosques and numerous villages were forcibly converted to Islam. Van and Zeitun, where armed Armenians fought back, saw less damage. Throughout all this, the British, French, and Russian envoys protested but refused to act. Except for a handful of armed men, led by popular leaders in Sasun, Bitlis, Van, and Mush who fought back, the majority of the Armenians were too stunned to react. Tens of thousands emigrated to the Arab lands, Europe, and the United States and the political demonstrations evaporated.

The Armenakan and Hnchak top ranks were decimated; the Dashnaks remained the only active party. European indifference moved the Dashnaktsutiun, who, up to then, had not participated in the public demonstrations organized by the Hnchaks. On August 26, 1896, twenty-six Dashnaks, armed with explosives and led by a very young Babgen Siuni, took over the Ottoman Bank in Constantinople and threatened to blow it up. They demanded full amnesty, the restoration of property, the immediate implementation of reforms, under the supervision of European officials, in the six provinces, and the introduction of a mixed Muslim-Armenian police force in western Armenia. During the siege, ten of the men were killed and the rest, after being assured by Western diplomats that their demands would be given consideration, left the bank and, under a safe-conduct guarantee sailed to Europe. The Turkish reaction was swift: the government instigated riots in Constantinople, in which some 6,000 Armenians were killed. The Turkish response to protests over this action was denial and blame on Armenian "terrorists."

The Revolution of 1908

Abdul-Hamid's police, in the meantime, was also active against the Turkish dissidents and intellectuals and arrested a number of their leaders. Between 1891 and 1896, the Young Turks created political cells in Europe. In 1895 another group, the Committee of Union and Progress (*Ittihad ve Terakki Cemiyeti*) was formed with the intention of organizing a coup. They were discovered and most of the leaders were exiled to Europe where they joined the Young Turks. In 1902, the Young Turks joined Armenian Dashnaks, Arabs, Albanians, Jews, and Kurds in the first Congress of Ottoman Liberals held in Paris. Although they agreed to work for a future constitutional state where all nationalities and religions would be accorded equal rights, they disagreed over European intervention on behalf of minorities (the Berlin Treaty's article 61) upon which the Armenians insisted and the Dashnaks refused to participate further. The Japanese victories over Russia and the 1905 Russian Revolution convinced the Turkish, Arab, and Iranian intellectuals that Westernization would put an end to their relative backwardness and allow them to emerge as truly independent states.

The alliance of Armenians and Iranian Azeris in the Iranian Revolution of 1906 brought the Armenians and Turkish revolutionaries closer and they began to plan joint activities against the government. Since earlier attempts by the Armenians to assassinate the sultan had failed, the Young Turks, led by the Committee of Union and Progress, moved to Thrace in 1906 to gather support among the officers of the army in Salonika. In 1907, during the second Congress of Ottoman Liberals, initiated by the Dashnaks in Paris, the Armenians and Turks, this time, agreed to work together for the overthrow of Abdul-Hamid and to create a modern state without European help. The Hnchaks, who had refused to attend either gathering, accused the Dashnaks of collaborating with the enemy. A year later, the army in Macedonia, under the command of the Young Turks, marched on Constantinople, deposed Abdul-Hamid (who retained his title of caliph) and established a constitutional government on July 24, 1908.

A few months later, a group of Armenian liberals and some members of the Armenian middle class, inspired by the Ottoman constitution and opposed to terrorist tactics sought to establish a different kind of political organization. The revolutionaries had already established themselves in Russia, Iran, and Turkey. This left the Armenian community of Egypt as the only powerful Armenian diaspora which had not been affected by revolutionary fervor. The Egyptian diaspora's political and socioeconomic position, as well as the British presence, created an ideal climate for the formation of a new political party which would advocate European liberal traditions and represent the Armenian middle classes of the diaspora. Gathering the remnants of the Armenakans and bringing together those few Hnchaks and Dashnaks who questioned their zealous leaders, these Armenian professionals founded the Armenian Constitutional Democrat Party (*Sahmanadir Ramkavar*) on October 31, 1908 in Alexandria. The party opened a branch in Constantinople, where they attracted many new members and where they later (1921) emerged, under a slightly different name, *(Ramkavar Azatakan)*, as one of the major Armenian political parties.

In the meantime, Armenians and Turkish leaders of the capital celebrated the end of Abdul-Hamid and applauded the new era of Armeno-Turkish cooperation. A number of Armenian intellectuals became members of parliament and a bright future was predicted. Even the Hnchaks, who had refused to cooperate with the Young Turks, decided to refrain from underground activities and to await reforms. The honeymoon lasted less than a year, however. Taking advantage of the revolution, Austria annexed Bosnia and Herzegovina, Bulgaria declared its independence, and Crete declared its union with Greece. Reaction in Turkey resulted in a coup and the return of Abdul-Hamid for ten days in April 1909. During those ten days and immediately after the return of the Young Turks, over 25,000 Armenians in Cilicia were killed by Turkish nationalists and reactionaries. Once order was restored, Abdul-Hamid was sent into exile, and his weak brother, Muhammad V, (1909-1918) became sultan and caliph.

Although several of the secondary culprits of the massacres were punished, the fact that some Young Turks in Cilicia had approved of and had participated in the act soured Armeno-Turkish relations. Despite this, the Armenian patriarchate and the Dashnaktsutiun, now the most prominent and visible Armenian political party, continued their cooperation with the Young Turks and Armenians enlisted in the Turkish army fought during the First Balkan War (1912). The leadership of the Young Turks was changing, however. Pan-Turkism racism, and militant nationalism was on the rise and its proponents, such as Zia Gökalp, were now part of the Central Committee of Union and Progress. The goal of pan-Turks was to Turkicize the minorities and to unite the Turkic people of Anatolia, Iran, Transcaucasia, Russia and Central Asia into a pan-Turkic empire. The idea gained more adherents following the departure of hundreds of thousands of Turkish refugees from the

Balkans during the 1908-1912 period. Turkish territorial losses in the Balkan wars and the declaration of independence by Albania ended the power of the remaining moderates and liberals in the government, and on January 23, 1913, a coup led by the ultranationalists gave dictatorial powers to a small group led by a triumvirate of Enver Pasha, as minister of War, Talaat Pasha, as minister of Interior, and Jemal Pasha, as the Military-Governor of Constantinople. Ignoring the provisions of the constitution, the new leadership ruthlessly suppressed all opposition.

The Genocide

Armenian leaders, fearful of these developments, and faced with the arrival of over 500,000 displaced and obviously anti-Christian *muhajirs,* or Muslim emigrants from the Balkans into western Armenia, once more began to look for outside assistance. In the meantime, however, the international political situation had changed drastically. In 1894 Russia made an alliance with France and in 1907 concluded an agreement with Britain by which they delineated zones of influence in Asia, thus forming the Triple Entente. The Central Powers, or the Germans, Austrians, and Italians, sought their own military and economic alliances against the Triple Entente. The Turks, having lost Britain, their traditional ally, looked toward Germany and were soon purchasing German arms, inviting German military advisors, concluding trade agreements, and planning the Baghdad-Berlin Railway.

By 1913, renewed Armenian political activity, as well as the tense international situation revived the Armenian Question, and Russia urged the powers to convene another conference. The Russian plan was to avoid another war. It had a number of provisions which put western Armenia under a non-Turkish governor, created a mixed police force, dissolved the *Hamidiye*, ended the settlement of Muslim immigrants from the Balkans in Armenian provinces, provided restitution for recent Armenian economic losses, and retained the revenues collected in Armenia for local projects, such as schools. Furthermore, it included Cilicia in this plan. Neither the Armenians nor Russia, however, advocated the separation of western Armenia from Ottoman Turkey.

German and Austrian objections, however, led to a number of compromises and by early 1914 an accord, accepted by the great powers, was signed by Russia and Turkey. The agreement included only a few of the original demands. Turkish Armenia was to be divided into two provinces, supervised by two neutral European governors-general, who would oversee the mixed police force and a number of administrative and fiscal reforms. Cilicia was not included in the plan. By the summer of 1914, Norwegian and Dutch governors had arrived in Turkey and Armenians, although disappointed, hoped that the long overdue reforms would finally be implemented in the six Armenian provinces. Even such mild reforms frightened the Turks, however, who saw in these reforms a gradual autonomy and eventual independence, as had occurred in the Balkan states.

Meanwhile, on the eve of World War One, a secret Turko-German alliance was negotiated with the understanding that the Germans would aid in the realization of the pan-Turanic dream. This meant that the Georgians, Russians, and especially the Armenians, the primary obstacle in uniting the Turkic peoples, had to be eliminated. Their elimination would also enable the Muslim emigrants from the Balkans, to settle in Armenian villages and to recoup whatever wealth they had abandoned in Eastern Europe. Moreover, the Turks felt that in order to create a Turkish bourgeoisie , the Armenian middle class had to be wiped out. Against a stern British warning, Turkey entered the war on the German side in fall of 1914. At the start of the war, Enver Pasha, as a first step in this plan, moved with a large army towards Transcaucasia and Iranian Azerbaijan. The winter campaign of 1914-1915 was a disaster for Enver, whose army suffered terrible losses on both fronts. He left the front and returned to the capital. To save face he blamed the Armenians in eastern Anatolia for his failure. The Central Committee now became very apprehensive about the Russian counteroffensive, which was surely to come after the winter thaw.

Immediately after the failed campaign, in February, Armenian soldiers were disarmed and relegated to work battalions. Armenian citizens, who had been permitted to carry arms following the 1908 revolution, were disarmed as well and many men were taken away to perform the most menial jobs in the army. In March the government decided to suppress or destroy the two main Armenian power centers, Zeitun and Van. The Armenians of Zeitun and a number of other towns in Cilicia were the first to be killed and deported. Although a few resisted and fled to the mountains, most of the population was driven to Deir el-Zor in the Syrian desert. Their property was immediately taken over by Muslim emigrants, mostly from Thrace and Bulgaria. The Armenians of Van province were next and by mid-April the Turks succeeded in killing or deporting most of the population of the province. The city of Van, with its 30,000 Armenian majority, was an exception, however. The Armenian quarter barricaded itself and, armed with a few weapons under the leadership of Aram Manukian and Armenak Erkanian, managed to

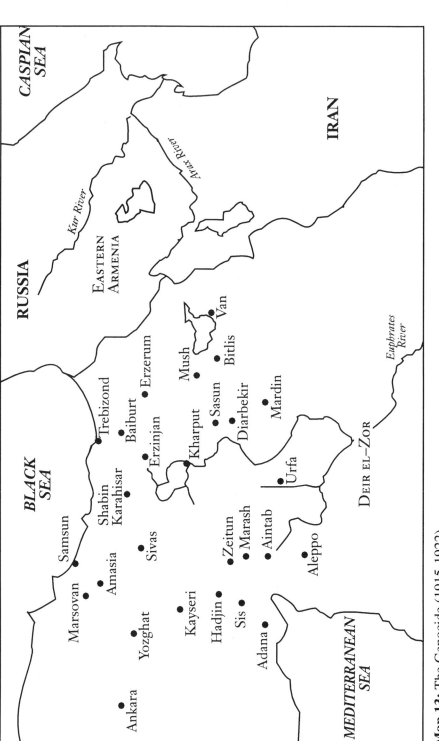

Map 13: The Genocide (1915-1922)

hold out until the arrival of Russian troops in mid-May 1915.

By the end of April the stage was set for the final solution to the Armenian Question. On the night of April 24, 1915, over two hundred Armenian writers, poets, newspaper editors, teachers, lawyers, members of parliament, and other community leaders in Constantinople were taken out from their homes at night and later killed. Among them were many of the writers who were born during or after the Armenian literary revival. By the end of the year, some 600 Armenian intellectuals and a few thousand workers had also been arrested and deported into the interior. One of the few noted Armenians to survive was the composer and folk song collector Komitas, who, after witnessing this catastrophe, suffered a breakdown from which he never recovered. Explicit orders were cabled to governors and military commanders of the six Armenian provinces to remove the Armenians by force from their ancestral homeland. The ethnic cleansing followed the same pattern in each province. First, all able-bodied men living in towns or villages were summoned to the municipal headquarters where they were held, or jailed for a short time. They were then taken out of town and shot. The old men, women, and children were then told that they had a few hours or days to leave for new locations. Although some were rounded up in churches which were then set on fire, the majority, guarded by special brigades composed of Turkish criminals and unemployed ruffians, were taken on long marches, where many died from lack of water, food, or exhaustion. Most of those who survived the march, died in the desert camps at Deir el-Zor. Women were raped and old men and boys were burned, maimed or beaten. Many young women were forcibly taken as wives or concubines by Kurds and Turks, and numerous children were also seized and brought up as Muslims. Suicides, torture, and murder decimated the ranks of the deportees who were being driven to Aleppo and Mosul. Few reached their destination, and according to most sources more than one million Armenians who lived in the six provinces perished. By 1916 the entire Armenian population of the regions of Van, Mush, Sasun, Bitlis, Erzinjan, Baiburt, Erzerum, Trebizond, Shabin Karahisar, Kharput, Sivas, Ankara, Diarbekir, Marsovan, Urfa, as well as Cilicia was eradicated (see map 13). Disarmed, outnumbered, surrounded, and without their able-bodied men, the Armenians went to their deaths with minimal resistance. A few individuals managed to fight back or to escape. The six Armenian villages perched on the side of Musa Dagh on the shores of the eastern Mediterranean, realizing the fate of their neighbors, decided to fight. They resisted the efforts of a large Turkish force for forty days and some 4,000 of them were eventually rescued by French ships. Their heroic stand was later immortalized by Franz Werfel in his novel *The Forty Days of Musa Dagh.*

Some Armenian Catholics and Protestants were shielded by missionaries, but a large number of them faced the same fate as their Apostolic brothers and sisters. The pleas of many foreign diplomats and missionaries, particularly the American ambassador Henry Morgenthau, who tried to intercede on behalf of the Armenians and to stop the carnage, were ignored. Although German and Austrian officials did not have a part in instigating the genocide, they were well aware of preparations for it and, although they witnessed or received news of the events, refused to do anything decisive about the matter (save for the German command in Smyrna). The Armenians of Constantinople and Smyrna were also included in the plan, but, except for the several thousand who were arrested early on, were spared primarily because of the presence of many European consulates and the intercession of American and German diplomats and military personnel. By the time it was over some 1.5 million people had lost their lives and the Armenian Question in eastern Anatolia had been resolved.

In comparing the Armenian genocide and the Holocaust of the Jews a few decades later, a number of common features appear. In both instances a dictatorial party was in control of the state and obedience to the state was an essential part of the national culture. Nationalism and racial homogeneity was advocated and the preparations for the elimination of specific minorities were coordinated, made in advance, and in secret. Deceptive methods were used to prevent resistance and officials who disagreed or hesitated were removed. Special brigades and committees were formed to supervise the plan and the military was used to carry out political decisions. Both Armenians and Jews were singled out as traitors and exploiters and their property was looted or confiscated. They both served as scapegoats for the failure of the dominant group. Medical experiments were carried out on both groups, although fewer Armenians were subjected to that horror. Both groups lost about sixty-five percent of their population. Revisionist historians have denied both events or have disputed and minimized the number of victims. A number of Turks and Kurds, like the "righteous gentiles," helped some Armenians to escape by warning, hiding, or letting them go. Those spared in both disasters suffered the guilt of the survivor and their literary responses were very similar. There are a number of differences, however. Due to technological advances, most European Jews were transported by train to the death camps and were killed in a highly organized fashion. The majority of Armenians were marched to their deaths, often naked, or left to die slowly in desert camps. More importantly, Armenians, unlike the Jews, were uprooted from their 3000-year old homeland. The present government of Germany, unlike that of Turkey, has acknowledged the Holocaust and has made attempts to pay reparations, impossible as that may be.

A handful of modern Turkish and American revisionist historians, adopting the official Turkish position, have denied the planned extermination of the Armenians, which was the first genocide of the twentieth century. They assert that Armenian political activities and especially the uprising in Van forced the state to remove the untrustworthy Armenians from the path of the advancing Russian army so that their treachery would not assist the enemy. There was no plan to exterminate the Armenians, they claim; rather they were simply being evacuated from the war zone. They also add that the Armenian population in Turkey, contrary to European and Armenian sources, was not slightly over 2 million, with more than half residing in western Armenia, but was somewhere around 1.3 million, with approximately 650,000 living in western Armenia. Finally, they add that although 300,000 Armenians perished at the hand of Kurds or died through unsanctioned actions of outlaws and hastily-organized deportations, most died from epidemics, lack of supplies, shelter, and other disasters of war, which killed more than two million Turks, some of whom were killed by Armenian armed bands.

Objective sources agree that only a minute percentage of Turkish Armenians offered any help to the Russians; the overwhelming majority remained loyal and some 100,000 enlisted or were drafted into the Turkish army. The revisionist historians ignore the facts that the deportations began earlier than the defense of Van and that Armenians from other regions, far from the war zone, were also deported and killed. The fact that the course of events was almost identical in each hamlet, village, or city in the Armenian provinces, irrefutably points to a well-organized plan. The revisionists also discount reports from German officials in Turkey, who clearly state that Enver Pasha's claim of only 300,000 Armenians dead was inaccurate and that the actual figure, according to their reports, was one million. There are thousands of official reports from American, Italian, and other neutral diplomats, as well as by the German and Austrian representatives, who were allies of the Turks. There are also Arab and even Turkish and Kurdish eyewitness accounts. Furthermore, accounts of various journalists, missionaries, and survivors makes the genocide undeniable. It is true that more Turks died during World War One, but they died as a result of war and not genocide. More Germans died in World War Two than did Jews, but of rather different causes, as well.

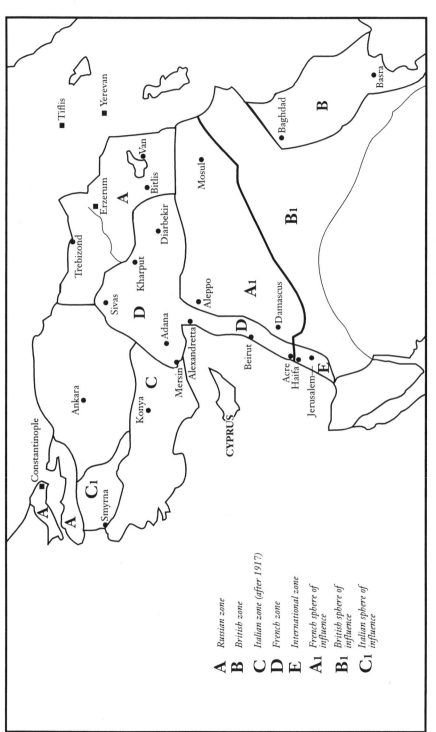

Map 14: The Sykes-Picot Plan for the Partition of the Ottoman Empire (1915-1916)

A   *Russian zone*
B   *British zone*
C   *Italian zone (after 1917)*
D   *French zone*
E   *International zone*
A1   *French sphere of influence*
B1   *British sphere of influence*
C1   *Italian sphere of influence*

By mid-1916 the Russian army had occupied most of western Armenia but there were almost no Armenians left there. Meanwhile, the Russian government, which had made an agreement for the future partition of Ottoman Turkey* (see map 14), changed its attitude towards the Armenians and western Armenia, and regarded the region as a military governorship where all lands and goods were to be used for the Russian army. Those Armenians who had escaped to Russia a year earlier were not permitted to return to their homes. The disbanding of Armenian volunteer units in the Russian army especially angered the Armenians. On a brighter note was the formation of the Armenian Legion, which was created in late 1916 from 600 Musa Dagh refugees. By 1917, volunteers from the Middle East, Europe, India, and the United States had enlarged the Legion into four battalions or 4,000 troops. The Armenian Legion fought well and was instrumental in the liberation of Palestine and Cilicia.

Armenian anger turned to hope when following the Revolution of February 1917, the Russian Provisional Government reversed the tsarist policy and not only allowed the repatriation of the Armenians but indicated that western Armenia would be administered as an autonomous region under Russian protection. Six months later, however, these hopes were dashed. Lenin, after the October Revolution, ordered the withdrawal of all Russian troops from Turkey and replaced them with an Armenian militia. As will be seen, the Treaty of Brest-Litovsk, signed between the Bolsheviks and Germany in early 1918, spelled doom for western Armenia.* Although the treaty involved the European front, the Turks pressured the Germans to include territorial gains for them as well. Not only was Russia to withdraw from the lands occupied during the war but it was forced to return Kars, Ardahan, and Batum, regions which Russia had gained in 1878. Lenin, wishing peace at any cost, agreed, and, although the Armenians insisted that the Bolshevik government did not represent the Russian Empire, the Turks advanced to occupy their territorial gains and by mid-April they had pushed the few thousand Armenian and Georgian volunteers back to the pre-1878 borders. In the meantime, civil war began in Russia, and Transcaucasia was left to its own fate.

*See chapter XIX.

IRAN & OTTOMAN EMPIRE	WESTERN & CENTRAL EUROPE	RUSSIA & EASTERN EUROPE	SOUTH & EAST ASIA	AFRICA & THE AMERICAS
Decline of Ottoman Empire accelerates (ca. 1800-1912)	Napoleon emperor (1804)	Annexation of Georgia (1801)	East India Co. in Singapore (1819)	Washington D.C. capital (1800)
Catholicos Arghutian (1800)	Tilsit Treaty (1807)	Alexander I (1801-25)	British take Burma (1824-26)	Jefferson president (1801-9)
Catholicos David (1801-7)	Napoleon abdicates (1814)	First Russo-Iranian War (1804-1813)	British take Mysore (1830)	Louisiana Purchase (1803)
Catholicos Daniel (1801-9)	Congress of Vienna (1814-15)	Gulistan Treaty (1813)	First Opium War (1839-42)	Slave importation prohibited (1808)
Muhammad ` Ali (1804-48)	Holy Alliance (1815)	Serbs gain partial autonomy (1817)	Hong Kong taken (1841)	Madison president (1809-17)
Hosein Qoli Khan (1807-27)	Metternich System (1815-48)	Nicholas I (1825-55)	Treaty of Nanking (1842)	Revolts against Spain in Latin America (1810-25)
Mahmud II (1808-39)	Troppau Confer. (1820-21)	Decembrist revolt (1825)	Treaty of Lahore (1846)	Treaty of Ghent (1814)
Catholicos Yeprem (1809-31)	Louis Philippe (1830-48)	Anglo-Russ. Treaty (1825)	Perry in Japan (1854)	Monroe president (1817-25)
End of Janissaries (1826)	Victoria (1837-1901)	Second Russo-Iranian War (1826-1828)	Treaty of Peshawar (1855)	Monroe Doctrine (1823)
Unkiar Skelessi Treaty (1833)	Communist Manifesto (1848)	Turkmenchai Treaty (1828)	Sepoy Mutiny (1857-58)	Adams president (1825-29)
Al-Afghani (1839-97)	Revolutions of 1848-49	Armenian Province (1828-40)	The British Raj (1858-1947)	Jackson president (1829-37)
Abdul-Mejid I (1839-61)	Franz Joseph I (1848-1916)	Russo-Turkish War (1828-29)	Treaty of Tientsin (1858)	Death of Bolivar (1830)
Tanzimat Era (1839-76)	Napoleon III (1852-70)	Adrianople Treaty (1829)	Treaty of Peking (1860)	Alamo (1836)
Straits Convention (1841)	Unification of Italy (1859-70)	Greece independ. (1829)	Shogunate ends (1868)	Van Buren president (1837-41)
Catholicos Nerses (1843-57)	Bismarck in power (1862-90)	Romania autonomous (1829)	Gandhi (1869-1948)	W. Harrison president (1841)
Nasr ad-Din Shah (1848-96)	First Socialist International (1864-1871)	Serbia autonomous (1830)	Compulsory military service in Japan (1872)	Tyler president (1841-45)
Anglo-Iranian War (1856-57)	Unification of Germany (1866-71)	Vorontsov viceroy of the Caucasus (1845-54)	Famine in Bengal (1873)	Polk president (1845-49)
Isma'il Pasha (1863-79)	Franco-Prussian War (1870-71)	Crimean War (1853-56)	Korea indep. (1876)	Liberia indep. (1847)
Young Ottomans formed (1865)	Vatican state est. (1871)	Alexander II (1855-81)	First Kaffir War (1877)	Taylor president (1849-50)
Suez Canal opens (1869)	Paris Commune (1871)	Peace of Paris (1856)	Satsuma revolt stopped (1877)	Fillmore president (1850-53)
Patriarch Khrimian (1869-73)	Third Republic (1871-1914)	Herzen's "Bell" (1857-1867)	Victoria procl. Empress of India (1877)	Pierce president (1853-57)
	Second Disraeli ministry (1874-1880)	Emancipation of serfs (1861)	Gandamak Treaty (1879)	Buchanan president (1857-61)
British control Suez (1875)	Second Gladstone ministry (1880-1885)	Sale of Alaska (1867)	First Indian National Congress meets (1886)	Lincoln president (1861-65)
Ottoman Constitution (1876)		Three Emperors' League (1872)		Civil War (1861-65)
Abdul-Hamid II (1876-1909)		Russo-Turkish War (1877-78)		

Table 4: 1800-1918

British occupy Egypt (1882)	Parnell imprisoned (1881-82)	San Stefano Treaty (1878)	Sino-Jap. War (1894)	French in Indochina (1887-1954)	Emancipation Proclamation (1863)
Armenakan party formed in Van (1885)	Congress on Africa (1884)	Populist movt. (1878-1884)		First general election in Japan (1890)	Gettysburg Address (1863)
Young Turks formed in Geneva (1891)	Boulanger Affair (1887-89)	Berlin Congress (1878)		Port Arthur leased to Russia (1898)	Arch. Maximillian (1863-67)
Catholicos Khrimian (1892-1907)	Kaiser William (1888-1918)	Bulgaria autonomous (1878)		Britain leases Kowloon (1898)	Johnson president (1865-69)
Union and Progress formed (1895)	Second Socialist International (1889-1914)	Alexander III (1881-94)		Boxer Rebellion (1900-1901)	13th Amendment (1865)
Armenian massacres (1895-96)	Suicide at Mayerling (1889)	Hnchak Party formed (1887)		Commonwealth of Australia (1900)	Dominion of Canada (1867)
Patriarch Ormanian (1896-1908)	Irish Home Rule rejected by Lords (1893)	Dashnak Party formed (1890)		Muslim League formed (1906)	Grant president (1869-77)
Crete revolt (1905)	Empress Elizabeth assassinat. (1898)	S. Witte (1892-1903, 1905-6)		"Open Door" agreement (1907)	Porfirio Diaz (1877-1911)
AGBU formed (1906)	First Hague Peace Conf. (1899)	Franco-Russ. Treaty (1893)		Japan annexes Korea (1910)	Hayes president (1877-81)
Iranian Revolution (1906)	King Umberto I assassinated (1900)	Nicholas II (1894-1917)		Chinese Republic (1911-49)	Scramble for Africa (1880-1900)
Young Turks move to Salonika (1906)	King Alexander and Queen Draga assassinated (1903)	Socialist Rev. Party (1901)			Garfield president (1881)
Turkish Revolution (1908)	Russ. Social Democratic Party split into Bolshevik and Menshevik factions (1903)	Trans-Siberian railroad completed (1903)			C. Arthur president (1881-85)
Sahmanadir Ramkavar Party formed (1908)	King Carlos I assass. (1908)	Anti-Armenian measures (1903-1905)			Gordon killed by Mahdi in Khartoum (1885)
Armenians massacred in Cilicia (1909)	Austria annexes Bosnia (1908)	Russo-Jap. War (1904-5)			Cleveland president(1885-89)
World War I (1914-1918)	Arch. Ferdinand assassinated in Sarajevo (1914)	Phleve assassinated (1904)			B. Harrison president (1889-93)
Armenian Genocide(1915-22)	World War I (1914-1918)	Revolution of 1905			Cleveland president (1893-97)
Sykes-Picot plan (1916)		Armeno-Azeri conflict (1905-7)			Hawaii annexed by US (1893)
Arab revolt (1916-1917)		Vorontsov-Dashkov viceroy of Caucasus (1905-16)			Spanish-American War (1898)
Balfour Declaration (1917)		First Duma (1906)			Boer War (1899-1902)
		Anglo-Russ. Accord (1907)			Sudan Convention (1899)
		World War I (1914-1917)			T. Roosevelt president (1901-1909)
		February Rev. (1917)			Taft president (1909-13)
		October Rev. (1917)			Wilson president (1913-21)
					Panama Canal opens (1914)
					US enters WW I (1917)

Table 4: 1800-1918. Continued

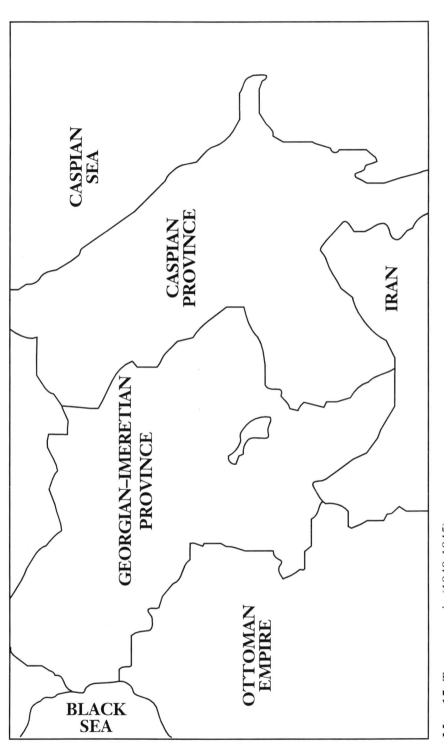

Map 15: Transcaucasia (1840-1845)

XIX

Subjects of the Tsar:
Armenians in Transcaucasia (1828-1918)

At the conclusion of the Second Russo-Iranian war, the Armenians hoped to establish an autonomous state under Russian protection. Tsar Nicholas I rejected the idea, but as a concession to Armenians and their supporters, the khanates of Yerevan and Nakhichevan were, for a short time (1828-1840) combined to form the Armenian Province (*Armianskaia oblast* or *Haikakan marz*, see map 11). The Armenians were soon disappointed, however, for Nicholas and his appointees in the Caucasus were conservatives who generally advocated Russifying the non-Russian areas of the empire and bringing them under the control of the central administration. In 1836 the Russians enacted a set of regulations known as the *Polozhenie*, which sought to oversee the affairs of the Armenian Church far more than the Iranians had ever attempted. A Russian procurator resided at Etchmiadzin to observe the activities of the Church. Whereas, in the past, the catholicos was chosen by Armenian clergy and lay representatives, under the *Polozhenie* they nominated two candidates, whose names were submitted to the tsar for final selection. The new catholicos would then swear allegiance to the tsar. Under the *Polozhenie*, however, the Armenian Church was recognized as a separate entity and retained a degree of autonomy denied the Georgian Church, which became subordinate to the Russian Orthodox Church. The Armenian clergy remained exempt from taxes and its property was secure. Moreover, the Holy See was given primacy over the Armenian dioceses in Georgia, eastern Caucasus, New Nakhichevan, Bessarabia, and Astrakhan. By 1840, the title of "Armenian Province" was offensive to Nicholas' sense of Russian nationalism and he abolished it. Eastern Armenia was now divided among the two new Transcaucasian provinces. The former territories of the khanates of

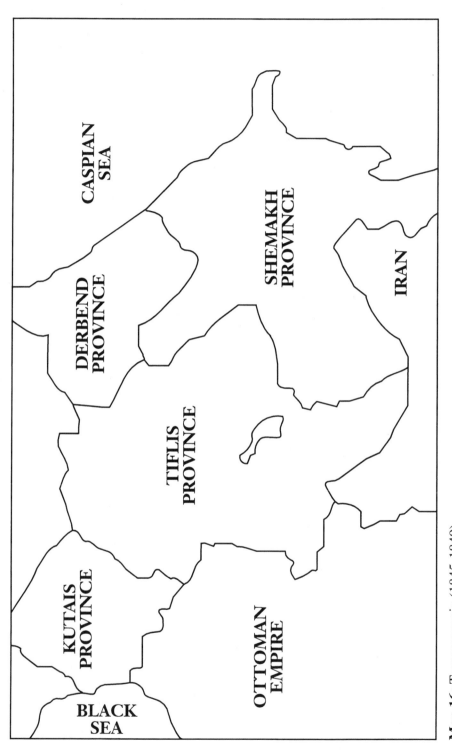

Map 16: Transcaucasia (1845-1849)

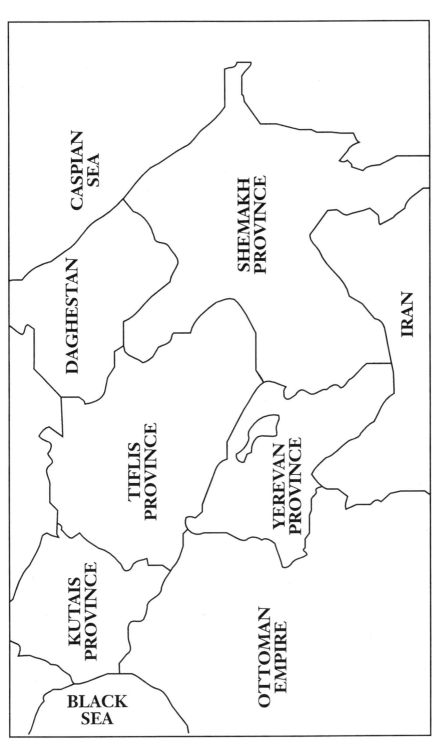

Map 17: Transcaucasia (1849-1868)

Yerevan, Nakhichevan, and Ganja became part of the Georgian-Imeretian Province, while Karabagh was included in the Caspian Province (see map 15).

Russian expansion in the nineteenth century added large territories and new ethnic populations to the empire. The main objective of the state was to incorporate these lands and to integrate its people into the Russian administration. The mountain tribes of the Caucasus continued to resist Russian occupation until 1859 and since the region was also a springboard for military campaigns against the Ottoman Turks, Russia appointed military men as the governors of Transcaucasia. Nicholas' administrators were divided into two broad groups, sometimes termed *regionalist* and *centralist*. While both advocated Russian rule, the regionalists were more sensitive to local traditions and hoped for a gradual transformation, while the centralists wanted a speedy Russification of all borderlands. Economically, the first group advocated improving the living conditions of the area, while the other urged its exploitation as a colony.

Socioeconomic Conditions and the Rise of the Armenian Middle Class

Initially, following the Russian conquest, socioeconomic conditions in eastern Armenia deteriorated. The new administration, unfamiliar with the region, relied heavily on Muslim officials and landlords. Trade declined and taxes were increased. Some Armenians even returned to Iran. The military importance of the Caucasus and the dissatisfaction with and hostility to the Russian administration on the part of the native population, eventually prompted the tsar to appoint a more capable and sensitive man as the first viceroy of the Caucasus. Count Michael Vorontsov arrived in 1845 and in his nine-year tenure managed to befriend the Georgians, Armenians, and even most Muslims. Realizing that the random territorial divisions had caused dissatisfaction, and in order to establish better control, he partitioned Transcaucasia into four smaller provinces: Kutais, Shemakh, Tiflis, and Derbend. These provinces were then subdivided into counties and districts. Most of eastern Armenia fell within the Tiflis Province (see map 16).

Vorontsov lowered tariffs and permitted European commerce to transit through Transcaucasia. Appreciating the Armenian expertise in trade, he granted their merchants and craftsmen special privileges. Armenian businessmen were classified as "respected citizens of the empire." They were exempted from military service, corporal punishment, and a number of taxes. To better gain the favor of Armenians, Vorontsov, in 1849, detached the regions of Yerevan and Nakhichevan (or the territory of the former Armenian Province) and created a fifth province, the Yerevan Province (see map 17).

Vorontsov's successors continued to reorganize Transcaucasia. In 1862 the Shemakh Province was renamed Baku Province and Derbend became the Daghestan Province. The Armenian district of Lori was severed from the Yerevan Province and became attached to the Tiflis Province. In 1868 a new province, Elizavetpol, was formed by taking lands away from the Baku, Yerevan, and Tiflis Provinces. Karabagh and Zangezur, as well as Ganja became part of the Elizavetpol Province (see map 18). In 1875, a minor change resulted in redistricting the Yerevan Province into seven districts. Following the Russo-Turkish war of 1877-1878, the Russians created two more provinces from western Armenian and western Georgian territories conquered from the Turks. The Batum and Kars Provinces were thus added to the Transcaucasian administration. The final change occurred in 1880 when a new district, the Borchalu, was created within the Tiflis Province (see map 19). The result of this shifting was that some provinces and districts had a mixed Georgian, Armenian, and Turko-Tatar population, a situation which was to have dire consequences in the twentieth century.

The arrival of thousands of Armenian immigrants, the policies of Vorontsov, and the industrialization of some of Transcaucasia's urban centers, created an environment in which the Armenians, with their commercial contacts and talents, performed far better than their Georgian or Turko-Tatar neighbors. In addition, Russian conquests had brought the Armenian communities in the Crimea, Poland, Bessarabia, Russia, Georgia, and eastern Armenia, including the Holy See of Etchmiadzin, under a single state. By the second half of the nineteenth century, an Armenian middle class had emerged and by the end of that century, Armenian tradesmen dominated Tiflis, Baku, Elizavetpol, and other urban centers of Transcaucasia. Like the Armenians in Constantinople, the urban Armenians became the most loyal subjects of the state. Unlike the Armenians in Turkey, however, the urban Armenians of Russia began to view Russian culture as somewhat superior to their own.

More than half of the Armenians of Transcaucasia, however, did not participate in the economic benefits of Russian rule. For the Armenian peasants, life remained much the same as before, with taxes and duties taking away most of their produce. As in Ottoman Turkey, class differences between urban and rural Armenians were pronounced. Until 1870, the peasants were serfs and much of their land was recognized as the hereditary property of local Muslim and Christian landlords, or belonged to the Church, which,

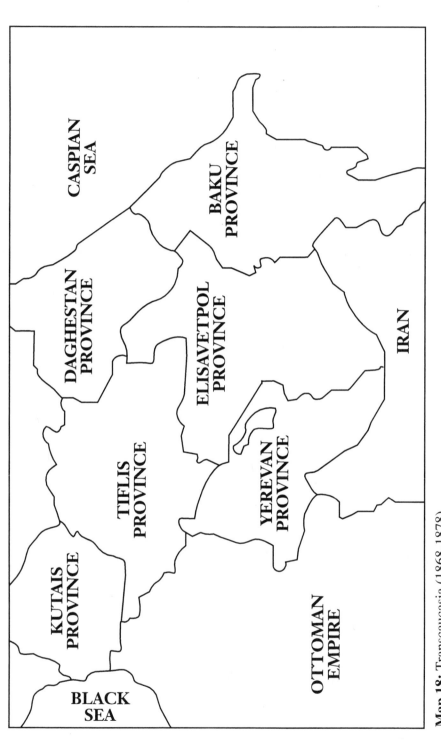

Map 18: Transcaucasia (1868-1878)

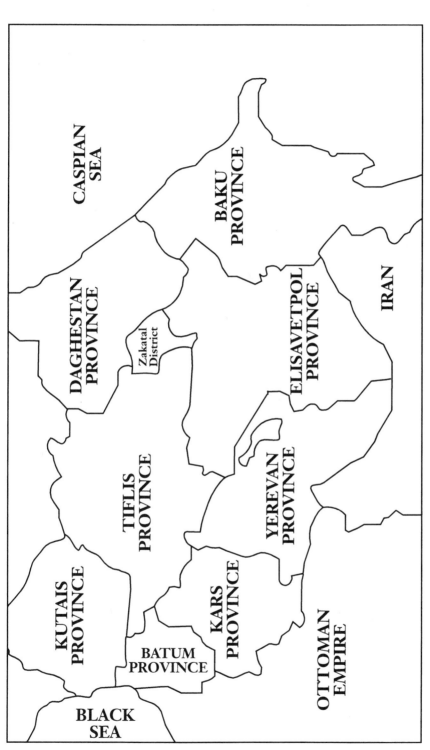

Map 19: Transcaucasia (1878-1918)

together with the state, was the largest landowner. The land reform of 1870 did not significantly alter these conditions. Although the peasants were permitted to own land, they had to purchase it from their landlords. Most peasants were too poor to do so and, therefore, there was little improvement in the life of the peasants during the imperial regime.

Immigration from western Armenia and the Russian annexation of Kars and Ardahan, as well as improved economic conditions, resulted in the increase of the Armenian population from half a million in 1840, to over one million in 1897, and slightly under two million in 1917. The Muslims continued to remain a majority in the cities of Nakhichevan and Ordubad. Yerevan only achieved an Armenian majority prior to the first World War. In all the other urban centers of the Yerevan province, Armenians held a solid majority, however. Although the cities of Yerevan and Alexandropol (later Leninakan, present-day Gumri) and the region of Alaverdi attracted some entrepreneurs, who established the wine and cognac industry, foreign trade, and copper mines, the Armenian middle class was concentrated, not in the few urban centers of eastern Armenia, but in Tiflis and Baku. Tiflis was the center of the Russian administration of the Caucasus and the Armenians formed the largest ethnic group there. Their middle class dominated trade, banking, bureaucracy, and crafts. Armenian artists, like Hakob Hovnatanian (1806-1881) painted numerous portraits of the Russian, Georgian, and Armenian elite of Tiflis. Armenian families with Russified surnames like Tumanovs, Gevorkovs, and Yegiazarov controlled the leather, tobacco, and textile industries. The mayor of the city and most of the city council was Armenian. It was Baku, however, that attracted new Armenian entrepreneurs. Besides the lure of its trans-Caspian trade with Iran, Central Asia, and Russia, Baku's oil deposits were among the largest in the world. By the twentieth century, Armenian magnates, led by Mantashev, owned thirty percent of the oil in Baku. While the Armenians rose to dominate bureaucracy, banking and industry, the Georgian nobility declined and fell into debt and the Muslim khans lost their political advantages. The differences among the ethnic groups created hostility and envy against the Armenians on the part of their Georgian and especially their Muslim neighbors.

The Armenian Cultural Revival

Urban Russian Armenians, like their counterparts in the Ottoman Empire, were among the first minorities to take advantage of the European influences which had entered Russia during the reign of Catherine the Great and

Alexander I. An Armenian printing press was established in St. Petersburg in 1780 and a number of European classics were translated at the end of the eighteenth century. By the second decade of the nineteenth century, Armenians had opened schools in New Nakhichevan and Astrakhan. The famous Lazarev Institute in Moscow, founded in 1815, had a renowned library and its own press. It concentrated on the study of Eastern languages and cultures, including Armenian, and educated a number of future Armenian intellectuals. Armenians enrolled in Russian and European academies and a number of them, such as the painter Aivazovsky (1817-1900) achieved great fame. Following the annexation of Georgia, the state opened a Russian school and a Russian Orthodox seminary in Tiflis. This prompted the Armenian Holy See, in 1813, to open a seminary in Etchmiadzin, which, by the end of the century, was transformed into the famous Gevorkian Academy. In 1824 Archbishop Nerses of Ashtarak, who was instrumental in establishing the seminary at Etchmiadzin and who had left for Tiflis to organize the liberation of the remainder of eastern Armenia, opened the Nersessian Academy, which became the main Armenian educational center in Transcaucasia. By the mid-nineteenth century, Armenians had some two dozen schools and a number of presses, including one in Karabagh.

The more liberal reign of Alexander II created new opportunities and enabled urban Armenians to come into contact with political and social developments in Europe and Russia. Like their counterparts in the Ottoman Turkey, a number of Armenian intellectuals sought to educate and to create a sense of nationality among their people. Armenian educators in eastern Armenia, however, faced the same problems and pressures their counterparts were experiencing in western Armenia. Church leaders tried to control the schools and the curriculum. In addition, some Russian officials were suspicious and tried to limit the influence of the West. The better educated, younger or married priests and lay instructors clashed with the establishment when they tried to replace faith and obedience to traditions with reason, science, modern literature, and new ideas about Armenian history. Nevertheless, during the next fifty years this younger generation succeeded in establishing in Russia some 500 schools with 20,000 students and some 1,000 teachers.

The immediate concern of the Russian Armenian intellectuals was the same as those in Ottoman Turkey: how to best educate and reach the majority of their people. A primary stumbling block was that the Church continued to use *grabar,* the classical Armenian language in all liturgical services and insisted on its use in all Armenian publications. A number of young teachers and journalists felt that Armenians were in need of a living literary language. Like the Armenians in the Ottoman Turkey, the Armenians of Russia decided to adopt a modern standardized means of expression.

Stepan Nazariants (1812-1879) was one of the earliest authors to write in the modern dialect. Khachatur Abovian (1805-1848) and Gabriel Patkanian's (1802-1889) entire literary output was in the vernacular, or *ashkharhabar,* dialect spoken in the Araratian region. Their efforts and those of their students eventually created the modern eastern Armenian literary language used today by the Armenians in Russia, Transcaucasia, and Iran. Abovian had studied at the University of Dorpat (present-day Tartu, Estonia) and returned to Armenia to become a teacher. His novel, *Wounds of Armenia* (*Verk Hayastani*) was a patriotic work which glorified the Armenian language and lamented the foreign domination of his native land. He clashed with both conservative Armenian priests and Russian officials, and mysteriously disappeared in 1848. Patkanian had been educated in Tiflis by his father, who himself had been educated in Venice by the Mekhitarians. The family moved to Astrakhan where his father taught at the Armenian school. After attending a Russian school, where he learned Russian and French, Patkanian taught at a number of schools in New Nakhichevan and in the Crimea, where he was ordained as a priest. He clashed with the conservative clergy and was exiled to a monastery. In 1846 he was permitted to teach at the Nersessian Academy where he also helped to publish the newspaper *Caucasus* (*Kovkas*). The newspaper, written in classical Armenian, emulated the Russian paper *Kavkaz,* also published in Tiflis. *Kovkas* had historical and biographical articles, as well as translations of European popular novels. By 1850, Patkanian published *Ararat,* the first newspaper in modern eastern Armenian, which was soon closed due to pressure from the Church, as well as the suspicions of the Russian censors.

Abovian's and especially Patkanian's influence and teachings were handed down to a new generation, among whom were Gabriel's son Raphael Patkanian (known by the pen-name Gamar Katipa, 1830-1892) and Gabriel's student Mikayael Nalbandian (1829-1866). Nalbandian studied theology, as well as Russian and Western languages and literature at the school run by Gabriel Patkanian in New Nakhichevan. He defended his teacher against Church leaders, and for this was forced to go to Moscow. He studied at the Lazarev Institute and Moscow University. The considerable lifting of censorship under Tsar Alexander II, allowed Nalbandian and his friend Stepan Nazariants to publish *Aurora Borealis*, a secular and anti-clerical newspaper, in 1858. Extremely anti-Catholic, Nalbandian even criticized the Mekhitarians and their influence on the Armenian cultural revival. He, and Stepan Vosgan (1825-1901) were the first Armenian intellectuals who were truly affected by the European revolutions of 1848 and who advocated that the Armenian national revival should not be dominated by the Church. Modern national schools, they felt, should be founded to educate those who truly constituted the nation, the common people. Towards the end of his life, Nalbandian visited London, where he met and was influenced by Russian socialists. He was arrested upon his return, exiled to southwestern Russia, and died in 1866.

Although in 1869 a small group of Armenian liberals in Alexandropol formed a society for the liberation of their homeland, Tiflis continued to remain the center of Armenian intellectual activity. Armenian conservatives, under the leadership of the director of the Nersessian Academy, Petros Simonian, published the newspaper *The Bee of Armenia*, which supported the traditional role of the Church as leader of the community. The majority of the Westernized Transcaucasian Armenians, however, embraced the newspaper *The Tiller* (*Mshak*), founded in 1872 by Grigor Artsruni (1845-1892). Artsruni and the editors of a number of other liberal Armenian newspapers in Russia pointed out that Russian rule had not only enabled a cultural revival but had provided the Armenians socioeconomic growth and security from invasion. An Armenian bourgeoisie, they added, had emerged and their children had the opportunity to study in Russia or abroad, join the Russian officer corps, or take part in the administration of the empire.

Armenian Populism, Socialism and Nationalism

Unlike the Armenian intelligentsia in Ottoman Turkey who had studied in Italy, Switzerland, and France and who were influenced by the French revolution, the philosophical ideas of Utopian socialists, and the Greek and Italian uprisings, Armenians in Russia had studied in Berlin, Leipzig, and St. Petersburg. They, together with the Russian intellectuals, were influenced more by German philosophical ideas. The Russian, and later the Georgian, intellectuals and revolutionaries, however, who were living on their ancestral land, gravitated more toward socialism, while the Armenians, scattered in numerous diasporas and, with most of their homeland and half of their people remaining under oppressive Turkish rule, leaned towards nationalism.

During the second half of the nineteenth century, eastern Armenian novelists and poets began to emulate the romanticism of the Western writers by glorifying patriotism, justice, and freedom. The novels of Raffi (Hakob

Melik-Hakobian, 1832-1888), Berj Proshiants (1837-1907), Mouratsan (1854-1908), Alexander Shirvanzade (1858-1935), Avetis Aharonian (1866-1948), and the poems of Raphael Patkanian and Smbat Shahaziz (1841-1901) stirred the younger Armenian generation. Like their counterparts in the Balkans, Poland, and Bohemia, they too adopted the concept of rebellion and resistance to foreign domination.

By 1880s Russian Populist ideas of going out among and learning more about the common people, and at the same time educating them and inspiring them with revolutionary ardor, reached Transcaucasia as well. Armenian intellectuals realized that conditions for their fellow Armenians living in eastern Anatolia were far worse than any hardships experienced in Russia. They realized, too, that the Armenians of Constantinople and Smyrna were too far removed from eastern Anatolia, and, like the Armenian grandees in Baku and Tiflis, had become too cosmopolitan. Like the Russian Populists, these young Armenians felt responsible for their fellow Armenians who suffered so close to them across the border. Giving the motto of the Russian Populists, who advocated "Going to the People," a nationalist turn, the Armenians, adopted the motto of *depi erkire* or "Going to the Homeland."

Armenian Populists did not adopt the peasant socialism, nor the revolutionary and later terrorist activities of the Russian Populists. Unlike their Russian counterparts, they were willing to accept Russian absolutism if it provided for the liberation of western Armenia. During the Crimean War Armenian volunteer units had joined the Russian army and Armenian officers like Bebutov and Loris-Melikov had performed heroically. The Russian occupation of a segment of western Armenia during that war had raised the hope that all of Armenia would be soon under Russian rule. The Russian withdrawal from western Armenia after the Peace of Paris had not diminished that hope. Twenty one years later, Russia, as we have seen, nullified the humiliating Treaty of Paris and embarked on the third and last Russo-Turkish war of the nineteenth century. Armenian generals Loris-Melikov, Ter-Gukasov, and Lazarev led the Russian armies into western Armenia. Since the Armenians of Transcaucasia were not subject to the draft until 1887, they once again volunteered and fought alongside the Russians to liberate their homeland. The Armenian volunteers felt that they were finally doing something for their people. By 1878 almost all of western Armenia was in Russian hands and Armenians once more began to imagine a united Armenia under Russian protection. During the peace negotiations, eastern and western Armenian religious, military, and business leaders and their Russian supporters used whatever influence they had to include the fate of the western Armenians in the final treaty.

As we have seen, article 16 of the Treaty of San Stefano stated that Russian troops would remain in western Armenia until the political reforms promised by the *tanzimat* were implemented there. Although article 61 of the Berlin Treaty dampened Armenian aspirations, it did allow Russia to annex a chunk of western Armenia and brought some 100,000 Armenians into the Russian Empire. Ignoring the assurances of European diplomats, more than 20,000 additional Armenians left Van, Bitlis, and Erzerum with the evacuating Russian army. Despite the Russian withdrawal from the rest of western Armenia, eastern Armenians saw Loris-Melikov's appointment as primeminister of the empire as further assurance that, in time, Russia would succeed in liberating the remainder of historic Armenia.

The assassination of Alexander II brought major changes to Transcaucasia. Alexander III engaged in a policy of Russification and active persecution of non-Russian nationalities. The Russian administration in Transcaucasia decided to target the Armenians. The successful Armenian middle class dominated the urban centers. The economic and, to some extent, the political power of the wealthy merchants and industrialists had created an Armenian elite which was envied and resented by the Russians, Georgians and Turko-Tatars of the region. In 1885 all Armenian schools were closed and replaced by Russian schools. When the Armenians began to organize underground classrooms, the government reopened the schools, but replaced many of the teachers, and Russified the curriculum.

The actions of the Russian government drove some Armenians to imitate Russian revolutionaries and adopt socialism and even anarchism. Six Armenians gathered in Geneva and in 1887 established the Hnchakian Revolutionary Party, later renamed the Social Democrat (Marxist) Hnchakian Party. They published a newspaper, *Hnchak* (Bell), a title borrowed from the Russian Social Democratic newspaper *Kolokol* (Bell) printed in Europe. Led by Avetis Nazarbekian and his fiancee Maro Vardanian, the party advocated an independent and socialist Armenia, to be gained through armed struggle. This state would then become part of the future socialist world society.

The Armenians in Russia, in the meantime, were not idle. Revolutionary circles formed in Yerevan, Karabagh, Moscow, St. Petersburg, and Tiflis. The latter became a major center of Armenian revolutionary activities when, under the leadership of Kristapor Mikayelian, it formed a revolutionary organization called *Young Armenia* and recruited members in Iran and Ottoman Turkey. By 1890, the Armenian revolutionaries decided to create an organization which would unify all Armenian revolutionaries, including the Armenakans and the Hnchaks, into a single political party, with socialism-nationalism as its main platform. Under the leadership of Mikayelian, Simon Zavarian, and Stepan Zorian they formed the Federation of Armenian Revolutionaries (*Hai Heghapokhaganneri Dashnaktsutiun*) in Tiflis. The Federation, from the very start, faced arguments between its socialist and nationalist factions. The Tiflis leadership was not sufficiently socialist to satisfy the Hnchak founders in Geneva, while the Geneva group was viewed as being more concerned with the success of international socialism than with the liberation of western Armenia.

The Hnchaks tried to recruit members in Russia and Turkey but could attract large numbers only in the more Europeanized circles of Constantinople and Cilicia. Most Armenians did not understand socialism and felt that its ideas could not be put into practice. Populist and nationalist slogans were closer to their heart. A number of compromises were sought, but by 1891 the Hnchak leadership in Geneva, feeling isolated, claimed that they had not agreed to an official union and went their own way. Following the massacres of 1895-96, the Hnchaks themselves split into radical and reformed (moderate) wings. The radical Hnchaks joined the struggle for the proletariat and the world revolution, and attracted members in the urban centers of the Ottoman and Russian empires, as well as in Europe and the United States. The reformed Hnchaks continued their populist orientation. Some of them were eventually absorbed into the Dashnaktsutiun, which, by subordinating socialism to national issues, managed to unite most Armenians and, despite some divisions involving the degree of socialism of the party, emerged as the most influential Armenian political party. The remaining reformed Hnchaks later joined the Ramkavars.

In 1892, in Tiflis, the Dashnaktsutiun, renamed the Armenian Revolutionary Federation (*Hai Heghapokhagan Dashnaktsutiun*), adopted a platform which called for the creation of a freely-elected government; equality of all ethnic and religious groups; freedom of speech, press and assembly; the distribution of land to landless peasants; taxation based on ability to pay; equal conscription; compulsory education; security of life and the right to work. The party would defend Armenians by arming the population, creating fighting units, conducting propaganda and espionage, and by killing corrupt officials, traitors, and exploiters. The Dashnak's program, in many ways, resembled the People's Will faction of the Russian Populist movement. Ironically, while the Marxist Hnchaks called for an independent western Armenia (and eventually eastern Armenia), the more nationalist Dashnaks and their newspaper *Flag (Droshak)* advocated autonomy within the framework of Ottoman Turkey.

At the start of the twentieth century there were over one million Armenians in Transcaucasia. Half of them were peasants who lived in the Yerevan province. There were also tens of thousands of Armenians who worked in the oil fields and factories of Baku, Tiflis, and other urban centers. Although the Russian Social Democratic Labor Party had succeeded in recruiting Russian, Georgian and even a few Muslim intellectuals and workers to form Marxist circles and to strike, they had attracted only a handful of Armenians. The Armenian Marxists were soon divided into those who, like Stepan Shahumian, joined the multinational Caucasian Union, followed orthodox Marxism and preached class struggle, and those who formed their own Armenian Social Democratic Workers Organization, referred to *specifist,* for it maintained that the Armenian situation was different from that of the rest of the workers in Russia. It required specific consideration of a national and cultural self-determination within the Marxist movement.

The split of the Russian Social Democrats into Menshevik and Bolshevik factions, in 1903, affected the Armenian Marxists as well. Some, like Shahumian, followed the Bolshevik path, others agreed with Menshevik ideas, yet others formed separate socialist circles. A small number of Armenians also joined the Socialist Revolutionary Party, a populist group which, like the Dashnaks, called for the socialization of the land. Unlike the Georgian intelligentsia, who overwhelmingly adopted Menshevik ideas, the majority of Armenians in Russia followed the Dashnak party.

The Armenian Church Crisis and the Armeno-Azeri Conflict (1903-1907)

Although the Dashnak platform advocated revolution and terror, it was against the overthrow of the Russian state and forbade attacking or killing Russian officials. A strong Russia was necessary if it was to aid in the liberation of western Armenia. Events in the first decade of the twentieth century, however, forced the Dashnaks to change their tactics and for the first time to actively oppose the Russian state. On June 12, 1903 Tsar Nicholas II, following the advice of Prince Golitsyn, the Governor-General of the Caucasus, abrogated the *Polozhenie* of 1836 and ordered the confiscation of Armenian Church property and the transfer of its schools to Russian jurisdiction. Golitsyn had accurately surmised that by removing the Church and the schools from Armenian control, Russification could progress more swiftly and the Armenian revolutionaries would lose their strength. The decree, in fact, had the opposite effect. Armenians united behind their Church, and citizens, who had remained outside the political and revolutionary activities, joined the Committee for Central Defense organized by the Dashnaktsutiun. Most other Armenian political parties joined the Committee as well. The Dashnaktsutiun revised its policy, adopted a more socialist outlook, and pledged to defend Armenian rights against the tsarist state. Catholicos Khrimian of Van (Mkrtich I, known as Khrimian Hairik, 1892-1906), a product of Armenian awakening in Ottoman Turkey, backed the Committee and refused to accept the decree.

The next two years witnessed violent demonstrations, strikes, and various acts of terrorism by Armenians which killed, maimed, or wounded hundreds of Russian officials, including Golitsyn, who was stabbed by three Hnchaks.

On January 9, 1905 there occurred in Russia an event which changed the entire picture. A large group of Russians gathered peacefully in front of the Winter Palace in St. Petersburg to petition the tsar to alleviate their unbearable economic conditions. They were fired upon and many died or were wounded. "Bloody Sunday"' as the event came to be known, began the 1905 revolution which, combined with losses in the Russo-Japanese War (1904-1905) and the general economic depression, spread the revolt to every corner of Russia. Faced with a dangerous situation, the tsar promised the creation of a *Duma* (representative legislature) and to initiate reforms. He also appointed Count Vorontsov-Dashkov (1837-1916), an astute and tactful man, and a relative of the first viceroy, to govern Transcaucasia. In August 1905 the tsar not only rescinded the decree of 1903, but expressed special affection for his Armenian subjects. The Armenian leaders immediately voiced their total support for the tsar and the viceroy. Both the Armenian activists and the Dashnaktsutiun had scored a major victory.

The revolution begun in 1905, however, continued its course for another two years. Fearful that the embers of the revolt would spread into Transcaucasia, some Russian officials, in order to distract the Caucasians from the political upheavals in Russia, provoked ethnic and religious conflicts in the region. Socioeconomic hostilities already existed there, and the Armenians, as noted, were envied by the less prosperous Georgian and Turko-Tatar population. By that time the Georgians had established their own socialist and nationalist parties. The Turko-Tatar population, which was at the lower end of the socioeconomic scale, and which angrily referred to itself as "soulless" (*bijanli*), had also awakened politically, and, influenced by progressive and nationalist ideas among the Russian Tatars, Iranians, and the Ottoman Turks, sought to establish an identity. On the eve of the new century, pan-Islamic and pan-Turkic ideas began to gain some adherents among the Muslims of Transcaucasia. Although a number of intellectuals favored religious ties to Shi`i Iran, most felt closer to Turkey. Some of their leaders adopted the term *Azerbaijani Turk,* the name of the people in neighboring Iranian Azerbaijan who spoke the same dialect. A decade later they would declare themselves independent and refer to the lands on which they lived, as Azerbaijan.

Russian administrative divisions, as we have seen, created combined pockets of Armenian and Azeri populations in a number of counties and districts. Encouraged by some Russian officials, spurred by age-old religious and ethnic conflicts, and angered by the economic disparity between them, the charged situation in Russia erupted into civil war between the Armenians and Azeris. The war lasted two years. The Russian army did not intervene to end the conflict until 1907, when the first Russian revolution had finally ran its course. Although the war caused thousands of casualties and much property damage on both sides, it had taught the Armenians that they need not always be victims. They were good fighters and the Muslims were not invincible. The Azeris, in the meantime, had gained a national consciousness.

The creation of the Russian Duma gave voice to another Armenian political group. Since the Dashnaks and Hnchaks had boycotted the elections, the four Armenians who were elected to the parliament were not members of any political party, but represented the liberal middle class elements of Tiflis, who had made peace with the tsarist officials and had totally rejected the revolutionaries. The Armenians in the First Duma were thus identified with the Russian Liberal Kadet party. By 1907, the tsar felt strong enough to dissolve the Duma. The Second Duma had five Armenian members all from the Dashnak and Hnchak parties. The Dashnaks had resolved their arguments and had adopted a more explicit socialist platform, and, in 1907, had joined the Second Socialist International. All five Armenian delegates voted with the other radical members of the Second Duma, which was dissolved the same year it convened. The tsar then changed the election law to favor the supporters of the regime. By the Third and Fourth Duma (1907 and 1912), only one representative from each national group was permitted to sit in the parliament. Hovhannes Saghatelian, a Dashnak, was elected by the Armenians both times.

Armenian revolutionaries lost their initiative after 1907. The minister of the tsar, Stolypin, and the secret police began to arrest suspect political leaders. Many were jailed until 1912, when conditions eased and they were finally brought to trial. Defended by Kerensky, the future premier of Russia, most were freed and others received light sentences. Meanwhile the majority of

Armenians had come to the conclusion that Russia was their only hope for the liberation of western Armenia. Vorontsov-Dashkov felt that he could use the Armenian middle class to pacify the region and assure its loyalty. Catholicos Gevorg V (1911-1930) petitioned the tsar not to ignore the fate of the Armenians in Ottoman Turkey. As Turkey moved closer to Germany, Russia, as we have seen, renewed its demands for implementations of reforms in western Armenia.

The outbreak of World War One created great hopes for the Armenians. Assured by the tsar, the viceroy, and the catholicos, they looked forward to the liberation of their homeland. Some 150,000 Armenians, or approximately 10 percent of the Armenians of Transcaucasia, joined the Russian armies. Since the majority of the Russian Armenians were dispatched to the European front, Vorontsov-Dashkov, with the help of the Church and community activists led by Alexander Khatisian, the Armenian mayor of Tiflis, recruited four units from among the Armenian immigrants from Turkey and a small group of Transcaucasian Armenians who were not drafted. The units were led by popular commanders such as Andranik, Dro, and Keri. A few months later, volunteers from Europe, Russia, and the United States created three more units.

In January 1915, the Russian army and the Armenian volunteers defeated the large Turkish army led by Enver Pasha and advanced into Anatolia. Although by June 1916 Russia had conquered western Armenia, the Armenian genocide, as we have seen, had left the region empty of its native inhabitants. International agreements, in the meantime, had altered the Russian attitude toward the Armenians.

The Sykes-Picot plan partitioned the Ottoman Empire among Britain, France, and later, Russia. Britain was to get most of the Arab lands, France was to control the regions of Lebanon, present-day Syria, Cilicia, and half of western Armenia. Russia was to receive the province of Trebizond, the rest of western Armenia, and Constantinople (see map 14). Not only was Vorontsov-Dashkov replaced, but the Armenian press was suppressed, Turkish Armenian refugees forbidden to return home, and the Armenian volunteer units made part of the Russian army.

Meanwhile, the Russian army were not successful in Europe. By February 1917, severe Russian defeats and a shortage of food resulted in another Russian revolution. The Provisional Government was soon led by Kerensky and Armenians, as we have seen, were assured that the new regime would create an autonomous Armenia under Russian protection. To show its good intentions, the new government began to redraw the map of Transcaucasia.

Districts with large Armenian concentrations, such as Karabagh, would be included in a new Armenian Province. The new representative government also permitted the return of some 150,000 Armenian refugees to rebuild their lives in western Armenia. The administration of Transcaucasia was also transferred to a committee of Armenians, Georgians, and Azeris.

Continued Russian losses and the defeatist propaganda of the Bolsheviks was of grave concern to the Armenians, who knew that a Russian withdrawal from western Armenia would bring Turkish armies to eastern Armenia. Armenian leaders in Transcaucasia, therefore, convened an assembly in Tiflis. Following the example of their Russian counterparts, the few Armenian Bolsheviks boycotted the assembly. Although the Dashnaks had the majority of delegates, the newly-formed Armenian People's Party (*Hai zhoghovrdakan kusaktsutiun*), a populist party which had replaced the Kadets as representatives of the Armenian liberal middle classes of Transcaucasia, had the second largest number of delegates. The Hnchaks, Socialist Revolutionaries, and nonpartisans had only a handful of representatives. A National Council led by Avetis Aharonian of the Dashnaktsutiun was formed, which, realizing the dangerous situation caused by Bolshevik activity urged the Provisional Government to expedite the release of the Armenian troops fighting in Europe so that they could return to Transcaucasia.

The October Revolution (October 25, by the Julian calendar, November 7 by the Gregorian calendar), ended the Russian representative government and replaced it with Bolshevik Commissars. Except for Baku, which was controlled by a Bolshevik Commune, chaired by Stepan Shahumian, the rest of Transcaucasia refused to recognize the new government. Instead they formed a federation with its own executive (*Commissariat)* and legislative body (*Seim*) composed of Georgians, Azeris, and Armenians. Although some of the Georgian and Azeri members contemplated the creation of a separate state, Armenians believed that the restoration of a democratic Russia was their only salvation. They were proved right, for by the end of 1917 the Bolsheviks removed the Russian army from Turkish Armenia and began negotiating for a separate peace with Germany. With the Russian armies gone, Armenian troops and volunteers, led by commanders such as Tomas Nazarbekian, Andranik, and Dro, together with a small Georgian force, were left to defend the front.

Knowing that the Azeris would not defend Armenian or Georgian territory, and wanting to test the commitment of the federation's members to defend each other, the Turks proposed to negotiate a peace. They soon found out that the Georgians were willing to sacrifice western Armenia, as long as their territory was not threatened. Outvoted and alone, the Armenians were forced to accept this compromise. A delegation composed of Georgians, Armenians, and Azeris departed for Trebizond to negotiate the handing over of western Armenia. Meanwhile, as we have seen, the Russians signed the peace treaty of Brest-Litovsk which gave up all of western Armenia, including the regions annexed to Russia after the Berlin Congress, to the Turks. Once in Trebizond, the Georgians and the Armenians now realized that by the treaty of Brest-Litovsk, the Bolsheviks had given away the Russian gains of 1878 and that the Turks now demanded the return of Kars, Ardahan, and Batum, in addition to western Armenian regions evacuated by the Russian armies. The Georgians hoped to save Batum by sacrificing Kars but the Turks were adamant. The delegation returned to Tiflis and although Azerbaijan refused to contribute troops, the assembly in Tiflis voted for war with Turkey.

The war did not materialize, however. The fall of Batum to the Turks forced the Georgians to accept the provisions of Brest-Litovsk, and together with the Azeri representatives and the disappointed Armenian delegates, declared their independence from Russia and the formation of the Transcaucasian Federative Republic (April 22, 1918). The Georgians claimed the most important administrative posts and ordered the Armenian army to surrender Kars. In order to save eastern Armenia, the Dashnaks, led by Khatisian and Hovhannes Kachaznuni, cooperated with the Georgian Mensheviks and remained in the federation. The representatives of Transcaucasia went to Batum to accept the Brest-Litovsk provisions, but were surprised to learn that the Turks now demanded Akhalkalak and Akhaltsikh, as well as the western half of the Yerevan province. Without waiting for a response, the Turks invaded and took Alexandropol. They then marched towards Tiflis and Yerevan. Germany, fearing a strain in Russo-German relations, told the Turks not to violate the Brest-Litovsk borders and sent a German observer to Batum who reported that the Turks were planning to kill all the Armenians in Transcaucasia and to create a unified Turkish state with Azerbaijan. When German pressures on Turkey proved fruitless, the Georgians once again abandoned the Armenians and put themselves under German protection. In order to do so, they had to withdraw from the federation. On May 26, 1918, the Georgians declared their independence and the German flag was raised in Tiflis. Two days later, the Azeris, declared the independence of Azerbaijan. Since Baku was in the hands of a coalition of Bolsheviks and Dashnaks -- strange bedfellows indeed -- they selected Elizavetpol (later Kirovabad, present-day Ganja) as the temporary capital and awaited the arrival of Turkish troops to liberate Baku. The Armenians were left on their own and on May 28, the National Council in Tiflis, in order to be able to negotiate with the Turkish delegation in Batum and save what was left of their homeland, had no choice but to declare the independence of Armenia.

TRANSCAUCASIA	RUSSIA	THE MUSLIM WORLD	EUROPE & THE UNITED STATES	AFRICA, ASIA, LATIN AMERICA
1918	**1918**	**1918**	**1918**	**1918**
Battle of Sardarabad	Bolsheviks dissolve Duma	Turkish armies collapse in	Wilson's 14 Points	Montagu's Report on Indian
Georgia, Armenia, Azerbaijan	Brest-Litovsk Treaty	Palestine	WW I ends	Constitutional Reform
declare independence	Capital moved to Moscow	Moudros Armistice	Czechoslovakia, Poland,	Mexico nationalizes oilfields
Batum Agreement	Red Army formed	Muhammad VI (to 1922)	Austria, Yugoslavia formed	
Andranik in Zangezur	Japanese in Siberia		**1919**	
Kachaznuni leads Arm. govt.	Assassin. attempt on Lenin		Armenian delegations in Paris	
Fall of Baku, Armenians	Civil War (to 1920)		Hoover heads US Relief	
massacred	Tsar and family murdered	**1919**	Prohibition Amendment	
Turks leave Transcaucasia,	Death of Plekhanov		Paris Peace Conference	**1919**
British land in Baku	First Constitution		First League of Nations meets	Amritsar Massacre
1919	**1919**	King-Crane Commission	Mussolini founds Fascists	German African colonies fall
Famine in Armenia	Third International (to 1943)	Italians land in Anatolia	Bela Kun's govt. in Hungary	to France & Britain
Armenian delegation led by	Red Army takes Crimea	Greeks land in Asia Minor	Versailles Treaty	Govt. of India Act passed
Aharonian leaves for Paris	Red Army takes Ufa	Mustafa Kemal defies Allies	St. Germain Treaty	Rowlatt Act passed
American relief arrives	War with Finland (to 1920)	(to 1922)	Curzon apptd. Foreign Sec.	War with Afghanistan
Armeno-Georgian territorial	Red Army takes Omsk	Wafd Party in Egypt	Immigration curtailed in US	Korea rebels against Japan
dispute	Red Army takes Kharkov	Sa'ad Zaghlul deported	Neuilly Treaty	Death of Botha
Armeno-Azeri territorial	Kolchak defeated	Turk. nationalist conferences	Wilson leaves Paris	Jan Smuts P.M. of South
dispute	Denikin fights on	in Erzerum and Sivas	Stambuliski rules Bulgaria	Africa (to 1924)
Khatisian leads Arm. govt.	Nationalization and foreign	French repress Arab nationa-	US Senate considers joining	**1920**
Harbord Commission	trade monopoly	lism in M. E. & N. Africa	League of Nations	Communist and nationalist
1920	**1920**	**1920**	**1920**	movements in South Asia
Armenia recognized	Odessa captured	Allies occupy Constantinople	US votes against League	Gandhi emerges as India's
Baku falls to Bolsheviks	Denikin and Warngel defeated	Provisional govt. in Ankara	San Remo Conference	leader (to 1948)
Bolshevik demonstr. in Arm.	End of Civil War	Treaty of Sèvres	Trianon Treaty	German colonies fall to Japan
Ohanjanian leads Arm. govt.	War Communism (to 1921)	Turks attack Armenia	19th Amendment	Civil War in China (to 1926)
Vratzian leads Arm. govt.	Famine (to 1922)	Turko-Bolshevik accord	League moves to Geneva	
Bolsheviks in Yerevan	War with Poland (to 1921)	Faisal king of Syria	Govt. of Ireland Act passed	
Alexandropol Treaty	Allied forces withdraw	French and British mandates		

Table 5: 1918-1921

XX

A Thousand Days:
The Armenian Republic (1918-1921)

Although the Armenian National Council had assumed dictatorial powers over the Armenian provinces on May 28, 1918, it did not make the declaration public until May 30. Even then, the announcement did not include the term "independence," for no one was sure if there was going to be an Armenia or, if there was, of its exact parameters. The Turkish armies had invaded eastern Armenia two weeks before and had perpetrated massacres in Alexandropol and a number of other towns and settlements. The Turkish forces had encircled the region of Yerevan and the end of historic Armenia was predicted. What saved Armenia was the heroic stand of Armenians of every age and rank, including women and the very old, at the battles of Sardarabad, Kara-Kilisa, and Bash-Abaran. On June 2, the news of Turkish defeats in these encounters and their withdrawal from Yerevan was confirmed; two days later, the Batum agreement was signed between the Armenians and Turks. It was only then that an independent Armenian republic was informally proclaimed in Tiflis.

Proclaiming a republic did not create it. While Aram Manukian and General Dro oversaw the defense of Yerevan, the Armenian National Council was in Tiflis, the capital of the newly-independent Georgian Republic. The disagreements among the leaders of the different Armenian political parties, all in Tiflis, precluded the establishment of a coalition government until the last day of June, when the continued objections of minor Armenian parties forced the Dashnak-dominated National Council to forgo democratic protocol and to form their own cabinet. The Armenian ruling body, unwelcome in Tiflis, left for Yerevan, which after the loss of Alexandropol was the only urban center left to the Armenians. On July 19 the Armenian govern-

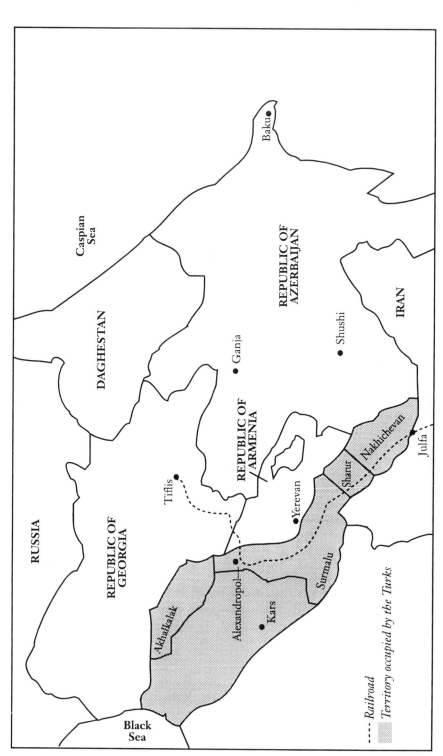

Map 20: The Armenian Republic after the Batum Treaty, June 1918

ment, led by prime-minister Hovhaness Kachaznuni, arrived in Yerevan and replaced the military command of Aram Manukian. The independent republic of Armenia had formally begun.

The Treaty of Batum had left Armenia a territory of some 4500 square rocky miles (see map 20) and 700,000 inhabitants, of which 300,000 were hungry refugees from western Armenia and 100,000 were Azeris and Kurds. The industrial center of Alexandropol and the fertile fields of Sharur and Nakhichevan, as well as most of the railroad lines, were not included in the republic. Loss of animals and farming equipment had also decreased agricultural productivity in the region. Yerevan, never a major center of the Russian Empire, was a dusty rural town with a few government offices and almost no industry. Landlocked and surrounded by hostile neighbors, the republic was also threatened by cholera and typhus epidemics. The majority of Armenian intellectuals, artisans, and entrepreneurs were in Tiflis, Baku, or in Russia. Lack of food, medicine, and the presence of armed bands who attacked in broad daylight did not promise a bright future for the new republic.

Feeling that elections could not take place under such conditions, an enlarged National Council acted as the parliamentary body *(Khorhurd)* instead. Democratic principles were not totally overlooked, however, for although the Dashnaks controlled the cabinet and had the most members in parliament, the other parties were represented and heated debates did occur. The Muslim and Russian minorities had their own representatives.

Independence had arrived unexpectedly. Most of the republic's middle-class leadership had been raised outside historic Armenia and had never even visited Yerevan. The next four months were spent creating some sense out of the chaos, becoming accustomed to living in squalid conditions, and in petitioning Germany to restrain the Turks from further demands. Meanwhile, Azeri and Turkish forces captured Baku in September and although many Armenians had fled the city, over 15,000 Armenians were massacred. The Turks then entered Mountainous Karabagh and the situation became ominous for that Armenian enclave, as well as for the Armenian Republic. General Andranik and his volunteers, who were in Zangezur, immediately set off to repel the Turks from Karabagh. Andranik, who had not approved of negotiating with the Turks in Batum, had broken with the Dashnak government, gone to Zangezur, and was in the process of driving the Azeris out of that region. Before anything could be resolved, however, the Turkish capitulation to the Allies brought an end to the world war in Transcaucasia and British forces arrived in Baku.

The Moudros Armistice required the Turks to evacuate their troops from

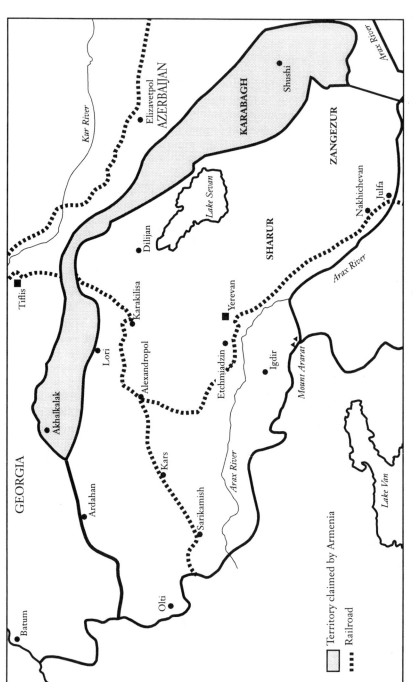

Map 21: The Armenian Republic, September 1920

Transcaucasia and Iranian Azerbaijan and to surrender the control of the Straits to the Allies. The Turks withdrew to their pre-war borders, enabling the Armenian forces, under the command of General Dro, to extend the territory of the republic soon after. With Russia amidst a civil war, the Armenians took Kars and the Georgians Batum, but the districts of Ardahan and Olti, which lay between the two and which were populated mainly by Armenians, were claimed by both Georgia and Armenia and, together with other territorial disputes discussed below, led to tensions between the two Christian neighbors (see map 21).

The Turkish defeat had a great psychological effect on the Armenians. Many who had been skeptical now realized that the republic had a chance of survival. A number of Armenian intellectual and financial leaders who had remained in Tiflis, decided to relocate to Yerevan and to offer their services to the republic. More importantly, the People's Party, which became the Caucasian equivalent of the Constitutional Democrat Party (Sahmanadir Ramkavar) and which represented the middle class, now decided to join the cabinet. The Dashnaks, who needed the expertise of middle-class professionals and who wished to demonstrate to the Allies that Armenia was not controlled by "radicals," embraced the liberals and gave them half, albeit not the most important, of the cabinet positions.

Despite the hopeful situation, Armenia now had to endure the severe winter of 1918-1919. Lack of bread, fuel, medicine, and shelter caused riots, epidemics, and famine. People ate grass, dead animals, and boiled leather; cases of cannibalism were reported as well. By the time it was over some 200,000 people had died from hunger, frost, and typhus. Aid did finally arrive, however. The American Near East Relief, organized by missionaries and headed by James Barton, raised millions for the "starving Armenians," and by spring, food, clothing and medical supplies began to arrive. More important was the aid given by the United States government. By the end of summer, the American Relief Administration, directed by Herbert Hoover, had sent some 50,000 tons of food, which saved thousands of lives and enabled the republic to plant crops. Nor was the Armenian government itself idle. It tackled the problem of creating judicial, health, and educational systems, as well as a tax structure and a state budget. The few industries, like the wine and cognac works of Yerevan, and a number of mills were nationalized. Telegraph and rail lines were repaired and new mines were explored.

Three issues remained foremost on the mind of the government: the Paris Peace Conference, which had begun in January 1919, and the territorial disputes with both Georgia and Azerbaijan. The conference in the French capital was to conclude peace terms with the German, Austro-Hungarian and Ottoman empires, to establish future peace through the creation of a League of Nations, and to hear the claims of various nationalities who, encouraged by points five and twelve, of the Fourteen Points set forth by President Wilson in his address to Congress (January 8, 1918), sought self-determination through autonomy or independence. The Armenian Republic dispatched a delegation headed by Avetis Aharonian. Its mission was to press the republic's claim to western Armenia or the six Armenian provinces in Turkey, as well as to convince the Allies to grant the republic an outlet to the Black Sea.

Upon arrival, the delegation met another Armenian group: the Armenian National Delegation, headed by Boghos Nubar Pasha, representing the western Armenians, as well as the Armenians of the diaspora. Most members of that delegation belonged to the Constitutional Democrat Party. Boghos Nubar's status among the European statesmen had enabled him to unofficially press a number of Armenian claims. He told Aharonian that Cilicia, with an outlet to the Mediterranean, must be included in the Armenian demands. The two delegations then united and presented a joint petition for an enlarged Armenian republic stretching from Transcaucasia to the Mediterranean. There were a number of complications attached to the Armenian claims, however. The Sykes-Picot plan had allocated Cilicia and half of western Armenia to the French. The Russian civil war was far from over and if the Whites were victorious, Russia, according to the same agreement, would end up with Trebizond and the other half of western Armenia. Moreover, Kurdish territorial claims conflicted with Armenian claims. Furthermore, the Turkish army in Anatolia was not disarmed and the small Armenian republic, with its lack of arms and resources, could not possibly defend an Armenia which would approach 100,000 square miles. It would need a mandatory power to assist it in such a transition. Although President Wilson was disposed to an American mandate, the Armenians had to await the outcome of two events: peace with Germany, which had to be concluded before any other issues could be decided upon; and the approval of the peace conference and the Covenant of the League of Nations by the United States Senate. Some of these obstacles were familiar to the Armenians, others were not. Armenia, like most of the smaller nationalities, was not given a seat at the conference and was, furthermore, not privy to the private discussions between David Lloyd George, the prime minister of Britain; Georges Clemenceau, the leader of France; and Vittorio Orlando of Italy.

The French, who were adamant in their desire to punish Germany, to recover territories lost in the Franco-Prussian War, and to receive war reparations, concentrated on the treaty with Germany. The Versailles Treaty was signed on June 28, 1919. A number of regions which Germany had gained in the eighteenth and nineteenth centuries were given to Poland and France. The control over some of Germany's industrial regions was temporarily passed to France. Germany lost its colonies, was limited in its armed forces, and was forced to accept the sole blame for the war, which saddled it with astronomical reparation costs. The humiliation embittered the German people, impoverished its economy, gave rise to both left- and right-wing parties, led to Hitler and the Nazis coming to power, and put Europe on the road to a second world war.

Having, in their opinion, reduced the threat of future German might, France and England were not in a hurry to resolve the partition of the Ottoman Empire. The Sykes-Picot plan had presented them with possibilities for colonial expansion in Asia Minor and the Arab lands. In addition, the British and the French were in an embarrassing situation. The former had given the Jews (in the Balfour Declaration) and the Arabs (through Lawrence of Arabia and others) conflicting promises of a homeland. The Kurds and the so-called Assyrians were also promised a degree of self-determination. Both powers had also given the Armenian leadership in Transcaucasia, Europe, and the Middle East their strongest and most sincere vows that the injustices of the past would finally be corrected. Armenian blood spilled in the massacres and the genocide, as well as on behalf of the Allies by the Armenian volunteer units in the Russian armies and in the British and French armies (The Armenian Legion) in the Middle East, would not be forgotten, they claimed. A large, independent Armenia protected by the Allies was to be their reward. The departure of President Wilson to America to present the European agreement to Congress, gave the powers the excuse to stop the peace process with the Ottomans and to iron out these difficulties. The fate of the rest of Europe, as well as Armenia, was to be decided in future conferences and treaties. Armenia and other oppressed nationalities awaited President Wilson's debate with the Senate over the Versailles Treaty, the League of Nations, and the Armenian mandate. In the meantime, political reality began to take precedence over promises, and the Russian civil war raged on.

During the next six months, Europe, while awaiting the American decision, disposed of the Austro-Hungarian Empire by means of the Saint Germain Treaty (September 10, 1919) in which the independence of Poland, Czechoslovakia, and Yugoslavia was recognized, and Austria lost territories to Poland, Italy, and Yugoslavia. The Treaty of Neuilly (November 27, 1919) punished Bulgaria with some loss of territory, as well as reparation payments and the loss of most of Macedonia, which fell within Greek and Yugoslav borders. The Hungarians, racked by economic problems, rebelled against their government and installed a Bolshevik regime under Bela Kun. The short-lived state went to war to keep Hungary intact. It was defeated a few months later and the new government signed the Treaty of Trianon (June, 4, 1920), by which Hungary lost Transylvania and other lands to Romania, Austria, and Czechoslovakia and was saddled with part of the Austro-Hungarian reparations.

Meanwhile, the situation in Transcaucasia was far from calm. The breakup of the region into three independent republics presented Armenia with its border issues to be resolved. These, as we have seen, had their origins in the nineteenth-century administrative divisions of the Russian Empire. The first was the Armeno-Georgian dispute over the districts of Akhalkalak and Lori, both of which had a solid Armenian majority and were part of historic Armenia, but which had been part of the Tiflis Province and were claimed by Georgia as part of its new republic. The dispute led to minor military conflicts between the two Christian states which were resolved by a compromise, whereby Armenia took control of half of Lori, with the other half becoming a neutral zone, and Georgia retained control of Akhalkalak.

The second problem was far more serious, involving territorial disputes between Armenia and Azerbaijan. In Armenian eyes there was little distinction between the Turkic Azeris and the Turks themselves. Azeri cooperation with the Turks during the 1917-1918 period also contributed to the Armenian Republic's view that Azeri nationalist and pan-Turkic statements were a threat to its existence. Furthermore, the Azeris saw Armenia as a smaller version of the Yerevan province of 1849. Azerbaijan considered itself the successor of the Baku and Elizavetpol provinces; therefore, in its eyes, Karabagh and Zangezur were Azeri territory. The northern parts of Armenia and easternmost parts of Georgia, which had pockets of Turkic people, were, in its view, part of Azerbaijan as well. The Azeris also claimed those regions of western Armenia which came to Russia after 1878. Basically, they envisioned a state from the Caspian to the Black Sea, with a small Armenia locked between it and Turkey. To complicate matters further, there were tens of thousands of Muslims living in the southern part of Armenia, as well as in Yerevan, and hundreds of thousands of Armenians lived in Mountainous Karabagh, Zangezur, and in the cities and suburbs of Baku, and Elizavetpol. During the last days of World War One, Armenian forces under the leadership of General Andranik, as we have seen, were ready to take Mountainous Karabagh. The war ended and the British asked Andranik to halt his advance and await the Paris Peace Conference. Armenians felt assured that their historic and ethnographic arguments would secure them Karabagh (map 21).

The British command in Baku, however, was pro-Muslim, due to the oil in Baku, which the British began to pump and sell as soon as they landed forces there. In addition, the British Empire had many Muslims who viewed the sultan as the caliph and expected a generous treatment of the defeated Turks. The British therefore backed the Azeri claims in Karabagh and Zangezur. Zangezur, which thanks to Andranik was fully under Armenian control, expelled the Azeri military and administrative personnel who arrived there, but Karabagh's refusal ended in massacres in a number of Armenian villages and a compromise. The Armenian-populated districts in Karabagh received internal autonomy, but, for the time being, were put under Azeri jurisdiction. From the very start the Azeris violated the agreement and an Armenian rebellion resulted in the burning of Shushi, the capital of Mountainous Karabagh, by the Azeris. The government in Yerevan was not strong enough to intervene and the Karabagh question, together with other territorial questions regarding Armenia, had to await the peace treaties.

At the same time, another problem hampered the internal affairs of the republic. Although there were a handful of socialists in the government, the political leadership, as stated, was shared by the Dashnaks, who controlled the top cabinet posts and the liberal People's Party, who composed the other half of the cabinet. Each had different philosophies. The People's Party was flexible in structure and advocated a more open government. The Dashnaks were well-organized and active revolutionaries, who occasionally used what some considered undemocratic methods against both Armenians and non-Armenians. Their party organization, especially their Central Bureau, was more rigid and demanded the full obedience of its members. The intellectual and political leaders of both groups had the welfare of Armenia and the Armenians in mind, but came from different social and economic backgrounds and sought to achieve it by different methods. The former were raised in the liberal traditions of the upper middle classes of Tiflis, Baku, Moscow, and St. Petersburg; while the latter were a product of the lower middle classes, as well as farmers and workers, who were influenced by the revolutionary fervor and national aspirations prevalent in Eastern Europe.

Prior to spring 1919, the liberals, whose programs (except for education and charity) were not geared to the uneducated and hungry Armenian crowds of Yerevan, hoped that despite the difficulties of living there, their presence in the government would benefit the Armenian masses by creating jobs and a more representative parliament. After six months, however, signs of strain between the two parties began to appear. The emergence of Boghos Nubar and his pro-liberal delegation in Paris emboldened the liberals in Yerevan, who felt that they had a larger voice than before. The final break came just prior to the first national elections. On the first anniversary of the republic, Khatisian, speaking for the government, announced the symbolic unification of eastern and western Armenia. The liberal coalition did not comment at that time but, a few days later, resigned from the government, claiming that Boghos Nubar and his party, who represented the western Armenians, were not consulted and that the Dashnaks were once again subverting democratic principles in an attempt to usurp the future government of a united Armenia.

The boycott by the liberals resulted in the overwhelming victory (90 percent of the vote) of the Dashnak party. The minor socialist parties had more constituents in Georgia, Azerbaijan, Russia, and Europe than in Armenia, and together managed to capture the remaining 10 percent. The socialists and liberals began to assert that the whole episode was staged by the Dashnaks to gain control of the republic. Khatisian, who formed the new government, however, realized that the charge could have major repercussions. In order to diffuse the situation, and out of conviction, he strove to include non-Dashnaks in various posts. He clashed with the Dashnak party Central Bureau, who did not agree with his policy but sought swift changes to strengthen the party and to push the social reforms which would win them the support of the masses. The Bureau chiefs feared that the masses would eventually lose their patience and join the Bolsheviks, whose propaganda and victories in the civil war were beginning to have an effect on the working and poorer classes in Armenia. The main clash between the party and the government came in late 1919 during the party congress. Khatisian maintained that if the party insisted on running the state, there would be no difference between them and the Bolsheviks. The government, he added, had to be independent from the party. The party had to implement its program through their representatives in the legislature. Party veterans, however, insisted that without party control, the state would not be able to survive the difficult days ahead. It was finally decided that members of the Bureau who entered the government would withdraw from active participation in the Central Bureau during their tenure. Although in practice this compromise did not work well, the gesture did avoid an all out confrontation.

The second year of the republic began on a promising note, with the railway and telegraph back in service and with a slight revival in industry. There were problems with inflation, with the Muslim population, feeding and housing the refugees, and most importantly, the distribution of land to peasants; something the Dashnaks had promised but had not yet implemented. This last item gave the Socialist Revolutionaries ammunition for recruiting some disgruntled peasants and the opportunity to gain more members in the future. A major problem was that the Armenian republic did not have the infrastructure of Baku or Tiflis. The war, as well as the short Turkish occupation of half of the province, had removed or destroyed animals and equipment. Agricultural projects, plans for dams, schools, veterinary medicine, reforestation, and other items were being set up for the long term and would bear fruit only in the future. Modern courts were being set up and rural self-administration was being organized. There were even efforts to introduce Armenian as the main language of the administration, but since most of the intellectuals used Russian, the government functioned in both languages. Elementary and secondary schools and a state university were opened in a number of urban centers, but a lack of fuel and financial restrictions kept school attendance sporadic. There was optimism, however, and postage stamps and currency were designed and issued. That same year President Wilson dispatched a commission headed by Major-General J. G. Harbord, who spent two months in western Armenia and the Armenian Republic to assess the possibility of a mandate. The commission cited equal arguments for and against an American mandate. They stated that although it was desirable from the humanitarian point of view, the cost would be very large indeed and would involve the United States in a mire of problems.

As long as the outcome of the Russian civil war was in doubt the European powers refused to recognize Armenia or the other Transcaucasian republics. At the start of 1920 the defeat of the White armies under General Denikin, made it clear that the Transcaucasian republics should be recognized as *de facto* states and be armed to resist the Bolsheviks. Lord Curzon, the foreign secretary of Britain, was in favor of supplying weapons to Armenia, but Winston Churchill of the War Office did not approve, arguing that any such arms would fall into the hands of Bolsheviks, who were sure to win.

In the meantime, the Armenian government had put all its hopes on Europe and the United States. In spring 1920, the United States Senate rejected the Versailles Treaty and the League of Nations. Since the mandates were to be administered by the League, the issue of an Armenian mandate was, for all intents and purposes, dead. Strong support for Armenia in the United States and in the Senate continued, however, and the Armenian

Republic and its envoy, Armen Garo (Garegin Pasdermadjian), were officially recognized. Complicating the situation for the Armenians was the fact that
the United States had never declared war on Turkey and thus, after Wilson's
defeat in the Senate, the United States withdrew from discussions on the partition of the Ottoman Empire. The delays in implementing a Turkish settlement proved disastrous for Armenia. During this time, the Turkish nationalists in the interior were organizing strong opposition to the Allied plans for
the partition of Turkey. The Turkish army had not demobilized or disarmed
and was being reorganized by Mustafa Kemal (later known as Atatürk) into
a capable force. At the same time, European, and later American, businessmen felt that they could reap greater profits from a viable Turkey and its
trade routes than with a starving, landlocked Armenia. Moreover, the colonial offices in Europe continued to consider what the feelings of Muslims in
their colonies would be if Turkey, the center of the caliphate, was treated as
Germany or Austria had been. Britain and France had no conflicting interests
in Anatolia, but had major disagreements regarding the Arab lands. Greek
and Italian ambitions conflicted in Anatolia, and the Greeks, with British
approval, had, in May 1919, landed troops in Smyrna. Since neither the
French nor the British had the means or the resolve to attack the Turkish
nationalists in faraway Anatolia, they hoped that the Greek invasion would
force the Turks to come to terms and accept the Allied proposals which were
being discussed informally.

The inability of the Armenians to defend themselves gave the European
Although there was sympathy for the Armenians, time was running out
for them. While the Senate was preparing for Wilson's defeat, the European
powers finally began the discussion of the peace treaty with the Ottoman
Empire in San Remo, Italy. In the meantime, news arrived that the thousands
of Armenians who had returned to Cilicia in 1918, were being massacred by
Turkish nationalists, who, outraged at the Greek landing, disregarded the
orders of Constantinople and considered themselves to be the true government of Turkey. The Turkish attacks, the refusal of the French to fight in
Cilicia and their eventual return of Cilicia to Turkey in exchange for keeping
Syria, would, in the end, spell the death of Armenian Cilicia. Those who
were not killed or captured had to once again leave their homes for Lebanon
and Syria.

The inability of the Armenians to defend themselves gave the European
powers an excuse to take Cilicia and half of western Armenia, that is, the
regions which were originally granted the French, out of any future Armenian state. There was still a chance that Constantinople or the Greek armies
would convince the Turkish nationalists to agree to a reduced Turkish state.

In the meantime, by April 1920, the Allies in San Remo agreed to give Armenia Van, Erzerum, and Bitlis, and an outlet to the Black Sea. The Allies realized that the agreement was a dead letter, for no one in Europe was ready to commit a force to help the Armenians in establishing control over such a large territory. Both the French and the British were now faced with the dilemma of how to fulfill their numerous pledges to the Armenians. Since the Bolsheviks had repudiated the Sykes-Picot plan, the British granted the Armenians the half of western Armenia that was promised to the Russians. The British felt that they had resolved their problem, and hoped that the Greeks and the Transcaucasian republics would succeed in repelling the Turkish nationalists and the Bolsheviks. Although the United States Senate had basically rejected the European agreements and the question of the League, sympathy for Armenia continued in the Senate. Some historians claim that it was Wilson's rash treatment of the Republican senators and his insistence that his entire proposal be accepted without amendments or reservations, as much as isolationism, that spelled the end of American involvement on behalf of Armenia. The French and the British, however, continued to hope that Wilson and the United States would still be willing to take the responsibility for Armenia. They asked Wilson to draw the final borders of Armenia, within the guidelines agreed in San Remo. Wilson, hoping that support for Armenia might still reverse the tide in the Senate, accepted. Although he did not submit the final boundaries of Armenia until November (see map 22), on April 18, 1920 the victorious powers announced at San Remo that an agreement was finally reached. Soon after, the Senate totally rejected the idea of an American mandate.

The fall of Adrianople to the Greeks in June 1920 forced Constantinople to accept the conditions of San Remo and three months after San Remo, on August 10, 1920 the Turks, European Allies, and the Armenians, represented by Avetis Aharonian and Boghos Nubar Pasha, signed the Treaty of Sèvres (see map 22). The treaty accepted the future Wilsonian boundary (which was to include the provinces of Van, Bitlis, Erzerum and an outlet to the Black Sea at Trebizond) and promised reparations and the restoration of property to the survivors of the genocide. It also agreed to the return of Armenian women and children who had been taken or adopted by Turks and Kurds. Finally, the treaty recognized the independence of Armenia and promised to punish those responsible for the Armenian genocide. The Armenians, in turn, promised to guarantee the religious and cultural rights of the Muslims who would remain in western Armenia. Thus, twenty-one months after the end of the World War, the conflict was officially over.

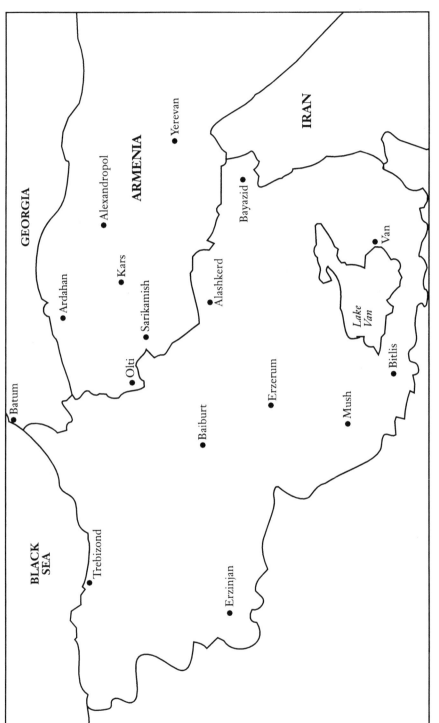

Map 22: Wilson's Armenia for the Treaty of Sèvres, 1920

By summer 1920, the Armenian republic had many reasons for hope and fear. In addition to the United States, Armenia was now formally (*de jure*) recognized by Belgium, France, England, Italy, Chile, Argentina, Brazil, and several other states. Armenian passports were considered valid and Armenian diplomats began to work in China, Japan, Ethiopia, Greece, Turkey, Romania, Yugoslavia, Bulgaria, Iran, Iraq, Germany, Belgium, Italy, France, and England.

Meanwhile, ominous clouds were forming. Mustafa Kemal, realizing that the agreements in San Remo would mean a weak, truncated Turkish state, announced that the government in Constantinople did not represent the Turkish people and that any agreements it signed were null and void. Since the Allied fleet was in Constantinople, Mustafa Kemal organized a counter-government in Ankara. An astute politician, a charismatic and capable leader, and a competent military commander, Mustafa Kemal made it known that he was only interested in keeping the homeland of the Turks, or Asia Minor; in other words, he did not insist on the territorial integrity of the former Ottoman Empire. The Balkans were already independent and the Arab lands could be severed. British and French governments would not lose their zones of influence and a strong Turkey would be preferable to them than weak Transcaucasian states which could fall prey to Bolshevism. Assured of Allied inaction, he then turned to resolve the Armenian Question and the Greek invasion.

Not able to fight simultaneously on two fronts, Kemal approached the Bolsheviks via Enver Pasha who had fled to Russia and who was working with the Bolsheviks to bring the Russian Muslims to the communists. Kemal assured the Bolsheviks that if they supplied him with arms, grain, and gold, he would bring Azerbaijan, with its numerous Turkish advisors and officers, to their side and would eliminate the "imperialist" Armenians. The Bolsheviks entered Baku at the end of April and were well-received by Azeri leaders, who, temporarily forgetting their former nationalistic fervor, portrayed themselves as the representatives of the working class. The fall of Baku forced the Yerevan government to send a mission to Moscow in May to convince the Bolsheviks that an independent and friendly Armenia would be better for Russian interests in the region. In the meantime, the Bolshevik movement had slowly arrived in Armenia and although a small minority, they were vocal and managed to create a minor uprising in May in Alexandropol, demanding the establishment of a Soviet republic. The reaction of the Dashnaks was swift: some of the Armenian Bolsheviks were executed; the rest fled to Baku. The main result of the short uprising was to end

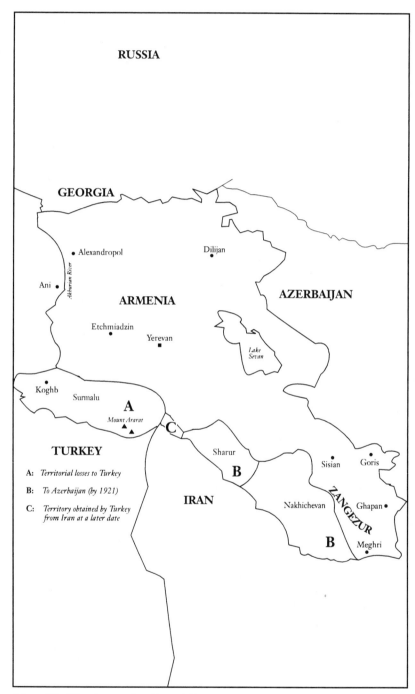

Map 23: The Armenian Republic after the Treaty of Alexandropol
(December 1920)

Khatisian's premiership and his policies. The Bureau of the Dashnaktsutiun took over the government with Hamazasp Ohanjanian as premier. After clearing out the Bolsheviks, the Bureau ordered the removal of all Muslims who did not accept the authority of the government. Many Muslims left the southern parts of the republic and although the socialists did not protest Dashnak policies, these actions alienated the liberals even further. The second anniversary of the republic was celebrated in quite a different spirit.

There are different interpretations on the events that followed. Sources sympathetic to the Dashnaks claim that the Bolsheviks gave the Armenians false assurances, while awaiting the results of the Soviet-Turkish negotiations in Ankara. Anti-Dashnak sources point out that the Yerevan government was to blame. The majority of the Dashnaks refused to work with Moscow. The Armenian government thus delayed its response to Moscow, forcing the Russians into making a deal with the Turks. Dashnaks counter that any agreement with Moscow would turn the West against them. Since the Treaty of Sèvres was not signed until August, they tried to delay a rapprochement with the Bolsheviks. The Hnchak view points out that the takeover of the Yerevan government by the Dashnak Bureau and the crushing of the young Bolshevik movement in Armenia not only ended any hopes of negotiations with the Bolsheviks, but made them forever distrust Armenian national aspirations.

In the meantime, the Bolshevik and Turkish negotiations continued. Although a number of Bolsheviks insisted that the Turks had to give Armenians some territory from western Armenia, the Turks refused to discuss the issue of borders and insisted that a treaty of alliance be negotiated without reference to borders. Stalin, who did not favor the Armenians, and Lenin, who was concerned about larger matters, agreed. Shortly after the Sèvres treaty, the Russians and Turks made an agreement in Moscow (August 20, 1920). It not only voided all previous treaties made by the imperial government but stated that any international treaty, such as Sèvres, not accepted by Ankara would not be recognized by Moscow either. To show the world their total rejection of Sèvres, the Turks, assured of Russian cooperation and non-interference, American neutrality, and European inaction, attacked Armenia in late September.

By mid-November, the Turks had recaptured the entire region they had controlled prior to their withdrawal in November 1918. The Russians, surprised by the rapid Turkish advance, feared the loss of the Georgian Black Sea ports and the only rail connection to Iran. They approached the Yerevan government and offered to intercede on their behalf. The Turks rejected any

Russian interference. The Dashnak Bureau, now blamed for the Turkish victories, gave up the reigns of government to a new cabinet, headed by Simon Vratzian. The cabinet was still dominated by Dashnaks, but had two Socialist Revolutionary members. At the end of November the Bolsheviks entered Armenian territory and insisted that Armenia's salvation lay in becoming a Bolshevik state, denouncing the Treaty of Sèvres, and cutting its ties to the West. The Turks continued their advance and captured Sharur and Nakhichevan. Faced with total annihilation, the Armenian government sent Khatisian to Alexandropol to negotiate with the Turks and appointed a team headed by General Dro to transfer the government to the Bolsheviks. On December 2 Armenia became an "independent" Soviet state and the Bolsheviks promised to restore its pre-September 1920 borders. Contrary to common belief, the Armenian Republic did not officially end on that date. Although the republic had changed its political leadership, Dashnaks, as well as other party representatives, were guaranteed freedom and continued to serve the state in a number of positions.

On the same day, Turkey demanded that Armenia immediately sign a treaty renouncing Sèvres and all claims to western Armenia, including Kars and Ardahan. In addition Armenia had to accept temporary Turkish jurisdiction in Nakhichevan and Sharur (see map 23). In return the Turks would guarantee the independence of the remaining portion of the republic. Khatisian, aware of Dro's negotiations with the Bolsheviks, delayed Armenia's acceptance until midnight of December 2. He then signed the Alexandropol agreement in the early hours of December 3. A small part of Armenia was thus saved from Turkish occupation. Since his government no longer existed on December 3, Khatisian calculated that the Bolsheviks would denounce the treaty as null and void and would demand that the Turks return to the former boundaries. At the same time the Dashnaks hoped that if the Bolsheviks did not keep their promises and tried to completely take over the republic, they could rely on the Turkish guarantee to repulse them. The Armenians thus hoped to use either the Russians or Turks to their benefit. It was a calculated move which ultimately failed.

A few days later, the Red Army, together with zealous young Armenian and non-Armenian Bolsheviks of the Revolutionary Committees arrived in Yerevan and, contrary to the agreement made with Dro, arrested numerous officials and officers. The period known as *War Communism,* with its harsh requisition, retribution, and attacks on traditional values, had arrived in Armenia and under the leadership of Sarkis Kasian and Avis Nurijianian, wreaked havoc for the next two months. The Bolsheviks and Turks then moved on to Georgia, the last independent region in Transcaucasia. With the Red Army gone, the population, fed up with War Communism, angry at the Bolshevik betrayal, and faced with the loss of western Armenia, rebelled in February 1921. Led by Dashnaks and armed non-partisans they ousted the Bolshevik Armenians and set up a National Salvation government with Vratzian as president.

Their victory was temporary, for after the Sovietization of Georgia, the Red Army returned in March and, by the beginning of April, the rebels were forced to withdraw to Zangezur where, under the leadership of Njdeh they fought on, declaring the region as the Independent Mountainous Armenia (Lerna-Hayastan). In the meantime, after the fall of Yerevan to the Red Army in March, the Turks and Russians, without any representatives from Armenia or Georgia, negotiated the fate of Armenia and the rest of Transcaucasia. As far as the Armenians were concerned, the terms followed the general line of the Treaty of Alexandropol, but with some significant changes. Nakhichevan and Sharur would not be returned to Armenia but would become part of Azerbaijan. In order for the Turks to be closer to Nakhichevan (they later exchanged a strip of land with Iran which gave them a common border with Nakhichevan) they demanded the district of Surmalu with Mount Ararat, which had never been part of western Armenia. The Russians, in exchange for Batum and parts of Akhalkalak and Akhaltsikh, which the Turks had occupied, agreed to give up Surmalu and Mount Ararat, the symbol of Armenia, to the Turks. Finally, it was agreed that the treaty would be later signed and ratified by the Transcaucasian republics. The Treaty of Moscow, signed on March 16, 1921, was the official end of the first Armenian republic, some one thousand days after its formal beginning.

ARMENIA & THE USSR	THE MUSLIM WORLD	EUROPE	THE AMERICAS	AFRICA/ASIA/AUSTRALIA
Treaty of Moscow (1921)	Reza Khan's coup (1921)	German mark falls (1921)	Harding president (1921)	First Indian parliament (1921)
NEP (1921-1927)	Faisal I (1921-33)	Mussolini march on Rome (1922)	Teapot Dome scandal (1923)	US-Jap. Naval Agr. (1922)
Treaty of Kars (1921)	Palestine mandate (1922)	Irish Free State (1922)	Coolidge president (1923-29)	Gandhi jailed (1922)
Miasnikian (1921-25)	Turkish republic (1922)	Beer Hall Putsch (1923)	Pan-American Treaty (1924)	Earthquake in Japan (1923)
Anglo-Soviet trade (1921)	Abul-Mejid II (1922-24) as	Zinoviev Letter scand. (1924)	Immigration Bill (1924)	Hertzog P.M. S. Africa (1924)
Rapallo Treaty (1922)	Caliph only	Locarno Confer. (1925)	FBI under J. Edgar Hoover	Hirohito emperor (1926-89)
USSR formed (1921)	Lausanne Treaty (1923)	Pilsudski's coup (1926)	(1924-72)	Parliament in Canberra (1927)
Death of Lenin (1924)	Ankara capital (1923)	German economic collapse	Inter-American Treaty of	Chiang Kai-shek (1928-49)
Britain recog. USSR (1924)	Transjordan indep. (1923)	(1927)	Arbitration (1929)	Emp. Haile Selassie (1930-74)
Hovhannesian (1925-27)	Kemal president (1923-38)	Kellog-Briand Pact (1928)	H. Hoover president (1929-33)	Jap. seize Manchuria (1931)
CPSU expels Trotsky (1927)	Qajar dynasty ends (1924)	Lateran Treaty (1929)		Gandhi arrested (1932)
Stalin in power (1928-53)	Caliphate abolished (1924)	Allied troops leave Rhineland	Dunning tariff (1930)	Japan withdraws from League
Hovsepian (1928)	Reza Shah Pahlavi (1925-41)	(1930)	Smoot-Hawley tariff (1930)	of Nations (1933)
First 5-Year Plan (1928)	Ibn-Saud (1926-1953)	German banks closed (1931)	Veterans Compensation Act	Philippines indep. (1933)
Trotsky leaves USSR (1929)	Republic of Lebanon (1926)	Gömbös in Hungary (1932)	(1931)	Washington treaties renoun.
Kostanian (1929-30)	Turkey adopts Latin alphabet	Hitler chancellor (1933)	Stimson Doctrine (1932)	by Japan (1934)
Collectivization in full force	and secular state (1928)	Reichstag fire (1933)	Federal Reserve est. (1932)	Siam's Rama VIII (1935-46)
(1930)	Passfield White Paper (1930)	Stavisky scandal (1933)	U.S. RFC est. (1932)	Italy invades Ethiopia (1935)
Khanjian (1930-36)	Const. named Istanbul (1930)	First concentration camps in	F. D. Roosevelt president	China-Japan war beg. (1936)
Second 5-Year Plan (1932)	Saudi Arabia (1932)	Germany (1933)	(1933-1945)	All-India Congress Party wins
Famine in USSR (1932)	Iraqis kill Assyrians (1933)	Hitler-Mussolini meet (1934)	20th Amendment (1933)	elections (1937)
Catholicos Khoren I (1933-38)	Balkan Pact (1934)	S.A. purged by S.S. (1934)	US off gold standard (1933)	Konoye P. M. of Japan (1937)
USSR joins League (1934)	Kemal named Atatürk (1935)	Dollfuss assassinated (1934)	U.S.AAA & FERA est. (1933)	Panay incident (1937)
Kirov assassinated (1934)	Persia named Iran (1935)	Hitler as Führer (1934-45)	TVA est. (1933)	US-Jap. tensions rise (1939)
Purges and trials (1934-38)	Arab High Committee (1936)	Nazis repudiate Versailles	Chicago World's Fair (1933)	World War in the Pacific
Stakhanov year (1936)	Montreux Con. (1936)	Treaty (1935)	PWA est. (1933)	(1940-45)
New USSR Const. (1936)	Saadabad Pact (1937)	Laval P.M. of France (1935)	US recog. USSR (1933)	Japanese victories (1941-42)
Amatuni (1936-37)	Royal Comm. on Palestine	Rome Pact (1936)	US Securities Act (1933)	US troops in N. Africa (1942)
Third 5-Year Plan (1938)	recomm. two states (1937)	Rome-Berlin Axis (1936)	21st Amendment (1933)	Casablanca Conf. (1942)
Harutiunian (1938-1953)	Sidqi assassinated (1937)		U.S. FFMC est. (1934)	Atom bombs dropped (1945)

Table 6: 1921-1991

ARMENIA & THE USSR	THE MUSLIM WORLD	EUROPE	THE AMERICAS	AFRICA/ASIA/AUSTRALIA
Stalin-Hitler Pact (1939)	Inönü (1938-1965)	Edward VIII abdicates (1936)	CWERA est. (1934)	Vietnam Republic est. (1946)
Eastern Poland annex. (1939)	Alexandretta to Turk. (1939)	Spanish Civil War (1936-39)	Social Security Act (1935)	Chinese civil war beg. (1945)
Molotov (1939-1957)	Von Papen in Turkey (1940)	Anti-Comintern Pact (1936)	Huey Long assass. (1935)	India indep. (1947)
War with Finland (1939-40)	War in North Africa (1940-3)	Chamberlain P.M. (1937)	Wealth Tax Act (1935)	Gandhi assass. (1948)
Baltic Rep. Annex. (1940)	Moh. Reza Shah (1941-79)	Anschluss (1938)	U.S. Neutrality Act (1937)	Chinese People's Rep. (1949)
Trotsky assassinated (1940)	Tehran Conference (1943)	Munich Confer. (1938)	US recog. Franco (1939)	Nationalist China formed in
Russo-Jap. neutrality (1941)	Arab League founded (1945)	Sudetenland taken (1938)	US economic boom begins	Formosa (Taiwan) 1949
Nazi invasion (1941-44)	Pakistan created (1947)	Franco (1939-75)	(1939)	Nehru president (1949-64)
USSR accepts Atlantic	Arabs reject division of	Anglo-Polish Treaty (1939)	U.S. OPA est. (1941)	Korean War (1950-53)
Charter (1941)	Palestine (1947)	W.W. II (1939-45)	Jap. attk. Pearl Harbor (1941)	Honolulu Conf. (1952)
Siege of Moscow ends (1942)	Israel created (1948)	Churchill elected P.M. (1940)	U.S. Savings Bonds (1941)	Mau Mau act in Kenya (1952)
Fall of Sevastopol (1942)	Transjordan named Hashemite	Hess flies to England (1941)	Jap. in US interned (1942)	Kenyatta arrested (1953)
Patriarchate re-established	Kingdom of Jordan (1949)	Jewish Holocaust (1942-45)	Gen. McArthur Chief Com.	Dien Bien Phu taken (1954)
(1943)	Israel admit. to UN (1949)	Allies land in Sicily (1943)	in Far East (1942)	Burma-Jap. Treaty (1954)
Siege of Stalingrad ends	Mossadeq in Iran (1951-53)	D-Day (1944)	Dumbarton Oaks Conf. (1944)	US-Nat. China Pact (1954)
(1943)	King Abdullah assass. (1951)	Hoxha in Albania (1944-85)	Eisenhower supreme comm.	Collectives in China (1955)
Moscow Conference (1943)	Turkey in NATO (1951)	Potsdam Conference (1945)	in Europe (1944-1952)	Great Leap Forward (1958)
Siege of Leningrad ends	Rev. In Egypt (1952)	Tito (1945-1980)	Truman president (1945-52)	Reforms in Congo (1959)
(1944)	King Hussein (1952-)	Italy a republic (1946)	UN Conf. in S.F. (1945)	US present in Vietnam (1963)
Yalta Conference (1945)	Germany agrees to pay comp.	Benelux union est. (1947)	UN World Bank est. (1945)	Kenya indep. (1963)
War against Japan (1945)	to Israel (1952)	Czech. Comm. State (1948)	NY est. UN headquart. (1946)	Tanzania formed (1964)
Cath. Gevorg VI (1945-54)	Republic of Egypt (1953)	Berlin airlift (1948-49)	Churchill's Iron Curtain	Zambia formed (1964)
Fourth 5-Year Plan (1946-51)	Shah leaves Iran (1953)	Rep. of Ireland (1949)	Speech (1946)	Rhodesia indep. (1965)
Treaties with Finland, Italy,	Nasser (1954-1970)	Fed. Rep. of Germany (1949)	Peron (1946-55, 1973-74)	Indira Gandhi (1966-77)
Bulgaria, Hungary and	Israel-Jordan border clashes	Dem. Rep. of Germany (1949)	Marshall Plan (1947)	Malawi republic (1966)
Romania (1947)	increase (1955)	W. Ulbricht (1950-71)	Taft-Hartley Act (1947)	Milit. coup in Ghana (1966)
Break with Tito (1949-55)	Baghdad Pact (1955-59)	Elizabeth II (1952-)	Cold War begins (1948)	Cult. Revolution (1966-76)
Fifth 5-Year Plan (1951)	Sudan indep. Republic (1956)	Commonwealth Conf. (1953)	NATO signed (1949)	Pueblo incident (1968)
General Party Congr. (1952)	UN truce between Israel, Leb.	Zhivkov in Bulg. (1954-89)	Sen. McCarthy 's anti-	Death of Ho Chi Minh (1969)
	Syria, Jordan (1956)		Communist camp. (1950-4)	

Table 6: 1921-1991 *Continued*

Death of Stalin (1953)	Israel invades Sinai (1956)	Vienna Treaty (1955)	McCarran Act (1950)	US bombs Cambodia & Laos (1971)
Malenkov (1953-56)	US aid to Israel (1956)	Invasion of Hungary (1956)	22nd Amendment (1951)	Gen. Idi Amin (1971-79)
Tovmasian (1953-60)	Pakistan Islamic Rep. (1956)	J. Kádár (1956-88)	Eisenhower pres. (1953-60)	Indo-Pakistani war (1971)
Catholicos Vazgen I (1954-94)	Nasser takes Suez Can. (1956)	Gomulka (1956-70)	Rosenbergs executed (1953)	Bangladesh formed (1972)
20th Party Congress, Stalin's crimes exposed (1956)	Br. & Fr. Attack Egypt (1956)	Cardinals Wyszynski and Mindszenty released (1956)	Potomac Charter (1954)	Ceylon Republic, renamed Sri Lanka (1972)
Khrushchev (1956-64)	Egypt retains Canal (1957)	Rome Treaty (1957)	Hammarskjöld in UN (1953)	Tanaka P.M. of Japan (1972)
Sputnik launched (1957)	Martial law in Jordan (1957)	Common Market (1958)	Bus boycott in Ala. (1955)	Marcos declares martial law in Philippines (1972)
Gromyko (1957-1985)	Israel withdraws from Sinai (1957)	De Gaulle (1956-70)	AFL & CIO merge (1955)	Nixon in China (1972)
Geneva & Disarm. Confer. fails (1960)	UAR (1958-61)	Cyprus a republic (1960)	M. L. King leads desegrega- tion movt. (1956-68)	Japan regains Okinawa (1972)
Zarobian (1960-66)	Revolution in Iraq (1958)	Berlin Wall Crisis (1961-2)	Eisenhower Doctrine (1957)	End of Vietnam War (1973)
Currency reform (1961)	Aswan Dam loan from USSR (1958)	Profumo crisis (1963)	AFL/CIO expels Teamsters (1957)	Famine in Africa (1974)
First man in space (1961)	Ayub Khan (1958-69)	Wilson elected P.M. (1964)	Alaska 49th state (1958)	Ethiopian Civil War begins (1975)
Rift with China (1963)	Lebanese conflict (1958)	Ceausescu (1965-1989)	Castro takes Cuba (1959)	Khmer Rouge take Cambodia (1975)
Atom. Test ban discus. (1963)	CENTO (1959)	France leaves NATO (1966)	Khrushchev in US (1959)	Communists take over South Vietnam (1975)
Brezhnev (1964-82)	Milit. coup in Turkey (1960)	Greek military coup (1967)	Hawaii 50th state (1959)	Mayaguez incident (1975)
Mikoyan retired (1965)	Milit. coup in Syria (1961)	Protests in Warsaw (1968)	U-2 incident (1960)	Pathet Lao in Laos (1975)
Economic pact w/Italy (1966)	Ben Bella (1962-65)	Czech. invaded (1968)	Kennedy-Nixon debate (1960)	N. Mariana Islands become US Commonwealth (1975)
Kochinian (1966-74)	UAR & Iraq union (1963)	Prot. and Cath. conflict in N. Ireland begins (1969)	Kennedy president (1961-63)	Chiang Kai-shek dead (1975)
Dipl. break with Israel (1967)	Saudi King Faisal (1964-75)	G. Pompidou elec. (1969)	Bay of Pigs (1961)	Fraser P.M. Australia (1975)
Kiev summit (1968)	Arafat leads Al-Fatah (1964)	W. Brandt elec. (1969)	R. Trujillo assass. (1961)	Vietnam united (1976)
Treaty of friendship with W. Germany (1970)	Revolution in Algeria (1965)	E. Heath elec. (1970)	Cuban Missile Crisis (1962)	Seychelles indep. (1976)
Demonstrations in Yerevan (1974)	Israel-Jordan clashes (1966)	Gierek (1970-1980)	U-Thant in UN (1962)	Port. Timor becomes part of Indonesia (1976)
Demirjian (1974-88)	Six-Day War (1967)	E. Honecker (1971-1989)	Civil Rights marches (1963)	Milit. coup in Thailand (1976)
Russ. Helsinki group arrested (1977)	Coronation in Iran (1967)	British direct rule on N. Ireland (1972)	Johnson president (1963-68)	Riots in South Africa (1976)
Brezhnev assumes title of president (1977)	Arafat chairman PLO (1969)	Two Germanies est. diplomat. relations (1973)	Malcolm X shot (1965)	
New Soviet Const. (1978)	Golda Meir (1969-74)	H. Schmidt elec. (1974)	Watts riots (1965)	
	Sadat (1970-81)	Turkey invades Cyprus (1974)	Anti-war protests beg. (1966)	
	Milit. coup in Turkey (1971)	Greece restores dem. (1974)	25th Amendment (1967)	
	Arab-Israeli clashes (1972)		Che Guevara killed (1967)	

Table 6: 1921-1991 *Continued*

ARMENIA & THE USSR	THE MUSLIM WORLD	EUROPE	THE AMERICAS	AFRICA/ASIA/AUSTRALIA
Treaty with Vietnam (1978)	Iran nationalizes oil (1973)	Portugal restores dem. (1974)	Martin L. King assass. (1968)	Death of Mao (1976)
Afghanistan invaded (1979)	Arab-Israeli War (1973)	Juan Carlos I (1975-)	R. Kennedy assass. (1968)	Gang of Four arrested (1976)
Sakharov banished (1980)	Oil embargo (1973-74)	Helsinki accords (1975)	Nixon president (1969-74)	War in Angola (1976-88)
Andropov (1982-84)	Rabin (1974-77)	Pope John Paul II (1978-)	Moon landing (1969)	Fukuda P.M. of Japan (1976)
Korean airline shot over USSR (1983)	Golan Heights truce (1974)	M. Thatcher elected (1979)	Chicago Eight trial (1969)	Djibouti indep. (1977)
Chernenko (1984-85)	Nixon in Middle East (1974)	Mountbatten assass. (1979)	Allende in Chile (1970-73)	US-China est. full diplom. relations (1978)
Sakharov hunger strike (1984)	US halts aid to Turkey (1975)	Birth of Solidarity (1980)	Kent State killings (1970)	Botha P.M. S. Africa (1978)
Gorbachev (1985-91)	Saudi King Khalid (1975-82)	Mitterand elected (1981)	Pentagon Papers (1971)	Vietnam invades Cambodia (1979)
Gorbachev-Reagan summit (1985)	Suez reopened (1975)	A. Papandreou elected (1981)	26th Amendment (1971)	Indira Gandhi (1980-84)
Glasnost/Perestroika (1987)	Lebanese Civil War (1975-89)	Jaruzelski in power (1981-89)	Waldheim in UN (1971)	Zimbabwe Indep. (1980)
Baltic and Karabagh movements begin (1988)	OPEC raises oil prices (1975)	Assas. attempt on pope (1981)	Watergate Affair (1972-75)	ANC more active (1981-93)
Harutiunian (1988-1990)	Begin (1977-83)	H. Kohl elected (1982)	SALT I (1973)	B. Aquino assass. (1983)
Earthquake in Armenia (1988)	Milit. coup in Pakistan (1977)	ECSC issues document (1983)	Nixon resigns (1974)	Golden Temple killing (1984)
Gorbachev president (1988)	Sadat in Israel (1977)	J. Popieluzko killed (1984)	Ford president (1974-76)	Rajiv Gandhi (1984-91)
Soviet open elections (1989)	Milit. coup in Afghan. (1978)	Gibraltar-Spanish border opened after 16 years (1985)	US Bicentennial (1976)	Hong Kong accord (1984)
Soviets leave Afghan. (1989)	Camp David Accord (1978)	Anglo-Irish Agreement (1985)	J. Carter president (1977-80)	C. Aquino pres. (1986)
Yeltsin leaves CPSU (1990)	Islamic Rev. in Iran (1979)	K. Waldheim elected (1986)	Panama Canal Treaty (1977)	Tokyo Summit (1986)
Mutalibov (1990-91)	Milit. coup in Turkey (1980)	O. Palme assass. (1986)	SALT II Treaty (1979)	Sanctions on S. Africa (1986)
Elchibey (1991-92)	Iran-Iraq War (1980-88)	V. Havel elected (1989)	Sandinistas (1979-90)	Macao accord (1987)
Gamsakhurdia (1991-92)	Iran releases hostages (1981)	Dem. in Poland (1989)	Grain embargo on Sov. (1980)	Tamil revolt Sri Lanka (1987)
Attempted coup (1991)	Mubarak (1981-)	Berlin Wall down (1989)	Reagan president (1981-88)	Strikes in S. Africa (1988)
CIS formed (1991)	Saudi King Fahd (1982-)	Ceausescu killed (1989)	Falkland Islands War (1982)	F. W. De Klerk (1989-94)
Armenia member CIS (1991)	Özal (1983-93)	Dem. In Hungary (1989)	Grenada invaded (1983)	Martial law in Tibet (1989)
USSR ends (1991)	Peres (1984-90)	German unification (1990)	Star Wars proposed (1983)	Tianamen Sq. killing (1989)
Armenia independent (1991)	Milit. coup in Sudan (1985)	L. Walesa elected (1990)	Irangate scandal (1986)	Revolt in Liberia (1990)
Ter Petrossian (1991-)	US bombs Libya (1986)	European Union (1991)	INF Treaty (1988)	Emperor Akihito (1990-)
	Intifada begins (1988)	Yugoslav breakup and factional war begins (1991)	Bush president (1989-92)	Civil War in Chad (1990)
	B. Bhutto (1988-1990)		Panama invasions (1989)	
	Gulf War (1990-91)		Malta Summit (1989)	

Table 6: 1921-1991 *Continued*

XXI

From NEP to Perestroika:
Soviet Armenia (1921-1991)

The heart of the former republic had been saved and was once again under Russian, albeit Soviet, protection and rule. By June 1921 most of Zangezur was either captured or, after being assured by Lenin's representative, the diplomatic Miasnikian, that Armenia would keep Zangezur and the rebels would be granted amnesty, had been pacified. The last Dashnak stronghold remained active in Meghri until July 13, when its members crossed the Arax into Iran. For the next seven decades Armenia was to have only one official party: the Armenian Communist Party. A number of minor socialist parties like the Socialist Revolutionaries, Mensheviks, and Specifists, either abandoned political activities, were later purged, or joined the Communist Party of Armenia.

A number of parties remained active in the diaspora. The smallest was the Hnchak party. Like European socialists and communists, the Hnchaks had factions who opposed the Soviets, but they ultimately lost and the party firmly supported almost all the policies of the new Soviet Armenia. A group of Armenian socialists, who called themselves the Progressive League (*Harachdimakan*), were not usually in agreement with Moscow, but generally found a common dialogue with the Hnchaks. A much larger party was the Armenian Democratic Liberal Party (*Ramkavar Azatakan Kusaktsutiun*). Although it was established in 1921, after the Sovietization of Armenia, the party was actually formed by merging the oldest and newest Armenian political groups, that is the Armenakans, reformed Hnchaks, the People's Party, and the Constitutional Democrats. The party was thus a combination of conservatives, liberals, middle class artisans, professionals, wealthy businessmen, and intellectuals. Although liberal and capitalist, the Ramkavars felt

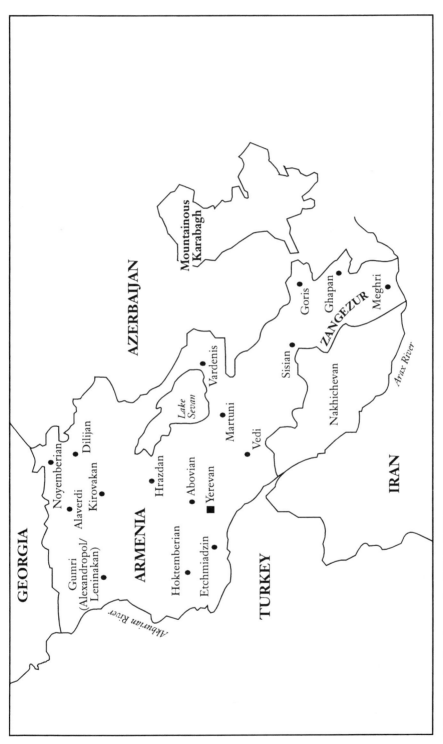

Map 24: Soviet Armenia (1921-1991)

that since, for the moment, Soviet Armenia was the only national state the Armenians had, and that since without Russian protection, Armenia, land-locked and surrounded by enemies, could not survive, it should be support-ed, communist though it might be. The largest and most active party, the Armenian Revolutionary Federation or Dashnaktsutiun, not only did not sup-port Soviet Armenia, but felt that they had been betrayed by the Bolsheviks. They vowed to work with the enemies of the Soviet Union and not to rest until historic Armenia was liberated.

NEP in Armenia

War Communism had turned many supporters of the Bolsheviks against them and on March 15, 1921 Lenin admitted that some Bolsheviks had become over-zealous. A new policy, one which would result in a slower tran-sition to communism was implemented. The policy, termed the New Eco-nomic Policy (NEP), did not abandon communist goals, but permitted some economic incentives, as well as joint-ventures with the West, or state capital-ism. Bolshevik officials who were more sensitive to local traditions and cul-tures replaced their zealous comrades. As we have seen, Miasnikian, a man close to Lenin, was dispatched to Armenia as First Secretary to pacify the region and to gently lead it into the Soviet fold. Armenia and the rest of Transcaucasia were to move even more slowly then Russia proper, Lenin wrote, toward socialism. Miasnikian, a seasoned party member, promised to try and regain some territory in the upcoming negotiations with Turkey, and was successful in pacifying Zangezur, which, with Lenin's backing, remained a part of Armenia. Moscow, it seemed, had finally realized that Zangezur was the only buffer between Turkey and the Turkic peoples of the Soviet Union.

Since the Transcaucasian states had to ratify the Treaty of Moscow, they met with Russian and Turkish representatives at Kars. The negotiations last-ed for almost three weeks and although the Soviet delegation tried to restore at least Ani and Koghb (present-day Tuzlucha) to Armenia, the Turks refused. The Treaty of Kars (October 13, 1921) resulted in the same borders agreed to in Moscow, borders which still separate Armenia and Georgia from Turkey today (see map 24).

Beginning in November 1919 and ending in December 1921, Turkish forces attacked Armenian and French positions in Marash, Sis, Hadjin, Urfa, and Aintab. The French refused to commit forces to defend Cilicia. First they abandoned half of the region, and at the end of 1921, in exchange for

Map 25: Mountainous Karabagh (1923-1991)

keeping Syria, the French diplomat Franklin Bouillion, handed Cilicia to the Turkish nationalists. Having resolved the Armenian Question in Cilicia and western Armenia, Kemal concentrated all his efforts on the Greek armies in Asia Minor. By the end of 1922 Turkish forces were successful in defeating the Greeks and pushing them out of Asia. The Armenian quarters of Smyrna were burned and the Armenian and Greek population were massacred or fled aboard Western ships to Greece. The final blow was to come one year later, when the European powers, setting aside their rhetoric, abandoned the Armenians and renegotiated the Treaty of Sèvres. The Treaty of Lausanne (July 24, 1923) did not even mention the Armenian Question. Turkey paid no reparations and was not blamed for any atrocities it had committed during the war. It agreed, however, to protect its Christian minorities—-few of whom, by then, remained in Turkey. The Straits were demilitarized and open to all ships in time of peace and neutral ships in time of war. Turkey, which was defeated in the World War, nevertheless, with Bolshevik assistance and at the expense of Armenia, had regained territories it had lost in 1878.

By 1924 Turkey had abolished the sultanate and caliphate and had become a republic with Mustafa Kemal as its first president. In just over a decade Kemal introduced the Latin alphabet, changed the names of many cities to Turkish, such as Istanbul for Constantinople and Izmir for Smyrna, encouraged the removal of the veil, granted women the vote, regained control of the Straits, secularized Turkey, began agricultural and industrial reforms through a five-year plan (loosely based on the Soviet model), forced the French to give up the sanjak of Alexandretta (1939), and overall managed to improve Turkey's image in Europe.

For the Armenians the uncertainty was finally over. They had managed to retain Zangezur and the presence of the new Russian state guaranteed Armenian security. As we have seen, more Armenians lived outside than inside Soviet Armenia, most of them in Tiflis, Baku, and in a number of cities in Russia. Economically the most backward of the Transcaucasian republics, with no major industry, Armenia needed the support of Russia and the help of her two larger neighbors, who controlled all the routes in and out of the landlocked republic. Armenia was therefore ready to become allied with the Russian Republic and to form a union with Georgia and Azerbaijan. In the meantime, Stalin, the commissar in charge of the Soviet nationalities, wanted to combine Transcaucasia into one unit and attach it politically and economically to Moscow. Georgia resisted such ties but in the end, realizing it would remain alone, agreed, especially since the border disputes between the republics had to be resolved. All three were rewarded in a fashion:

Armenia received Lori, but Georgia received Akhalkalak; Armenia retained Zangezur, but Azerbaijan received Karabagh and Nakhichevan. Nakhichevan, a part of the Yerevan Province, had a Muslim majority, while the mountainous region of Karabagh, had a solid Armenian majority. As a concession to protests from Armenian communists, Mountainous Karabagh (Nagorno Karabakh in official Soviet terminology) was classified as an autonomous region within Azerbaijan, and Nakhichevan was made an autonomous republic subordinate to Azerbaijan (see map 25).

In spring 1922 the three republics formed a federal union, which gave them some autonomy vis-à-vis Moscow. Although Stalin was not satisfied with this arrangement and wanted their total subordination, Lenin insisted that the republics retain a degree of autonomy. By fall of that year the USSR (Union of the Soviet Socialist Republics) was created. The Transcaucasian Federal Union was dissolved and a Transcaucasian Federated Republic took its place. Russia (which also included Turkestan, or the five present-day Muslim republics of Central Asia) Ukraine, Belorussia, and Transcaucasia formed the USSR. Each republic had its own constitution, modeled after that of the Russian Republic. Local communist parties became subordinate to the party chiefs (Central Executive Committee) in the Kremlin, which, in turn, controlled the Presidium. The budget of individual republics was part of the all-union budget. Foreign policy, foreign trade, civil and criminal legislation, education, health services, and the army, were unified for the entire USSR. In the case of Transcaucasia, the federation decisions were subordinate to Moscow's. Armenia, as the junior member of the federation, had to occasionally give in to its stronger neighbors, but Miasnikian's closeness to Lenin's and Stalin's representative in Transcaucasia, and Georgia's resistance to Moscow, gained Armenia some leverage.

The years of NEP had a great effect on Armenian economy and culture. One of Lenin's major decisions prior to his illness was the concept of "nativization" (*korenizatsiia*), which was to encourage the various nationalities to administer their own republics. All local newspapers, schools, and theaters would use the native language of the republic. The language and culture of each republic was to be supported by the state. Lenin surmised that this was the only way to bring the republic's intellectuals into the party and to convince the nationalities that Russian chauvinism was a thing of the past and that communism would treat all equally.

Armenians from other regions were encouraged to immigrate. Armenian intellectuals from Tiflis and Baku, faced with the cultural nativization of Georgia and Azerbaijan, moved to Yerevan. Immigrants from Europe and the Middle East arrived as well. Yerevan's population doubled and some industry began to be developed, although the population of Armenia remained predominantly agrarian. For the first time Armenian became the official language of the republic. All illiterate citizens up to age fifty had to enroll in schools and learn their own language. Special schools were created to produce teachers. Schools were opened in the cities and villages and a State University was founded in Yerevan. A science institute was established and after more than five hundred years, Armenian once again was used in scientific publications and lectures. The many dialects of the immigrants and locals created a problem, hence the dialect spoken in Yerevan became the standard literary language and a simplified orthography was devised as well. Historians, linguists, composers, painters, sculptors, novelists, and poets, such as Leo, Adjarian, Abeghian, Spendarian, and Sarian, came to Armenia and were given state support for pursuing their art on their native soil. A conservatory of music, national theater, and a film studio were established as well. Religion was not condemned but anti-religious propaganda was rigorously advocated by the state. The urban population, still small, was less religious than the peasant masses. Although the catholicos recognized the Soviet Armenian republic, there was an uneasy relation between the Church and the leaders of the Armenian Communist Party. Finally, the traditional role of women was changing, much to the chagrin of Armenia's men. Abortion, divorce, and a female presence in the work force were introduced. Nationalism and anti-Soviet sentiments were not tolerated, but nativization, and the departure of Muslims to Azerbaijan, created a more homogenous Armenia. Armenian language, literature, and the arts, within the limits imposed by communism, continued to unite and revitalize the nation. Between 1920 and 1937 Armenian writers and poets such as Tumanian, Issahakian, Derian, Armen, Yessayan, Mahari, Totoventz, Alazan, Zorian, Bakunts, Demirjian, and Charents managed to combine socialism with their nationalist temperament and to revive the eastern Armenian literary tradition of Abovian and Raffi.

In the meantime, political changes were occurring in Armenia. At the end of 1923 the Dashnaktsutiun officially ended its presence in Armenia and its members, together with independent socialists, were thrown out of the Communist Party and government posts; some were arrested as well. Miasnikian, who died in a plane crash in 1925, was succeeded by Ashot Hovhannesian, who was purged in 1927. He was replaced by Haik Hovsepian, who lasted one year and was replaced for the next two years by Haigaz Kostanian.

Stalin and the Armenians

In Russia, the three years following Lenin's death in 1924 witnessed the rise of Stalin and the demise of Trotsky. Meanwhile, NEP had not produced its desired effect. Industry was not growing sufficiently and low agricultural prices were forcing the peasants to hold back their produce. By fall 1928, food shortages in the cities put an end to the arguments of those who favored the continuation of NEP. Stalin, who had aligned himself with Bukharin, a NEP supporter, in order to destroy Trotsky, Kamenev and Zinoviev, now rid himself of Bukharin. As Stalin consolidated his power, people loyal to him were promoted, the rest demoted or removed. In spring 1929 Stalin's *Socialism in One Country*, as an alternative to NEP, and his five year plan to industrialize Russia were put into motion. In order to support rapid industrialization, the peasants had to join collective farms and give up their grain and animals to the state.

The result was peasant resistance. Farmers killed their animals and destroyed their crops rather than surrender them. Close to one million animals were killed in Armenia alone. In the long run, resistance was futile and after threats, arrests and executions, as well as such measures as the state-organized famine in the Ukraine, Armenian peasants, like all others, were collectivized. The harsh conditions on the farms and in the villages forced many to the cities and a new working class emerged. Industry burgeoned under heavy state sponsorship and central economic planning. The entire economy was under state control. Armenia's working classes grew and soon made up one-third of the population. The peasants rose in the party ranks as well and the whole nature of the party began to change. The next step was to purge anyone who questioned or opposed the new order. Old communists were replaced with Stalin's protégés and henchmen. In 1930 Stalin made Aghasi Khanjian the head of the Armenian Communist Party. His efforts on behalf of Armenia and his concern over Karabagh made Khanjian a popular leader, which caused him to become unpopular with Beria, the powerful Georgian leader, a close friend of Stalin and the unofficial watchdog in Transcaucasia. In 1936 Khanjian was called to Tiflis and there "committed suicide." Khanjian was replaced with Haik Amatuni, who purged Armenia of Khanjian's supporters. A year later, Amatuni and his group were purged for not being diligent enough in cleansing Armenia of the enemies of communism. Mikoyan and Beria now arrived in Yerevan and appointed Grigor Harutiunian from Tiflis, a henchman of Beria's, to head Armenia. Almost the entire cadre of Armenian top rank communists, as well as many intellectuals, were arrested, executed, or exiled to Siberia. Among them were Kasian, Nurijanian, Hovsepian, Amatuni, and Charents. By 1939 the purges were over and Stalin and the secret police (NKVD) had eliminated all opposition. The older Marxist generation of mostly non-working class intellectuals was replaced by a younger generation, either working class or career bureaucrats, loyal to Stalin, and who remained in power until the early 1980s. The state had eliminated all resistance and had a monopoly over every aspect of the political, socioeconomic and cultural life of its citizens.

Another blow to Armenia, as well as to other nationalities, was the end of nativization. Russian became compulsory for all students. Students were encouraged to enroll in the new Russian schools that had opened in Armenia. Anyone wishing to be promoted or advance in Moscow felt that Armenian schools, although not illegal, would lead them to a professional a dead end. Russian words replaced certain Armenian terms as well. Nationalism was condemned and replaced with Soviet patriotism, itself a form of Russian nationalism. The novels of Raffi were condemned as nationalistic. Many of the most talented writers, such as Yessayan, were arrested and died in prison. According to one scholar, the purges totally halted the eastern Armenian literary revival. The Church was not spared, for anti-religious activities increased and when Catholicos Khoren I (1933-1938) was reportedly strangled in Etchmiadzin, no new catholicos was elected. Abstract art was condemned and Socialist Realism became the norm for all the arts. In time Russians took over some of the top positions in government and began viewing themselves and being viewed as superior to non-Russians.

The Second World War brought many changes to Armenia. The Nazi danger forced Stalin to reconcile with the Church and seek the support of all nationalities to save their collective homeland. The works of Raffi were once again published, churches and the printing press at Etchmiadzin were opened and a new seminary was permitted to train priests. Some priests were allowed to return from Siberia as well. Nazi atrocities frightened people into forgetting the abuses of the past and rally around the state. The fear of Turkey led Armenians to reject any other possible action. Turkey was flirting with the Nazis and von Papen's missions to Ankara were not ignored. Most able-bodied Armenian men were at the front, as was the Red Army, and there would be little protection against an attack from Turkey. The memories of similar circumstances during World War One were still alive.

A small group of Dashnaks in Eastern Europe, on their own initiative, joined the Nazis (not out of sympathy for Hitler, but against Communist

Russia) to liberate Armenia, but the majority of Armenians at home and the diaspora were opposed to Hitler and joined the American armed forces, the French Resistance, and particularly the Red Army, where half a million Armenian troops engaged in the heaviest battles, produced sixty generals, and four out of the ten marshals of the Soviet Union, including Marshal Bagramian. Armenian losses approached 175,000 in a war which, according to new data, took more than 30 million Soviet lives. By the end of the war a new Catholicos, Gevorg VI (1945-1954), who, as a bishop, had cooperated with the Soviets in the war effort, was elected and allowed to live in Etchmiadzin. The Church and the state started a repatriation campaign. Many Armenians in the diaspora, especially the Ramkavars and Hnchaks, supported the return to the homeland. The repatriation brought over 100,000 Armenians, mostly from Greece and the Middle East. Most of these were the immigrants who had been displaced during the 1915-1922 period. Their arrival in a socialist state which was devastated after the war was not particularly welcomed by the local population, who resented sharing the little that was left after the war. They were condescendingly referred to as *aghbar* (which can best be rendered as "the poor relations"). By 1948, with the advent of the Cold War, their inability to adapt themselves to Soviet-style living and thinking made them suspect and many were exiled to Siberia.

The Armenian Question was raised again by Stalin, who demanded the return of Kars and Ardahan, or as he viewed them, the Russian territories gained in 1878 and lost in 1921. Turkey, which had good relations with the Soviets until the mid-1930s, had a rapprochement with the Nazis and, after the war, was internationally isolated. Stalin's motive had nothing to do with the Armenians, for reportedly the territory was to be added to the Georgian republic. Rather, the Armenian Question was merely used as a cover for Stalin's expansionist policy in the Middle East (also manifested in the Soviet actions in supporting Iranian Azerbaijani communists in 1945-1946). The repatriation of Armenians and the publication of works on the Armenian genocide was thus sanctioned by Moscow. The policy forced Turkey to seek aid from the United States. Turkey was brought into the Western Alliance and eventually joined NATO and the Armenian Question was shelved. Kremlin's policy towards the Armenians changed as well. Repatriates were suspect and books on the genocide ceased to be published. By 1950 Communism in China and the Korean War had put an end to cooperation with the former Allies and had increased the Cold War mentality. As in the ancient, classical, and medieval periods, Armenia was once again caught between two super-powers. In the event of war, American missiles in western Armenia (eastern Turkey) would be deployed against eastern Armenia and vice-versa. Contact between Armenia and the diaspora virtually ceased and Stalin began to tighten the reigns on any expressions of national culture. Raffi was again banned and modern writers and composers, such as Aram Khatchaturian, were told that their works were too nationalistic and lacked a working class spirit. A new purge removed suspected "Dashnaks" from Armenia to Central Asia.

Stalin's policies had a major socioeconomic impact on Armenia. As industry was encouraged, peasants began to arrive in the cities and the urban population increased. Armenia slowly changed from a peasant economy into an industrial one, a process which continued until the late 1970s. Yerevan changed as well. The dusty town was transformed into a major urban center. Designed by city-planner and architect Tamanian, boulevards were laid out and an opera, museums, national archives, and government buildings and boulevards were constructed, many from the red, red-orange, yellow, and lilac-colored volcanic tufa stone which gives Yerevan its distinctive look. The planned Soviet economy was designed to sustain the mutual inter-dependence of the republics by assigning the production of specific products to each region. Armenia and other small republics were to feel the full impact of these measures upon their independence four decades later.

Khrushchev and the Armenians

Stalin's death in 1953 opened a new era for Armenia and the rest of the Soviet Union. The first step towards this was to remove the pervasive control of the secret police. Beria was shot and the top NKVD henchmen in the Soviet Union, including Armenia, were removed. Suren Tovmasian became the new head of the Armenian Communist Party and held power until 1960. Tovmasian was a part of Stalin's bureaucracy and thus little changed politically in Armenia during his tenure. On the social and cultural levels changes did occur, however. Nikita Khrushchev's attack, backed by Anastas Mikoyan, a top-ranking member of the politburo, on Stalin's cult and crimes, enabled the rehabilitation of dead communists such as Khanjian and Charents, the release of thousands from the Siberian gulag, and the re-publication of Raffi and Patkanian. Stalin's body was removed from Lenin's tomb on Red Square, his large statue in Armenia was toppled and eventually replaced by one of Mother Armenia. Armenian language and culture were once again accepted by the party and a new nativization emerged. Armenians from other parts of the USSR came to Yerevan, as did a number from Iran. Political conditions improved for the former repatriates and some were even permitted to emigrate.

Khrushchev's changes in the economic sector were significant for Armenia as well. Large collective farms were divided into smaller ones. Armenia was permitted to plant other crops besides grain. Tobacco, vegetables, grapes and other fruits, more suitable to Armenia's soil and climate were planted. Local ministries responsible to Moscow were given more decision-making authority and better-educated managers. For decades the Soviet consumer had sacrificed material goods for the industrial growth and defense of the country. The peasants and workers of all nationalities craved relief from these depravations. In the Khrushchev era consumers goods began to appear and farmers were permitted to cultivate small plots for their own personal use. The production of livestock and various irrigation projects increased Armenia's agricultural output. A lack of land, however, meant that Armenia's farms produced less than its neighbors', and that Armenia had to rely on other republics for its food. Armenia's strength was in the industrial sector, which surpassed that of Georgia and Azerbaijan. Soviet Armenia had started with 80 percent of its population engaged in agriculture and seven decades later ended with close to 80 percent of its population living in urban centers and engaged in heavy industry, management, and services. Khrushchev's efforts to dismantle the Stalin bureaucracy and launch experiments in the economic and political sectors began a power struggle in the early 1960s. Iakov Zarobian, who was not associated with the old regime, was put in charge in Armenia. A new group of intellectuals and managers arose who, although subordinate to Moscow, frequently had the welfare of Armenia uppermost in their minds. A new kind of nationalism, a certain pride of Armenian abilities, skills, and achievements had emerged by 1965 which was to have a major cultural and political effect on Armenia over the next two decades.

Brezhnev and the Armenians

The ouster of Khrushchev in 1964 moved the Soviet Union into a long period of stagnation. Reforms and experimentation abruptly halted and under the leadership of Leonid Brezhnev, many Stalinist bureaucrats or *apparatchiks* were slowly brought back to the Kremlin as well as to the rest of the country. By 1966 Anton Kochinian, a typical party functionary, was put in charge of Armenia. The door opened by Khrushchev, the demand for consumer goods and artistic freedom, as well as national pride, could not now be completely shut. Rather, Brezhnev's system began an era of "benevolent neglect." Local party bosses, all loyal to Moscow and protégés of Stalin's bureaucrats, were allowed greater autonomy in running the affairs of their republics. As long as the production quotas were fulfilled and there was no turmoil, the center interfered little in local matters. As a concession to Armenian national senti-ments and the more emancipated intelligentsia, party leaders slowly permit-ted the construction of monuments to the heroes of Sardarabad, the victims of the genocide, General Andranik and Vardan Mamikonian. Numerous books on Armenian history and literature were printed. The Armenian geno-cide and the history of the 1920s were discussed far more openly than before, albeit, still with some restrictions. A new generation of writers and artists such as Baruir Sevag, Gevorg Emin, Hovhannes Shiraz, Minas Avetisian, and Hagop Hagopian began a new era in Armenian arts. In the 1970s a Soviet census revealed that over 99 percent of Armenians in the republic considered Armenian, rather than Russian, their national language. Even the Kurds, Assyrians and Azeris living in Armenia spoke Armenian. No other republic had as high a percentage of inhabitants who considered their national language as their primary mode of communication. By the 1970s Armenians constituted 90 percent of the population of the republic, a higher percentage than any other ethnic group living in their own republic. The troubling fact remained, however, that despite this, Armenians, after the Jews, were still the most dispersed nationality in the USSR. Only two-thirds of the Armenians of the USSR lived in Armenia, with the remaining one-third, primarily in Georgia, Azerbaijan, and Russia. Hence, while Armenians in Armenia were glowing with national pride, outside the republic, many Armenians were becoming Russified.

Tourism became a significant part of Soviet Armenia's economy, Arme-nians from the diaspora were encouraged to come to the homeland and see its progress first hand. Hotels and museums were opened and exchange pro-grams were established. A special Committee for Cultural Relations with Armenians Abroad was formed and symbolically housed in the building of the last independent Dashnak government in Yerevan. Even Dashnaks were welcome to come to see the great changes for themselves. Armenian text books were printed for Armenian schools in the diaspora and sent free of charge, as well as newspapers, periodical and other books printed in Yere-van.

Industry continued to make major inroads in Armenia and more people moved to the cities. The Medzamor nuclear plant was built in the 1970s to satisfy the need for heat and electricity not only in Armenia but in Georgia and Azerbaijan. As Armenian industrial output increased and surpassed that of Georgia and Azerbaijan, so did its pollution and the damage to its environment. Mount Ararat, shrouded behind a brown veil of smog, could rarely be seen from Yerevan and cancer was on the increase. Every major river in Armenia was declared ecologically dead and poorly planned projects resulted in the lowering of Lake Sevan's water level.

Another distressing development fostered by Brezhnev's policy of benevolent neglect were the cliques and power bases formed by the local communist bosses. Corruption became rampant and a second economy developed, a black market that catered to those who could afford foreign goods or needed favors. Absentee workers appeared on payrolls and some individuals held more than one job. Stealing supplies and goods from the government became commonplace. Inferior structures were built and inferior products made simply to satisfy quotas. Cement and steel was diverted from schools and other state buildings to private houses and paint, doors, windows, toilets, and other items were stolen and sold or used by private contractors. Projects which were economically or ecologically detrimental to Armenia were approved by the party bosses, providing that they benefited personally. Speculation and bribery became commonplace. An individual's network of relations and contacts became far more important than training, knowledge, or talent. Even universities were not immune and professors were known to give high grades in exchange for goods. Those intellectuals and entrepreneurs who could not function under Yerevan's cliques migrated to other republics where their abilities were rewarded and where they achieved high positions in local administrations. At the same time this freer atmosphere also created a new intelligentsia, who despised the prevailing situation and who felt that the corruption, emigration of talented individuals, pollution, and general loss of ethics had put Armenia on the road to disaster. Corruption in Transcaucasia and Central Asia surpassed that found in all other republics and eventually reached proportions which even the Kremlin could not ignore. Anti-Soviet activities on the part of a few dissidents resulted in the removal of Kochinian in 1974 and brought in Karen Demirjian, who was educated in Russia and whose job was to "clean up" the republic. In the early part of his administration, Demirjian cracked down on corruption, but soon after that it was business as usual; by the early 1980s Demirjian and his clique had themselves become part of the problem, rather than its solution. Demirjian's promises, however, had raised the hopes of honest intellectuals and they now demanded concrete changes. A number were given a role in the administration and an uneasy alliance began.

In 1978, during the debate over a new Soviet Constitution, thousands of

Armenians petitioned Moscow for the separation of Mountainous Karabagh and Nakhichevan from Azerbaijan. When Moscow considered changing the constitution and removing the native languages as the official languages of the republics, Armenians, together with the Georgians, protested vehemently and defeated the proposition. Armenian words soon began replacing Russian official terms. Armenian nationalism had resurfaced, but, unlike nationalism in the Baltic states and Georgia, it was not directed against the Russians but against the Turks, and as long as it was not too overt, the Demirjian government allowed its expression. April 24 became an official day of mourning and several items about conditions in Karabagh and the destruction of Armenian monuments in Nakhichevan were published. The Armenian Question was also raised unofficially in some circles. The Church under Catholicos Vazgen I (1954-94) became very active and the catholicos visited many communities in the diaspora. In Armenia, new churches were built, old churches and historical monuments restored, and liturgical works appeared. Armenian priests from abroad came to study at Etchmiadzin and Armenian lay men and women from the diaspora, mostly from the Middle East, especially those with Hnchak and Ramkavar affiliations, arrived to study at Yerevan University.

Political Dissidence in Soviet Armenia

What most Armenians in the diaspora were not aware of was the beginning of a dissident movement in Armenia, which had manifested itself as early as 1967. Tired of communism and dissatisfied with the futile and sometimes self-serving activities of the Armenian political parties in the diaspora, a group of young Armenians formed a secret party in Armenia, ironically on the 50th anniversary of the Bolshevik Revolution. The National Unity Party demanded the return of Nakhichevan, Mountainous Karabagh, and western Armenia and the creation of an independent democratic state. In 1974 it managed to publish illegally one issue of a journal and stage a protest where its members burned Lenin's picture on the main square in Yerevan. Kochinian was blamed for not suppressing the movement and was dismissed and the secret police arrested some of the Armenian activists. The group soon split into two factions. One, led by Stepan Zatikian, advocated terrorism against the Soviet regime and reportedly placed a bomb in the Moscow subway. Some of its members were arrested and executed. The others, moderates, became active as a human rights group, monitoring civil rights on behalf of the Helsinki Accord of 1975. They demanded a degree of self-determination and the freeing of Karabagh from Azeri control, an end to corruption and industrial and nuclear pollution. Karabagh remained the most volatile issue, however. With 80 percent of its population Armenian, it remained under Azeri jurisdiction, which, contrary to their promise of autonomy, had bound it to Baku. Some 125,000 Armenians were, for all intents and purposes, cut off from their culture. The refusal of Yerevan, Baku, or Moscow to act on the Karabagh question, solidified Armenian opposition.

Gorbachev and the Armenians

Brezhnev's death in 1982 ushered in an era of unprecedented change. Yuri Andropov, the head of the KGB, replaced Brezhnev and began tightening state control over the society and attempted a serious crackdown on corruption. Upon his death in 1984, his successor, Konstantin Chernenko, who was elected by the older members of the Central Committee, made a half-hearted attempt to reverse Andropov's disciplinary measures. It was too late, however, for the country was lagging behind the West economically and technologically. A new educated leadership, who had traveled or studied abroad, felt that the whole fabric of Soviet society had to change if it was to compete successfully against the West in the twenty-first century. Chernenko's death, a year later, presented an opportunity for the new intelligentsia to assert themselves. Mikhail Gorbachev, who had the support of the new generation of communist leaders, was elected to lead the country along a very different path. Gorbachev, a "new communist," planned a complete revamping of the Soviet system. He proposed to reconstruct the economic system (*perestroika*), permit free social expression (*glasnost*), and initiate political decentralization (*demokratizatsiia*). Although he opposed the separation of the minorities from the USSR, Gorbachev did promise greater political and cultural autonomy to them.

In early 1988, Armenians in Mountainous Karabagh, encouraged by Gorbachev's declarations and prompted by a number of statements made by Armenian leaders in Armenia and Russia, demonstrated peacefully and demanded to be made part of Armenia. On February 20, the Karabagh Soviet voted overwhelmingly to transfer the region to Armenia. The same day a huge demonstration followed in Yerevan. In the next few days more demonstrations were held in Yerevan and Stepanakert, the Soviet era capital of Mountainous Karabagh. Neither the Moscow nor the Yerevan hierarchy responded. The response came from Azerbaijan, when, during the last three days of February, the Azeris in Sumgait, an industrial town north of Baku, were permitted to carry out a pogrom in which they killed, raped, maimed, and burned hundreds of Armenians and destroyed their property. The pogrom, encouraged by Baku and conducted in full sight of the police, bore shades of the 1895-1896 massacres. Moscow's inaction regarding Sumgait infuriated the Armenians throughout the Soviet Union and turned them against Gorbachev. For the first time in many decades, Armenian nationalism, although primarily against the leadership in the Kremlin, had become anti-Russian in tone. There were unsubstantiated reports that these incidents were welcomed by Gorbachev who wished to discredit the corrupt apparatus in Transcaucasia and Central Asia, which was firmly entrenched and opposed his reforms.

In mid-1988 Demirjian was replaced with Suren Harutiunian, who had served in Moscow and who was unaffiliated with the so-called Mafia in Yerevan. Harutiunian was viewed as just another communist serving a system that had lost its credibility with the Armenian public. By the end of the year the Armenian intelligentsia was split: some of them asked the crowds to calm down and to rely on Gorbachev's reforms to bring about gradual change. They stated that the traditional Armenian doctrine was to rely on Russia. Others, led by the Karabagh Committee, the Union for National Self-Determination, the National Union, all based in Yerevan, and the Crane Committee in Karabagh, realizing that Moscow was not going to consider any historical, demographic, cultural, and even legal arguments in favor of uniting Karabagh with Armenia, demanded more immediate changes, but not secession. Following violent clashes between Soviet troops and demonstrators in Yerevan, Harutiunian lost whatever support he may have had. Although Moscow admitted that Azeris had violated the constitutional rights of the Armenians in Karabagh, and that representatives from Moscow would be dispatched to assess the situation, the rejection by the Supreme Soviet of Karabagh's request to join Armenia increased the tensions. Mass rallies and strikes took place in Yerevan and counter demonstrations in Baku. By the end of 1988 a nightly curfew was imposed throughout Armenia. As the communist government lost credibility, the Karabagh Committee gained respect and in effect became a second government.

At noon, on December 7, 1988 a terrible earthquake struck northwest Armenia killing over 25,000 people and leaving hundreds of thousands injured and homeless. Gorbachev was in New York. His immediate return and the international press coverage that followed brought world attention to Armenia. The Karabagh Committee, led by Ashot Manucharian, Levon Ter Petrossian and Vazgen Manukian, challenged the authority of the state by organizing its own relief effort and despite the catastrophe, continued to demand a resolution to the Karabagh problem. Its eleven members were arrested on orders from Moscow, martial law was declared, and Gorbachev, as well as the catholicos and a number of Armenian intellectuals, urged calm and promised to look into the situation in Karabagh.

In January 1989 Moscow did send Arkady Volskii, who took over the administration of Karabagh from Azerbaijan. In the meantime, Gorbachev was faced with a dilemma. If he sided with more radical reformers, like Boris Yeltsin, the ex-party chief in Moscow, he would be forced to establish a more democratic state and decrease the power of the party. Such an action would inevitably lead to complete independence for some republics, particularly the Baltic states. If he sided with the conservatives, he would have to enforce party discipline, maintain the status quo, and crack down on nationalist dissidents. The struggle divided the USSR. Although the new elections had brought more liberals into the Supreme Soviet, Gorbachev was still forced to maintain a delicate balance among those who wanted faster change, those who preferred a slower pace, and those who opposed any change at all.

By May 1989 Moscow realized it had no choice but to release the members of the Karabagh Committee, who were viewed as national heroes. In the meantime, a general strike in Karabagh aggravated the Azeri rail blockade of Armenia, delayed supplies for earthquake reconstruction, and caused some food and fuel shortages. Meanwhile, the Armenians of Azerbaijan (some 250,000) began to emigrate to Russia and Armenia. By fall the various Armenian dissident and national groups formed the Armenian National Movement or *Hayots Hamazgayin Sharzhum*. For the next five months, the National Movement, led by the scholar Levon Ter Petrossian, and the communists, led by Harutiunian, coexisted. By the summer of 1989 the idea of independence became more and more popular. Some Soviet Armenian dissidents, as well as the Dashnaktsutiun in the diaspora, advocated the restoration of historic Armenia (which included Karabagh, Nakhichevan, and western Armenia). Some Armenians continued to insist that Armenia's salvation lay with the Russians and that pan-Turkism was a greater threat. The leadership of the Armenian National Movement led by Ter Petrossian did not agree. He viewed the question of the restoration of western Armenia, and even Nakhichevan, as unrealistic and untimely. Armenia could not achieve such a goal without the support of a major power, which historically had been proven as disastrous. Karabagh was different, however, he maintained. The Armenians of Karabagh, not the Armenian republic had demanded self-rule. This was not a territorial issue but a self-determination issue. Volskii had to consider the wishes of the Armenian Council of Karabagh which represented the people. In the meantime, Azerbaijan continued its demands for the ouster of Volskii and the restoration of Azeri control over Karabagh. In November the Supreme Soviet voted in favor of Azerbaijan and returned Karabagh to Azeri control.

By the end of 1989 the fall of East European regimes encouraged clashes between nationalists and communists in Azerbaijan and Georgia, and began serious secessionist activities in the Baltic states. Moscow's pro-Azeri stand began a secessionist movement in Armenia as well. The Azeri nationalist leaders could not, or did not, control the masses in Baku and Ganja, and in January 1990 mobs organized pogroms, which killed and maimed Armenians and looted their property in those cities. Russia sent troops to Baku and the remaining Azerbaijani Armenians had to leave all their belongings and flee to Russia or Armenia. Armenians responded by attacking Azeri farmers who lived in Armenia and forced tens of thousands to leave for Azerbaijan. Both sides thus found themselves with numerous refugees. All efforts at negotiations failed and the situation was becoming out of control.

Moscow, fearing Azeri nationalism and Islamic resurgence, far more than Armenian frustrations, used the civil violence in Baku to install Ayaz Mutalibov, a communist, as the new president of Azerbaijan. During the next four months Azerbaijan received Moscow's blessing to crush Armenian resistance in Karabagh. Russian forces were deployed to remove Armenians from their villages and to resettle Azeris in their place. Armenia's total loss of faith in Moscow resulted in major gains for Armenian National Movement candidates in the May elections. The Soviet Armenian flag was replaced with the tri-color of the former independent republic and May 28 became the national day of the Armenian Republic. The Kremlin reacted by giving Baku more control over Karabagh and sending tanks to Yerevan. The Armenian capital and its residents were in a state of shock. The action backfired, and by August, Levon Ter Petrossian was elected as head of the Armenian parliament and announced that, in a year's time, Armenia would have a referendum on the issue of independence. Ter Petrossian was careful to avoid confrontation, however. The use of the word *on* as opposed to *of* independence, as well as Ter Petrossian's conforming to the letter with the requisite process of the Soviet Constitution, meant that Armenia was the only state in the union to follow a true democratic and free, multi-party election, which required two-thirds of the vote for secession. Many Western observers felt that the government of Armenia, by meticulously following every clause and by-law, had prudently created a situation by which Gorbachev could not attack it by sending special forces, as he had done in Lithuania. It would also force the world to recognize Armenia's independence if the referendum went against Moscow. Finally, the Armenian communists had been totally discredited and the National Movement quickly took control of Armenia. Unlike the 1918-1921 period, there was no internal strife during the transition. Despite Moscow's efforts to create conflict in order to justify its military presence, Armenian communists surrendered their posts without a struggle and the new parliament did not take advantage of its opportunity to retaliate against its former leaders. No other republic can boast of such an orderly transition. Ter Petrossian's early months as the head of parliament were spent in disarming those Armenians who, frustrated by the Azeri blockade and the forced deportation of Armenians from Karabagh, had not only taken over police stations and army barracks and threatened the civil order, but sought a conflict with Azerbaijan, a war which Armenia could not win.

During the first eight months of 1991 the Azeris, helped by the Russian army, weapons, and equipment, subjected the Armenians of Karabagh to ferocious bombings and attacks, which, according to a British journalist and historian, resembled Nazi reprisals in occupied Europe. Never, since the anti-Armenian measures of 1903-1907, had there been such violent anti-Armenian feeling on the part of the Russian government. Soviet helicopters and tanks killed, disarmed, and removed Armenians from the Shahumian and Hadrut regions of Karabagh. Numerous villages were depopulated and Azeris even bombed the cities of Goris, Ghapan, Sisian, and Meghri in Zangezur, inside the Armenian republic. The world press, the United Nations, and the major powers stood silent while Armenian men, women and children were surrounded and bombed in Karabagh, and as relief to refugees from Azerbaijan, Karabagh, and the earthquake zone was hampered by the Azeri blockade. Conditions in Armenia reminded some of the situation in 1920, when the republic was under siege.

Gorbachev, meanwhile, tried to save the Soviet Union by creating a treaty which would bind the republics to Russia. But only the Slavic and Muslim republics were ready to sign it. Armenia, Georgia, Moldova, and the Baltic states refused. Armenia paid a high price for its refusal, for Russian troops continued to aid Azerbaijan and the blockade tightened through the first half of 1991. Since Armenia had exported most of its products to Russia and imported much from its neighbors, it now had to face shortages. In spring, Georgia declared its independence and Azerbaijan followed that summer. Armenia was once again left alone to decide its course.

Before the new union treaty could be signed, however, the hard-liners, who did not want a fractured Soviet Union, carried out a coup on August 1991. Although Azerbaijan's president Mutalibov welcomed the coup, and Georgia's new leader, Zviad Gamsakhurdia, remained uncertain, Armenia categorically refused to recognize the coup. It is ironic that Armenia, despite all of Gorbachev's anti-Armenian policies, retained its democratic principles and supported the USSR's legal president against the hard-liners. The coup did not succeed and on September 20 the national referendum in Armenia overwhelmingly (99 percent) voted for independence and on September 21, 1991, the Armenian parliament by a vote of 213 to 0 declared a sovereign state outside the Soviet Union. On September 23, a new Armenian republic was born.

XXII

The New Spiurk:
The Armenian Diaspora in the Last Hundred Years
(1895-1994)

By the end of the nineteenth century, the Armenian communities outside the Ottoman and Russian empires, with the exception of Iran and Egypt, had either assimilated religiously and culturally, or had lost their economic and political influence and were generally reduced to insignificant clusters in a number of urban centers across the old world. The massacres of 1895-1896 and the anti-Armenian policies of Sultan Abdul-Hamid forced many Armenians to emigrate from Anatolia. Some joined the communities in Europe and the Middle East, others journeyed to the Americas. The Armenian genocide created hundreds of thousands of refugees who eventually settled both in the old and new worlds. Although a significant number repatriated to the Armenian republic in 1918-1919, many, as we have seen, fled in 1920-1921, or were deported by Stalin in 1936-1939. A second wave of approximately 100,000 repatriates arrived in Soviet Armenia in 1945-1948 and a third, much smaller group in 1953-1965. By 1985, however, nearly half of the post-war repatriates had emigrated to the West. Revolutions and civil wars in Asia and North Africa, throughout the four decades following the Second World War, resulted in the diminishing of the Armenian communities there and the growth of the Armenian diaspora in Europe, Australia, and the Americas. The historical events of the last one hundred years have thus resulted in a pattern whereby new Armenian immigrants have rejuvenated older diasporas by reviving their Armenian identity. At present Armenians, together with the Jews, are the only significant nationality/religious group which have more members living in the diaspora than in their own country. It is estimated that out of the more than seven million Armenians in the world barely over three million live in the Armenian republic. Like the Jews, Armenians are to be found in almost every country of the globe. The following brief account will survey those communities which can be described as being politically or culturally active.

Armenians in Eastern Europe

The large Armenian communities of Eastern Europe no longer exist. In Poland, the last Armenian Catholic archbishop died in 1938 and most of the remaining Armenians were killed during the Second World War. Lvov, now part of Ukraine, still maintains an active Armenian community centered around its fourteenth-century church. The world wars and the communist regime virtually ended Armenian presence in Hungary. The Armenians of Romania and Bulgaria, received many refugees from the political upheavals in neighboring Russia and Turkey in the years 1915-1922. Following the Second World War Communism closed most of the private enterprises owned by these Armenians. Many Romanian Armenians left for Europe and the United States, while large numbers of Bulgarian Armenians repatriated to Soviet Armenia. In the 1960s, they, too, began to leave for Europe and the United States. Some 5000 Armenians remain in Romania and are concentrated in Bucharest, Constantza, and Tulca. The 10,000 Bulgarian Armenians live primarily in Sofia and Plovdiv. Both communities maintain Armenian centers and churches.

The Armenian Community of Cyprus is also the product of refugees who arrived during the 1895-1922 years. In 1926 the Melkonian Educational Institute was founded to educate and shelter the orphans of the genocide. During the Lebanese civil war, the Melkonian had many students from that war-torn country. Today a large number of its students are Bulgarian Armenians. The 1974 Turkish invasion of Cyprus seriously affected the Armenian community, for most of the Armenian quarter of Nicosia, with its clubs, school, and church, fell into the Turkish-occupied sector. The same was unfortunately true of Famagusta, whose Armenian church and monastery of Surb Makar have been left in ruins and converted to a store. The Cyprus community, which had over 15,000 members before the invasion, has been reduced to only 2,000, with the rest emigrating to the West. Prior to 1895 there were only some 500 Armenians in all of Greece. About 150,000 Armenians arrived after the massacres and the genocide, especially following the expulsions of the Christians from Smyrna in 1922. After the Second World War, thousands left for Armenia, North America, Australia, and Europe. A number of churches, including an Armenian Evangelical church, serve the 10,000 Armenians in Greece, most of whom live in Athens.

Armenians in Western Europe

The Armenian communities of Western Europe had also declined by the end of the nineteenth century. The arrival of refugees from Russia and the Ottoman Empire expanded some established centers and created new ones as well. Of all the Italian cities which had Armenian communities, Venice has remained the only one with a significant Armenian presence, due to the Mekhitarians of San Lazzaro and their Murad-Raphaelian school on the main island. The Armenian communities of Belgium and Holland experienced Europe's world wars firsthand. During the First World War, many Armenians, who were still Turkish citizens, left Belgium for Holland to escape the German onslaught and from fear of being sent back to Turkey to be drafted. Most returned after the war and a chair in Armenian studies was established in the University of Brussels in 1931, with the famed professor Nicholas Adontz as its first chairholder. The community in Holland had all but disappeared, when it got a minor influx from the Armenians who had left Dutch Indonesia in the 1950s after the nationalist government took over there. More Armenians came to Holland from Iran, Turkey and Lebanon in the 1980s and eventually managed to repurchase the Armenian church in Amsterdam, which had been closed in the 1850s. Although barely 10,000 strong, the Armenian communities of Belgium and Holland are culturally active.

France is the only Western European nation to have received a major influx of the survivors of the massacres and genocide, as well as refugees from the political upheavals in the Middle East. Members of the Armenian middle class of Egypt, Syria, Lebanon, and European Turkey who had been educated in France or in local French schools, and who spoke French as a second language, settled in France during the 1930s. In the Second World War, Armenians served in the French army and in the Resistance. Following the war, many Armenians, who escaped the political and military revolutions in the Arab world emigrated to France. The French community not only has grown to some 250,000, but has become the most active Armenian community in Europe. Some thirty-five Armenian churches, twenty of them Apostolic, serve the Armenians who are concentrated in Paris, Marseilles, Lyon, and Nice. Armenian newspapers, organizations, schools, and institutions of higher learning thrive as well, including the Mekhitarian school in Sèvres.

The French-Armenian community has produced artists such as Aznavour, Carzou, and Jansem and scholars such as Sirarpie Der Nersessian. The widely-respected scholarly journal *Revue Des Études Arméniennes* is published in Paris.

A number of post-World War II communities have appeared in Western Europe as a result of political upheavals in the Middle East and are growing steadily due to recent Armenian emigration from the former Soviet Union. The most active of these are in Austria, England, Germany, Scandinavia, and Switzerland. There had been a few Armenians in Austria as early as the seventeenth century and the first coffee-house in Vienna was reportedly established by an Armenian. A number of Armenians from the Polish army had settled in Vienna after they helped to repulse the Turks in 1683. The arrival of the Mekhitarians in 1811 opened the doors to a small number of students from Russia and Turkey. England received a few Armenian merchants from the sixteenth to the eighteenth centuries who in 1780, set up an Armenian press in London. Others arrived after the First World War. Geneva is one city in Switzerland that has a significant Armenian presence. Six churches and a number of cultural centers serve the 50,000 Armenians who live in these communities.

Armenians in the Middle East

The Armenian communities in the Middle East experienced their greatest change in the last one hundred years. The Armenian communities in the Arab world received a large percentage of the refugees and survivors of the massacres and genocide. They increased the numbers of the Armenians in Egypt, Greater Syria, Mesopotamia, Sudan and Ethiopia. The European mandates enabled the Armenians to make advances in the economic and administrative sectors and to establish cultural and political associations. Egypt, with its strong Armenian community, was the guiding head of the Armenians in the Arab world until the mid-twentieth century. At the start of the twentieth century the Egyptian Armenians found a new leader, Boghos Nubar, the son of Nubar Pasha. Boghos had studied agriculture and engineering in Switzerland and France. Upon his return, he had served as the director of the Egyptian railways and had supervised the irrigation plan for the Sudan. He had become a banker and corporate officer in a number of companies and, like his father, was granted the title of *pasha*. The massacres of the Armenians in 1895-1896 in Turkey and especially the Armeno-Azeri clashes in Transcaucasia, beginning in 1905, had a sobering effect on the Armenian middle class of Egypt. Liberals and disenchanted socialists felt that there was a need for a world-wide Armenian philanthropic organization. On Easter day (April 15), 1906, ten Armenian professionals met at Boghos Nubar's mansion in Cairo and drafted the by-laws of the Armenian General Benevolent Union (AGBU).

Although initially there were some plans for the AGBU to also act as a political assembly, the idea was immediately abandoned—-that role was soon taken up by the Sahmanadir Ramkavar party. The AGBU's mission was to help the Armenians in historic Armenia by establishing or subsidizing schools, libraries, workshops, hospitals, and orphanages. It was to provide the peasants with land, seeds, animals, and tools and to assist in time of fire, famine, earthquakes, and other natural or man-made disasters. The aid was for all Armenians, regardless of religious or political affiliation. By 1913 the AGBU had 142 chapters in Europe, America, Africa, and the Ottoman Empire. During the genocide it lost all of its eighty chapters in the Ottoman Turkey. The first decade after the First World War was spent locating orphans and creating orphanages and hospitals. Refugees had to be sheltered and when the Near East Relief withdrew from the Arab lands, AGBU and other Armenian organizations replaced it. The emergence of many new communities, most in dire need, diverted the efforts of Armenian cultural and philanthropic organizations to select parts of the Middle East, Europe and the Americas. As the Bolsheviks consolidated their power in Armenia, it became increasingly difficult for outside organizations to work there, and although the AGBU managed to help Armenia, it concentrated its efforts in the diaspora. At the end of the British protectorate of Egypt in 1922 the AGBU headquarters moved to Paris and after the Second World War to the United States.

The departure of AGBU did not adversely affect the Armenian community of Egypt. The role of the Armenians in the Egyptian government, as well as prosperous Armenian businesses, helped that country remain a major Armenian center, where numerous schools, churches, and newspapers guided the 40,000 Armenians living in Cairo and Alexandria. The political changes in Egypt following the military uprising in 1952 and the economic policies of Egyptian president Nasser after 1956, forced the emigration of many Armenians to Europe, Australia, and the United States. At present there are only some 5000 Armenians left in Egypt, primarily in Cairo. Despite the decline of its Armenian community, Egypt remains an important and active Armenian cultural center.

The much smaller community in Ethiopia received new immigrants at the start of the century and built a church and a number of schools. The Ethiopian Armenians gained favor with Emperor Haile Selassie and an Armenian, Kevork Nalbandian, even composed the former national anthem of Ethiopia. The military revolution there (1974), which nationalized Armenian businesses, reduced the community from some 1,000 to 150 members. The Armenians of Sudan were centered in Khartoum where they built a church. The civil war in Sudan, which began in the late 1980s has drastically reduced the numbers of that community as well.

The Armenian communities of Palestine and Jordan, which were never large, also attracted some refugees from Turkey who laid the foundations for new centers in Jerusalem, Haifa, and Amman. The short-lived security during the British Mandate soon gave way to Arab-Jewish strife. Following the establishment of the State of Israel in 1948 and the Arab-Israeli wars, many Armenians emigrated to Europe, United States, and more peaceful centers in the Middle East. The majority of the Armenians of that region are primarily involved in the religious and scholarly activities surrounding the Armenian patriarchate of Jerusalem.

Most of the Armenian survivors of the massacres and genocide settled in modern Syria, mainly in Aleppo. The new arrivals were aided by Armenian and American missionary and philanthropic organizations and succeeded in invigorating the earlier settlements and creating one of the most active Armenian diasporas in the twentieth century. In many ways the Armenian schools, churches, centers, and hospitals in Syria, especially in Aleppo and its environs, became the inspiration and models for the Armenian communities of Beirut, Baghdad, Jerusalem, and Amman during the second half of the twentieth century. Until the end of the Second World War, the region was under British and French mandates. Fortunately the area did not become a theater of war during the Second World War and actually benefited from the material and personnel which were concentrated there to repulse the Germans from North Africa. Armenians, Assyrians, Christian Arabs, and a number of non-Sunni Muslim sects such as the Druzes, `Alawis, and Isma`ilis, were favored by and cooperated with the Europeans. Syria's independence in 1944 did not threaten the well-being of the Armenian community which continued to grow to some 75,000. The revolution of 1958 and the creation of the United Arab Republic with Egypt, as well as the military coup of 1963, not only hurt Armenian businesses, but restricted Armenian cultural activities. Some emigrated to Lebanon, others to the United States. Luckily, Syria soon abandoned the political and economic programs of Egypt and starting in 1971 President Hafez al-Assad reformed the extreme policies of the Ba`th

Party and created a more tolerant Syria, where social programs and businesses have striven to sustain the large population growth of the country. The
`Alawis are in charge of major government posts and the Armenians are
treated well. In Aleppo alone there are some 40,000 Armenians who utilize
Armenian centers, ten schools, a hospital, and organize numerous communi-
ty-sponsored events. The community in Damascus has also grown in the last
quarter of a century and new Armenian businesses have managed to stop the
flow of emigration. In fact Armenians from Lebanon, Iraq, and Kuwait, who
have fled turmoil in those countries, have settled, temporarily or permanently, in Damascus. Syria, with over 100,000 Armenians has, at present, the
largest Armenian community in the Arab world.

The Armenians of Lebanon were, for a time, the most important Armenian community outside of the Soviet Union and the United States. The core
of the modern community also arrived as a result of massacres and genocide
in Turkey. By 1926 there were some 75,000 Armenians in Lebanon and the
Lebanese Constitution granted them and other minorities civil rights, which,
in time, enabled the Armenians to elect their own members of parliament.
The country's geographic location and the security offered by the French, as
well as its Christian-dominated government, attracted more Armenians there
and in 1930 the catholicosate of Cilicia moved to Antelias, outside of Beirut.
Armenian Catholic and Evangelical Churches also established centers in
Beirut. In 1939 the sanjak of Alexandretta, which includes Musa Dagh, was
transferred to Turkey. As a result 30,000 Armenians moved into Syria and
Lebanon. The Armenians of Musa Dagh settled in the highlands of Anjar.
Armenians rose swiftly to economic and social prominence, and Lebanon's
liberal government made it possible for all Armenian political parties to
establish themselves. During the short-lived Lebanese civil strife of 1958 the
Armenians split and sided with both factions. By 1974 there were over
200,000 Armenians, who had two dozen churches, some seventy schools,
including institutions of higher learning, such as the Haigazian College,
founded in 1955 by the Armenian Missionary Association of America and
the Union of the Armenian Evangelical Churches in the Near East. In addition there were more than fifty athletic, compatriotic, and benevolent organizations, and numerous literary and cultural periodicals and newspapers. The
Lebanese civil war from 1974-1989 took its toll and although Armenians
remained neutral and much of their community infrastructure remained
undamaged, thousands left for safer shores, especially the United States.
Some 75,000 have remained and thanks to their neutrality and the efforts of
their leaders, have played a role in the Syrian-backed National Accord Docu-

ment, and are once again enjoying the benefits of Lebanon's unique situation. Forty-seven Armenian schools and numerous associations and organizations, including an Armenian Fund for Economic Development are putting the community on the road to recovery with members in parliament and the central government.

The Armenians in Iraq arrived primarily in the 1920's and, during the British mandate, established communities in Baghdad, Mosul, and Basra. Armenians were engaged in private businesses, worked in technical, administrative and financial positions for the British Petroleum Company, or participated in the trade between the Persian Gulf and the Mediterranean. Even after Iraq achieved its independence in 1932, the British presence did not end and the Armenians continued to enjoy the benefits of Iraq's economic rise, especially since they, unlike the Assyrians and Kurds, did not engage in anti-government and nationalist activities and were viewed as loyal citizens. Armenian businesses, churches, schools, and organizations grew until there were some 35,000 Armenians in that country. The revolution of 1958 and the subsequent radical policies of the Ba`th Party forced the migration of many Armenians from Iraq to Lebanon, Kuwait, United States, and the Gulf States. During the Iran-Iraq War (1980-1988) Armenians were drafted and killed both in the Iranian and Iraqi forces. The difficult political and economic conditions, combined with the disastrous Gulf War, spelled the doom of the Armenian community of Iraq. Many emigrated or have temporarily abandoned the unstable situation. Less than 10,000 Armenians remain in Iraq today.

By the twentieth century, Iran, like Egypt, was a major center of Armenian life in the Middle East. As we have seen, by the end of the nineteenth century, there were some 100,000 Armenians in Iran. The proximity of the Armenians in Iranian Azerbaijan to Transcaucasia and eastern Anatolia brought them under the influence of the political activities of Russian and Turkish Armenians. Armenakan, Hnchak and Dashnak cells opened in Tabriz and Salmas and a number of Armenian revolutionaries sought refuge from the tsarist and Turkish police there. The massacres of 1895-1896 brought Armenian refugees to northwestern Iran. The Revolution of 1905 in Russia had a major effect on northern Iran and, in 1906, Iranian liberals and revolutionaries, joined by many Armenians, demanded a constitution in Iran. Although the shah signed the document, his successor dissolved the *majlis* or parliament and it was only in 1909 that the revolutionaries forced the crown to give up some of its prerogatives. The role of Armenian military units under the command of leaders such as Yeprem Khan and Keri, in the Iranian

Constitutional Movement is well-documented.

Thousands of Armenians had escaped to Iran during the genocide. The Turkish invasion of Iranian Azerbaijan during World War One devastated a number of Armenian communities in that region, such as Khoi. The community experienced a political rejuvenation with the arrival of the Dashnak leadership from Armenia in 1921. The establishment of the Pahlavi dynasty began a new era for the Armenians. The modernization efforts of Reza Shah (1924-1941) and Mohammad Reza Shah (1941-1979) gave the Armenians ample opportunities for advancement. Armenian contacts with the West and their linguistic abilities gave them an advantage over the native Iranians. They soon gained important positions in the arts and sciences, the Iranian Oil Company, the caviar industry, and dominated professions such as tailoring, shoemaking, photography, auto-mechanics, and as well the managing of cafes and restaurants. Immigrants and refugees from Russia continued to increase the Armenian community until 1933. World War Two gave the Armenians opportunities to increase their economic power. The Allies decided to use Iran as a bridge to Russia. Western arms and supplies were shipped through Iran and Armenians, with their knowledge of Russian, played a major role in this endeavor. The Hnchaks, especially, were active and the Iranian Communist Party had an Armenian contingent. The majority of the Armenians remained loyal to the Dashnaks, while the minority, who had communist sympathies, either went underground or left with the Iranian Socialists when they fled to Russia in 1946. In 1953 the Iranian and few Armenian communists made a brief comeback during the Mossadeq period, but the return of the shah, once again decimated their ranks. Most Armenians, under Dashnak leadership, however, had remained neutral or loyal to the regime and were rewarded by the shah. For the next quarter of the century Armenian fortunes rose in Iran, and Tehran, Tabriz, and Isfahan became major centers with some 250,000 Armenians. The shah trusted and liked his Armenian subjects and Tehran, like Beirut, became a major center of Armenian life. Armenian churches, schools, cultural centers, sports clubs and associations flourished and Armenians had their own senator and member of parliament. Thirty churches and some four dozen schools and libraries served the needs of the community. Armenian presses published numerous books, journals, periodicals, and newspapers, such as *The Wave* (*Alik*). The better educated upper classes, however, were fewer in number and, compared to their counterparts in Lebanon, were relatively unproductive culturally.

Although the Islamic Revolution has ended the second golden age of the Armenian community in Iran, the community has not lost its prominence altogether. Ayatollah Khomeini's restrictions, the Iran-Iraq War, and the economic problems resulting from Iran's isolation, forced the exodus of 100,000 Armenians. The current government is more accommodating and Armenians, unlike the Kurds and Iranian Azeris, have their own schools, clubs, and maintain most of their churches. The fall of the Soviet Union, the common border with Armenia, and the Armeno-Iranian diplomatic and economic agreements have opened a new era for the Iranian Armenians.

The genocide, as we have seen, destroyed western Armenia and numerous other Armenian centers in Turkey. By the Second World War, Constantinople or Istanbul was the sole urban center with an Armenian presence. In 1945, an arbitrary property tax on the minorities impoverished many Greek and Armenian businessmen. Ten years later, mobs looted and burned Greek and Armenian businesses in Istanbul. At present there are some 75,000 Armenians in Turkey, the majority of whom live in Istanbul, where conditions, despite cultural pressures and occasional hostile acts, are not as unfavorable as one may imagine. Twenty schools, some three dozen churches, and a hospital maintain a strong Armenian identity. A number of Armenian newspapers, including the daily *Marmara* continue to publish, and Armenian organizations go about collecting donations and sponsoring cultural activities. The Armenian patriarch is also invited to official Turkish state ceremonies. Major problems include the lack of a seminary, Armenian institutions of higher education, and linguistic assimilation.

Armenians in South Asia and Australia

By the twentieth century the Armenian communities in South Asia had declined to a few thousand. Calcutta remained the only viable Armenian community in the region. In the 1920's, Armenians who had fled the Russian Revolution, civil war, and the Bolsheviks, began to arrive in Harbin, in the Chinese province of Manchuria, and in Shanghai. An Armenian Church was constructed in Harbin and Armenian merchants and artisans opened businesses in China and Southeast Asia. The Armenians worked closely and, at times, intermarried with, the Europeans of China. World War Two devastated the remaining Armenian centers in the region. The Japanese rounded up all Europeans in China, Burma, Indonesia, Philippines, Malaysia, and Singapore, including the Armenians. Those who survived the ravages of the war were soon faced with the discriminatory policies of the nationalist or socialist governments which followed the decolonization of South and Southeast Asia. The communist takeover of China in 1949 resulted in the emigration of its entire Armenian community, some of whom went to South America. Out of the once-successful community, some 1,000 Armenians remain in South and Southeast Asia, with a good part of them in India, especially in Calcutta, which still has an active Armenian school, club, and church.

Such major upheavals forced the Armenians of South Asia to leave in droves and seek refuge in Australia, where a number of them had already immigrated during the 1920's. Political changes and economic hardship in Eastern Europe and the Middle East brought more immigrants to Australia (and a few to New Zealand), which in the 1990s boasts an Armenian population of some 35,000, mostly in Melbourne and Sydney, where churches, clubs, and newspapers have created an active community.

Armenians in South America

The Armenian community in South America, like that of Australia, arose in the early twentieth century, as a result of immigrants who had survived the genocide. Although they settled in various parts of the continent, the majority went to Argentina, Brazil, and Uruguay, with some moving to Venezuela and Mexico. Unlike their compatriots who had emigrated to Europe or other parts of Asia, Armenians in the Americas had no previous connections, commercial or cultural, to aid them in acclimatizing to such a different culture. But, by the 1940s each of these countries had Armenian teachers, engineers, doctors, and lawyers. In addition, Armenian craftsmen opened their own businesses and, thanks to the economic boom in the region, became affluent. Their economic successes prompted other Armenians to relocate there from Greece and the Middle East and by the end of the 1980s there were some 70,000 Armenians in Argentina, 20,000 in Brazil, and 15,000 in Uruguay, concentrated in Buenos Aires, Sao Paulo, Rio de Janeiro, and Montevideo respectively. The numbers are somewhat deceiving, however, for with the exception of the Argentine Armenians, the Armenians of South America are not a cohesive community. A dozen churches (including Catholic and Evangelical), a number of schools, newspapers, and clubs and AGBU chapters have been established, but assimilation is taking its toll and hyper-inflation, as well as political instability, have resulted in emigration to North America.

Armenians in North America

Sources mention that in the first half of the seventeenth century, an Armenian called Martin, who was originally from New Julfa, came to Virginia via

Amsterdam. The genesis of the Armenian community in North America, however, began more than two centuries later. When American missionaries established schools in Turkey in the second half of the nineteenth century, they enabled some Armenians to come to the United States and attract more Armenian immigrants to the "promised land." A small group of Armenians thus settled on the East coast and built a church in 1891 in Worcester, Massachusetts. America was too far and too expensive for most to reach, however, and it was only after the massacres of 1895-1896 that a large contingent of Armenian men, realizing they had little to lose, took a risk and traveled to America. By 1900 some 15,000 had arrived. Between 1900 and 1916 some 70,000 Armenians immigrated to the United States. Statistics indicate that a great majority were men under 45 who were skilled and literate, and who had left their wives and families to seek their fortune. Before the closing of the gates in 1924, some 23,000 additional Armenians arrived in North America. Altogether over 100,000, the overwhelming majority from Turkey, settled in the United States and Canada. In 1948 a few thousand Armenians arrived from Europe under the Displaced Persons Act. Known as D.P.'s, they included Armenians who had fled western Russia with the retreating German armies. More Armenians arrived in the late 1950s and early 1960s, following the political problems in the Middle East.

The early immigrants to the United States had settled in the urban and industrial centers of the East coast, primarily in New York, Massachusetts, Connecticut, and New Jersey, with a few settling in the Midwestern cities of Detroit, Chicago, and Cleveland. The only Armenians who did not follow this pattern were those who, at the end of the nineteenth century, settled in the San Joaquin Valley in Central California. Here, they engaged in farming and grape-growing particularly around Fresno. For the next half century Fresno Armenians suffered terrible discrimination from the natives. Signs saying "No Armenians," appeared in store windows and real estate offices. The Fresno community, nevertheless, expanded until the Depression when San Francisco and Los Angeles began to attract new immigrants. Until the 1960s the east coast and the midwest received the largest percentage of Armenian immigrants. As customary with other immigrant groups, the first two generations worked very hard to establish themselves in the new land. Some tried to assimilate as soon as possible, others clung to their traditions. They saved money to bring their families over and to open small businesses. Their literacy and skills meant that they would move upward whenever possible. Discrimination, which was great in some places and at certain times, did not deter the Armenians, who had lived through much worse.

In the 1970s and 1980s some 80,000 Armenians from Soviet Armenia, some of whom had repatriated there in the late 1940s, taking advantage of détente and relaxed emigration laws created primarily for Russian Jews, came to North America. In addition Armenians fleeing the civil war in Lebanon, the fundamentalist Islamic Revolution in Iran, and the Iran-Iraq War, relocated there as well. The 1988 earthquake and the deteriorating conditions in Armenia and in the former Soviet Union brought thousands more to North America. The great flood of Armenian immigrants in the last three decades, however, has preferred the greater Los Angeles area, which alone holds approximately 250,000 Armenians. There are at present some 1 million Armenians in the United States and 100,000 in Canada (primarily in Toronto and Montreal), giving North America the largest concentration of Armenians outside Armenia.

By the third generation American Armenians had produced numerous doctors, lawyers, engineers, and academics, as well as very successful entrepreneurs. Armenian politicians, sports figures, composers, actors, artists and authors such as Alan Hovhannes, Rouben Mamoulian, Arshile Gorky and William Saroyan created a sense of pride among the new generation of American Armenians. With well over 100 churches, numerous schools, associations, academic and cultural societies, magazines, newspapers, as well as active and influential organizations, the Armenians in North America are a force to be reckoned with.

Literary Activity in the Diaspora

The Armenian genocide, as we have seen, wiped out almost the entire cadre of Armenian intellectuals in Turkey. What had taken a century to develop was destroyed in a month. A small group managed to survive, however, and, according to one expert, formed a sort of a transition generation. France and the Arab Middle East became the new home of western Armenian literature. By 1930 a group of young men such as Shahnur, Topalian, Shushanian, Beshiktashlian, Aharon, Sarafian, and Nartuni had created a new circle in Paris. Their poems, short stories, novels, and essays rejected the past and predicted a bright future. World War Two, however, soon ended this short-lived revival.

A number of writers chose the Middle East as their new home. Among them were Shant, Oshakan, and Tekeyan. Shant wrote romantic plays and became an educator. Oshakan returned to Constantinople in 1920 and together with Tekeyan, Zarian and others, signed a literary manifesto and started the periodical *Bardzravank*, with the goal of reviving Armenian literary activities. For the next two years they published their work in the periodical, as well as in the daily newspaper *Chakatamart*. In 1922 the Turkish nationalists reached Constantinople and the circle was disbanded. Tekeyan and Oshakan left Turkey and traveled in Europe and the Middle East. Tekeyan ended up in Cairo and Oshakan in Jerusalem. Tekeyan's works analyzed modern Armenian literature, while Oshakan's writings, according to one scholar, were really literary responses to the catastrophe of the genocide. By the second half of the twentieth century, the western Armenian literary revival had run its course. Although a few of the European and Middle eastern Armenian writers immigrated to the United States, the major literary output was in Eastern Armenian and was being produced in Soviet Armenia.

Diasporan Politics

The establishment of Soviet Armenia resulted in bitter political divisions among the Armenians of the diaspora. The Dashnaks, who were the dominant party, made an all-out effort to assume the leadership of the diaspora. The Hnchaks generally supported the Soviet Union. The Ramkavars decided to accept the *status quo* in Armenia, and sought to preserve the Armenian identity in the diaspora through educational, cultural, and charitable activities. After the Sovietization of Armenia, the Hnchaks and the Ramkavars accused the Dashnaks, especially their Central Bureau, of having ruled the republic like a dictatorship. Dashnak policies and intractableness, they asserted, not only had resulted in the loss of the republic, but in the loss of additional territories to the Turks and Azeris. The Hnchaks and Ramkavars separated themselves from the history of the first republic and, either mistakenly or from fear of political reprisals in Soviet Armenia (which had been given a different flag) rejected the tricolor of the republic (red, blue, and orange), and identified it as the emblem of the Dashnak party. At the same time, the Dashnaktsutiun claimed sole possession of the flag and the historical record of the republic. The Dashnaks accused the Hnchaks of being Bolshevik lackeys and the Ramkavars of being out of touch with the masses and the realities of Armenian history. They portrayed the Ramkavars as liberal businessmen who, ignoring the struggle for the independence of historic Armenia, concentrated their efforts on social and cultural activities.

A closer examination reveals that all sides ignored many facts in this polarization. Until mid-1920 the government of Armenia, except for top cabinet posts, had non-Dashnaks among its members. The tri-color was not a party flag but stood for the entire republic. Realizing that Bolshevik ideology, as it was preached at the time, had no room for Armenian nationalism, the Dashnaks put all their hopes in the Allies and President Wilson. In addition, the Dashnaks believed that the Allies could and would enforce the Treaty of Sèvres, while the Bolsheviks, who were not party to the treaty and were negotiating with Turkish nationalists, would reject it. Their ultimate disappointment was one shared by all Armenians. On the other hand, the Hnchaks and, especially, the Ramkavars, rather than being out of touch, were simply pragmatic and created the possibility of a dialogue with the Bolsheviks which, at times, enabled the diaspora to provide crucial assistance to Soviet Armenia. In addition, the liberal yet cautious policies of the Ramkavars directed their middle class wealth to causes which greatly benefited the large Armenian diaspora.

The reportedly unsanctioned assassination of Archbishop Levon Tourian in New York in 1933 by Dashnaktsutiun members, split the community even further. Other developments, however, such as the invitation to repatriate to Soviet Armenia and the Soviet efforts to regain Kars and Ardahan, did much to unite it. The disappointing results of both of these latter endeavors, and the ensuing Cold War once again split the community along party lines. The Cold War split had even more damaging effects. Armenian communities in the non-communist diaspora took sides. As the United States and its allies organized to limit the expansion of communism, they attracted, financed, and at times recruited to their cause national groups such as Armenians, Poles, Ukrainians, Latvians, Estonians, and Lithuanians. The Dashnaks, who had a revolutionary and socialist history, because of their opposition to the Soviet Armenian government, gained the trust of the West, while the Hnchaks were suspect by the West and anti-communist states. The Ramkavars were caught in the middle. Although they were accused by the Dashnaks of supporting Soviet Armenia, they argued that their support was based not on ideology but on patriotism and cultural ties to the fatherland. Although the Armenians in Eastern Europe and East Asia did not have to face this rift, the large and politically active Armenian communities in Lebanon, Iran, and the United States were particularly affected by the post-war ideological conflict.

With the death of the catholicos of the Holy See of Cilicia in 1952, the Dashnaks managed to elect a candidate who favored their principles. When the catholicos of Etchmiadzin, influenced by Soviet Armenian officials and the anti-Dashnak parties in the diaspora, refused to recognize the election, the Church split as well. This ecclesiastical division polarized the diaspora communities even further and Armenian groups fought, betrayed, and killed each other in Iran in 1953 and Lebanon in 1958, with the Armenian Hnchaks and communists supporting the anti-shah and anti-Maronite factions, and the Dashnaks joining the pro-Western coalitions. The Cilician See, meanwhile, began to extend its jurisdiction beyond Lebanon, Syria, and Cyprus and founded separate prelacies in communities where the Dashnaks had gathered support, especially, in Iran, Greece, Canada, and the United States.

By the mid-1960s the Armenian diaspora had established itself economically in every corner of the globe and the ideological differences within it were no longer the main topic of concern. Secure and accepted by their host countries, other issues occupied the communities, particularly, the fear of assimilation. Armenians in the Muslim world found it relatively easy to maintain their culture, but in the Christian world, especially in Europe and the United States, Armenians were intermarrying in large numbers, a phenomenon which some referred to as a "White Massacre." Armenians in America, in particular, considered themselves Americans and had no desire to repatriate to Armenia, even a free one. They had changed from being Armenian to feeling Armenian. Traditional Armenian values were being challenged throughout the diaspora as well. Divorce rates were on the increase and the young were uninterested in traditions which had become foreign to them. Like most Jews prior to the creation of modern Israel, the Armenians began to see the diaspora as a permanent situation. The Soviet Union appeared there to stay and the United Nations was not going to reopen the Armenian Question; worst of all, the Turkish government maintained its silence or outright denial of the atrocities perpetrated against the Armenians.

In 1965, on the fiftieth anniversary of the genocide, Armenians everywhere, including Yerevan, demonstrated their frustration and began to demand justice. A number of Turkish diplomats were assassinated by Armenians, who, influenced by national liberation movements around the world, considered terrorism the only way to awaken the conscience of the world. In 1975, a group of young men calling themselves the Armenian Secret Army for the Liberation of Armenia (ASALA) began to operate in Lebanon and cooperated with other national liberation factions. Despite their failure and, according to many, damage to the Armenian image, they succeeded in awakening a number of young Armenians into action. The Dashnaktsutiun, which had lost some young members to the ASALA, soon created its own force, the Justice Commandos of the Armenian Genocide, who were even more successful in targeting Turkish organizations and diplomats. The two groups occasionally clashed as well. The Turkish response to these developments was a repeated denial of the genocide by their government and historians.

Turkish and several Western academics, who had received grants from the Turkish government, went so far as to accuse the Armenians of having massacred Turks. Such actions not only rallied the particularly active Armenians, but brought out those who had removed themselves from Armenian affairs. Following the 1988 earthquake and the rapid political changes in the Soviet Union, most Armenians in the diaspora set aside the divisions of the past and political and church factions began to cooperate informally.

Independence caught the Armenians in the diaspora unawares. Initial euphoria was soon followed by uncertainties and debate, for with an independent republic the entire role of the diaspora had to be reexamined. Although some immediately lunged into supporting the republic with all their financial resources, others complained that such efforts were draining all the funds and were detrimental to important projects and activities in the diaspora. The churches connected with the Cilician See had to now justify their continued role and pressures for an ecclesiastical union began to surface. Finally, the very existence of diasporan political parties became superfluous. The Dashnaktsutiun, the largest and most active and the Hnchakian, the smallest and least active party in the diaspora were especially at a loss. With the demise of the Soviet system, the latter had lost some credibility, but since its membership had become almost hereditary, they continued their political activities. The former, however, had a serious dilemma. For seventy years the *raison d'être* of the Dashnak party had been the attainment of a free, non-communist Armenia. Armenia was finally free, but it was not the Dashnaks who had accomplished that task. The Ramkavars, whose policy favored a liberal and moderate state, and whose cultural ties to Armenia were greater than the Dashnaks, saw a chance to become the most influential party in the diaspora. The 1991 election in Armenia was, therefore, of vital importance to the future of the Armenian political parties of the diaspora.

XXIII

On the Map:
The Armenian Republic (1991-1994)

The election campaign in the newly-formed Republic of Armenia was peaceful but full of heated arguments. Levon Ter Petrossian's version of an independent Armenia did not coincide with that of some of his colleagues, who vehemently disagreed with his policies on the many critical issues facing the country, particularly his willingness to come to some sort of a compromise on Karabagh. A number of former Karabagh Committee members, either resigned from the government, left the Armenian National Movement and formed separate factions, or declared their candidacy for the presidency. An earlier dissident party, the National Self-Determination Union and its leader, Paruir Hairikian, stated that Armenia had to cut all its ties with the Soviet Union and had to declare its full independence after the upcoming referendum. The diaspora parties also registered for the upcoming presidential elections. The Ramkavars, out of conviction, as well as political pragmatism, endorsed the candidacy of Levon Ter Petrossian. The Hnchaks, desperate to have a voice in the new government, backed Ter Petrossian as well. The Dashnaktsutiun, basically agreed with Hairikian's platform, but in a calculated move, presented its own candidate, the venerable actor Sos Sargisian. The major problem with the diaspora parties was the fact that, like all national institutions existing abroad, they had never relied on public elections. Their leaders were elected by relatively small inner circles and did not have to answer to a large constituency. The Armenian press in the diaspora, with some exceptions, was also financed by the three political organizations and followed party lines. In some ways, in fact, the diaspora parties and press were similar to the defunct Soviet system.

On October 16, 1991 barely a month after independence, Armenians went to the polls to elect a president. Levon Ter Petrossian, representing the Armenian National Movement, won 83 percent of the vote. The other candidates had a poor showing indeed, with the National Self-Determination Union and Dashnak candidates together managing only 12 percent (with the Dashnaks an amazingly low 4.4 percent of the vote), and the various other parties and individuals totaling 5 percent. Neither the Dashnaktsutiun nor the communists could accept their defeat. The former had lost its pre-eminence and the latter its privileges. The two old antagonists, ironically, found common cause against Levon Ter Petrossian's government.

Receiving a clear mandate did not mean that the government of Levon Ter Petrossian would be free from internal or external pressures. The major internal problem was the virtual blockade of Armenia by Azerbaijan and the plight of the hundreds of thousands refugees from Azerbaijan and the earthquake zone. The other domestic issues involved the implementation of free market reforms, the establishment of democratic governmental structures, and the privatization of land. The external concerns involved future relations with Russia, Turkey, Georgia, and Iran. In addition, Gorbachev's post-coup efforts to maintain a restructured Soviet Union meant that the new republic would not be recognized by the West. The immediate concern, however, was the conflict with Azerbaijan over Mountainous Karabagh and the political uncertainties in Georgia, which contained 400,000 Armenians. In some ways the scenario of 1918 was repeating itself.

Meanwhile, Gorbachev continued to support Azerbaijan in order to pressure Armenia to join his new union. Ter Petrossian's first job was to calm Moscow's concern about future Armenian relations with Russia. A day after the elections, faced with numerous Azeri attacks on Karabagh and Armenia, he signaled his willingness to come to some understanding with Moscow. Still refusing to join a political union, Armenia nevertheless signed the economic treaty, which created a free-trade zone and an agreement to coordinate food, industrial, and energy supplies. Gorbachev had gained some leverage and, in exchange, offered to mediate a cease-fire in Karabagh. Azerbaijan, advancing on all fronts in Karabagh and sure that Armenia and Karabagh would soon come to their knees, refused to accept the invitation. Ter Petrossian had scored a political victory, however. He had indicated that, despite its independence, Armenia was not severing its ties to Moscow. He also demonstrated to the West, and to many Armenians in the diaspora, that his government was not impulsive, but was willing to move cautiously and gradually towards resolving conflict.

Ter Petrossian's next step was to assure Turkey that Armenia had no territorial claims against it and that it desired neighborly diplomatic and economic relations. The same message was sent to Georgia, Iran, and Azerbaijan. Rather than espousing an ideologically dogmatic and biased outlook, Armenia was to have a pragmatic and flexible foreign policy. As far as Karabagh was concerned, Armenia once again reiterated that the conflict was not between Armenia and Azerbaijan, but between the Armenian enclave of Mountainous Karabagh and Baku. It was a question of human rights and self-determination which had to be resolved by direct communication.

In the long run, Armenian efforts to establish political and economic relations with Turkey did not materialize. The Turks not only maintained a virtual blockade of Armenia but insisted that the issue of Karabagh had to be resolved before anything else could be discussed. The Azeri blockade had resulted not only in food and fuel shortages, but, since 1989, had virtually halted supplies for earthquake reconstruction. The closing down of the Medzamor Nuclear Energy Plant in 1989 meant that Armenian citizens, including the many refugees, would have to face another difficult winter. The political and economic situation in Russia and Georgia indicated that Armenia, aside from the trickle of foreign aid, had to rely mainly on its own efforts. Ter Petrossian's policies vis-à-vis Turkey were severely criticized by the Dashnaks and his lukewarm relations with Moscow were criticized by the Hnchaks and communists.

Gorbachev still hoped to salvage the former USSR and proposed the creation of a Union of Sovereign States. He received a verbal agreement from the leaders of seven republics, which included Azerbaijan, but excluded Armenia, Georgia, the Baltic states, and, most importantly, Ukraine. Azerbaijan's president, Mutalibov, continued to cooperate with Gorbachev and received Russian military aid to squeeze Karabagh into submission. In early November 1991, Azerbaijan shut its gas pipelines into Armenia. At the same time Turkey became the first country to recognize Azerbaijan. By the end of November, emboldened by its military and political successes, Azerbaijan's parliament, urged by its National Front, which had gained many supporters, abolished Karabagh's autonomous status and voted to take direct control of the enclave. The State Council in Moscow realized that such an action would not only force Ter Petrossian to abandon his moderate position, but would elicit a strong reaction from the European Parliament, which had been sympathetic to Armenia. Ignoring Gorbachev's idea of a buffer zone, the State Council ordered Azerbaijan to repeal its decision. Mutalibov, who feared the National Front and who was sure that Karabagh would soon be overrun, urged the parliament to change its mind. Turkey, who did not want a renewed

Russian presence in the region, also advised the National Front to back down and Iran offered to reconcile the two sides.

In the meantime, Georgia was also being punished for refusing Gorbachev's offer to join the Union of Sovereign States. Gamsakhurdia, the popular intellectual dissident, who had been jailed by the communists and who had become president of Georgia in spring 1991, faced major problems with the enclave of Southern Ossetia, which had declared its desire to join Northern Ossetia in the Russian Republic. Ossetia had began its separatist movement in 1990 but had been admonished by Moscow, which counted Georgia among its union members. In 1991, a year later, however, independent Georgia's actions resulted in Russian military aid to the Ossetians, who began a war against Georgia. Gorbachev, who was discouraging the Armenian separatist movement in Karabagh, was encouraging the same movement in Southern Ossetia. Gamsakhurdia's extreme nationalism and heavy-handed rule did not help matters and actually antagonized other Muslim minorities, like the Abkhazians. Eventually his low regard for democratic principles sparked a rebellion by the national guard which, by the end of the year, had put Gamsakhurdia in a precarious position.

Events moved faster than anyone had predicted, however. Gorbachev's plan for the Union of Sovereign States never materialized. On December 1, 1991 Ukraine voted for independence and on December 8, the leaders of Russia, Ukraine, and Belarus set up a commonwealth which invited other former Soviet republics to join as independent states. Gorbachev had been outmaneuvered by Yeltsin. Armenia immediately announced that it would join the commonwealth and on December 21, together with eight other republics, including Azerbaijan, formally joined the Commonwealth of Independent States (CIS). On December 25, 1991 Mikhail Gorbachev resigned as president and the Union of Soviet Socialist Republics was officially dissolved.

The change of leadership, not welcomed in Azerbaijan, was greeted with great enthusiasm by Armenia. Mutalibov was a hard-line communist, who was willing to obey Moscow's bidding as long as it kept him and his clique in power and supported Azerbaijan's efforts to destroy the Armenian movement in Karabagh. With Gorbachev's exit he joined the CIS and tried to ingratiate himself to Yeltsin, but his past actions, especially his support for the August coup and his treatment of ethnic Russians in Baku, made him unpopular.

The end of the USSR once again forced Armenia out into the international arena. On March 2, 1992, Armenia was recognized as a sovereign state and became a member of the United Nations. Armenian diplomatic missions were hastily opened in countries where there was an Armenian community to give financial and practical aid to the new diplomats. Soon after, passports, stamps, and eventually a new currency were introduced. Although the refugee situation, food, medical, and fuel shortages, the Azeri blockade, the civil unrest in Georgia, a hostile Turkey and the emergence of partisan politics, reminded many of the 1919-1920 era, there were significant differences. Russia, with all its problems, was not amidst a civil war. Armenia had a more organized and more representative government, was protected by the UN Charter, and had a better infrastructure than the first republic.

With Gorbachev's exit, Russian troops were withdrawn from Karabagh, the Karabagh Armenians began to fight back and, a year later, had not only recaptured most of the enclave, but had taken Kelbajar, which was outside the region (see map 25). The Azerbaijan Popular Front, which, like the Armenian right, had advocated a total break with Russia, and, in addition, had demanded closer ties with Turkey, began to gain new followers in the government. The Azerbaijani parliament refused to ratify the CIS treaty and forced Mutalibov's resignation. A caretaker government of National Front and communist ministers tried to govern until the new presidential elections in late spring. Two months later, however, the communist-dominated parliament, fearing the loss of power, voted to restore Mutalibov, who immediately declared a state of emergency and canceled the forthcoming elections. Riots by armed supporters of the National Front forced him to flee a day later and in early June, a leader of the National Front, Abulfez Elchibey, a scholar, won the election and became the new president of Azerbaijan. His absolute refusal to join the CIS and his closeness to Turkey not only worried Russia but Iran, as well.

Meanwhile, Gamsakhurdia could not contain the rebellion against him and, in early January 1992, fled Tbilisi. Eduard Shevardnadze, who had been the communist chief of Georgia for thirteen years (1972-1985), and who had later been part of Gorbachev's cabinet and foreign minister of the USSR, returned to Georgia. His refusal to join the CIS gave the Abkhazian minority an opportunity to declare that it wanted to join the CIS. Moscow, in order to reassert itself in the region and to halt Turkey's influence, gave some aid to the Abkhazians who managed to resist the Georgians and repel the Georgian army. By fall 1993, Georgia had decided that it was prudent to join the CIS and to begin negotiations with Abkhazia.

In the meantime, Elchibey's nationalist policies and pro-Turkish attitudes had alienated not only Russia and Iran, but had initiated a separatist movement by the Lezgis and the Taleshis, the former Sunnis and the latter of Iranian stock. Armenia, as a member of CIS, could rely on Russia far more than Azerbaijan, which was not. By summer of 1993, the Armenians of Karabagh had taken over Shushi, as well as the entire corridor between Armenia and Karabagh (see map 25). The Azeri army and the opposition decided to remove Elchibey. At this juncture Heidar Aliev, the former communist chief of Azerbaijan (1969-1987) and member of the Politburo in Gorbachev's time, took advantage of the situation. He had bided his time in Nakhichevan where he had established closer ties with Turkey. Two bridges were put across the Arax, connecting Nakhichevan to Turkey; the Turkish president had visited the region, had promised economic aid, and had warned Armenia not to attack Nakhichevan. By late summer Aliev, favored by Moscow over Elchibey, was at the helm of the republic and the democratically-elected Elchibey had sought refuge in Nakhichevan. In early fall, Azerbaijan became a member of the CIS and by October 1993 Moscow was once again the main broker in the Caucasus. With Moscow's leverage in the Caucasus reinstated, Russia's role has changed to that of a mediator and big brother. Unlike the past, however, there are no statements on territorial integrity of the ex-Soviet republics. It seems that Moscow prefers the war of attrition.

Although Armenia has done well on the diplomatic front and the struggle in Karabagh has, for the time being, turned in favor of the Armenians who have captured Aghdam and Fizuli (see map 25), the terrible economic conditions resulting from the Azeri blockade, the 1988 earthquake, ethnic cleansing in Azerbaijan, and the unstable political situation in Georgia, have created half a million refugees and emigrants. By the summer of 1994, an estimated 750,000 (from Azerbaijan, Georgia, and Armenia) had temporarily or permanently left for Russia, North America, Australia, and Europe. The winter of 1992-1993, in particular, was very harsh. The nuclear plant of Medzamor remained shut and fuel was so short that schools, offices, factories and hospitals had to close due to lack of heat and electricity. Aid from America, Europe, and the Armenian diaspora was of great assistance, but the mortality rate among children and the old was high. The birth rate fell as well. Thanks to better organization on the part of the government, and more aid from Armenian organizations in the diaspora as well as foreign governments and agencies, the winter of 1993-1994 was comparatively easier. Meanwhile, reconstruction of the earthquake zone is progressing. Improvements in medical care, private apartments, a new constitution, a free press, several political parties, and trade activities indicate a bright future. Despite protests from environmentalists, Armenia, terribly short of energy, is planning to renovate and restart the Medzamor Nuclear Plant. Hyper-inflation and the economic woes in Russia, as well as the continued Azeri blockade, the inability of Georgia to protect the crucial transport routes to Armenia, and the human and material cost of the conflict in Karabagh, has slowed the economic recovery. Armenians sincerely hope for the resolution of the Karabagh conflict. They have stated that they will be willing to give back all the captured territory outside Mountainous Karabagh, save the Lachin corridor, in exchange for serious guarantees and an independent status for Karabagh. Difficult economic conditions have brought out the opposition in force, however. Although the Dashnaks have not attracted many additional members, the communists and former members of the Armenian National Movement have gained some recognition. Demirjian and Harutiunian, who led Armenia in the Soviet era, and Vazgen Manukian, a former colleague of Ter Petrossian are occasionally mentioned as possible candidates for the next presidential elections.

Armenia, with its historical ties to Russia, a homogeneous population, and an active diaspora, may be Russia's favorite in the Caucasus. Levon Ter Petrossian is the only leader who has not been stained by communism and, despite some unsubstantiated accusations, has not been seriously implicated in any corruption scandal. Moreover Armenia has a far more democratic government than Georgia and especially Azerbaijan. In addition, Armenia serves as the buffer between Turkey and the Turkic groups in Transcaucasia and Central Asia. Finally, Georgian nationalist and Azerbaijani pro-Muslim declarations have had a distinct anti-Russian character which makes Armenia more desirable to Russian nationalists and the military. The importance of the Caspian and Black seas and Azeri oil may sway the Russians to loosen their ties with Armenia, however. Yeltsin, after crushing the opposition in parliament and sending tanks to the Russian White House, has continued to grapple with major domestic problems. Civil unrest in Russia would seriously affect landlocked and besieged Armenia. The Yerevan government is well aware of similar conditions which ended the first Armenian republic. Unlike the past, however, Armenia is keeping its options open. History has, one hopes, taught Armenia and its people that vigilance, moderation, and caution must replace blind faith and dogma.

1. Mekhitarian Center, San Lazzaro, Venice

2. Armenian Cathedral, New Julfa, Iran

3. Gandzasar Monastery, Mountainous Karabagh

4. The Armenian Church, Madras, India

5. The Armenian Church, Singapore

6. The Armenian Church, Dhaka Bangladesh

7. The Armenian Church,
Cairo, Egypt

8. The Armenian Church, New Nakhichevan (Rostov, Russia)

9. The Armenian Church, St. Petersburg, Russia

10. Lazarian Institute, Moscow, Russia

11. An Armenian Church, Tiflis, (Tbilisi) Georgia

12. Samuel-Murad Armenian School, Sèvres, France

13. Murad Raphaelian Armenian School, Venice, Italy

14. Armenian Church (Czernowitz, Moldavia),
Chernovtsy, Ukraine

15. Holy Cross Monastery, Crimea, Ukraine (photo C. Mutafian)

16. View of Zeitun, 1912 (courtesy of ALMA)

Bibliographical Guide

General

Academy of Sciences of Armenia, *The History of the Armenian People*, vols. V-VIII (in Armenian).Yerevan, 1967-1981; *The Cambridge History of Iran*, vols.VI-VII. Cambridge, 1986-1991; *The Cambridge History of Islam*, 2 vols. Cambridge, 1970; A. G. Abrahamian, *A Concise History of the Armenian Diaspora*, 2 vols. (in Armenian). Yerevan, 1964-1967; C. E. Bosworth, *The Islamic Dynasties*. Edinburgh, 1967; G. A. Bournoutian, "Armenian," in *An Ethnohistorical Dictionary of the Russian and Soviet Empires*, J. S. Olson, ed. London, 1994; G. Dédéyan, ed., *Histoire des Armeniens*. Toulouse, 1982 and *Les Arméniens: Histoire d'une Chrétienté*. Toulouse, 1990; T. Kh. Hakobian, *Armenia's Historical Geography* (in Armenian). Yerevan, 1968; and *History of Yerevan*, vols. II-IV: 1500-1917 (in Armenian). Yerevan, 1959-1981; R. G. Hovannisian, ed., *The Armenian Image in History and Literature*. Malibu, 1981; Leo, *Armenian History*, vols. III-IV (in Armenian). Yerevan, 1969-1984; T. F. Mathews and R. S. Wieck, eds. *Treasures in Heaven: Armenian Illuminated Manuscripts*. New York, 1994; M. Miansarof, *Bibliographia Caucasica et Transcaucasica*. Amsterdam, 1967; V. N. Nersessian, *Armenia* (Bibliographical Guide). Oxford, 1993; V. Oshagan, ed., A. Paolucci, gen.ed., *Review of National Literatures: Armenia*. New York, 1984; H. Pasdermadjian, *Histoire de l'Arménie depuis les origines jusqu'au traité de Lausanne*. Paris, 1949; A. Salmaslian, *Bibliographie De L'Arménie*. Yerevan, 1969; M. Sarkisyanz, *A Modern History of Transcaucasian Armenia*. Nagpur, 1975; R. G. Suny, ed., *Transcaucasia: Nationalism and Social Change*. Ann Arbor, 1983; C. J. Walker, *Armenia: The Survival of a Nation*. New York, 1990.

Chapter XII - Armenians in Asia Minor:

K. Bardakjian's chapter on the Armenian patriarchate, H. Barsoumian's chapter on the *amira*, and B. Braude's chapter on the *millet* system in B. Braude & B. Lewis, eds., *Christians and Jews in the Ottoman Empire*, vol. I, New York, 1982, form much of the new research on these topics. M. S. Anderson's, *The Eastern Question, 1774-1923*, New York, 1966 and J. A. R. Marriott's, *The Eastern Question: A Study in European Diplomacy*, Oxford, 1951, remain the standard works on that subject. H. F. B. Lynch's, *Armenia: Travels and Studies, vol. II: The Turkish Provinces*. London, 1901 and S. Mardin, *The Genesis of Young Ottoman Thought: A Study in the Moderniza-tion of Turkish Political Ideas*, Princeton, 1962 are thorough studies on their respective topics. S. Shaw's early study, *Between Old and New: The Ottoman Empire under Sultan Selim III, 1789-1807*. Harvard, 1971 is a pio-neering work on Selim's reforms. The following are works on specific peri-ods or movements described in the chapter: L. Arpee, *The Armenian Awak-ening: A History of the Armenian Church, 1820-1860*. Chicago, 1909; V. Artinian, *The Armenian Constitutional System in the Ottoman Empire, 1839-1863*. Istanbul, 1988; N. Berkes, *The Development of Secularism in Turkey*. Montreal, 1964; T. A. Bryson, *American Diplomatic Relations With the Mid-dle East, 1784-1975*. Metuchen, N.J., 1977; R. L. Daniel, *American Philan-thropy in the Near East, 1820-1960*. Athens, Ohio, 1970; R. Davison, *Reform in the Ottoman Empire, 1856-1876*. Princeton, 1963; J. Etmekjian, *The French Influence in the Western Armenian Renaissance*. New York, 1964; W. J. Hamilton, *Researches in Asia Minor, Pontus, and Armenia*. Zurich, 1984; B. Jelavich, *The Ottoman Empire, the Great Powers and the Straits Question, 1870-1887*; and *History of the Balkans, Vol. I: Eighteenth and Nineteenth Centuries*. Cambridge, 1993; R. Kasaba, *The Ottoman Empire and the World Economy: The Nineteenth Century*. Albany, N.Y., 1988; Lord Kinross, *The Ottoman Centuries: The Rise and Fall of the Turk-ish Empire*. New York, 1977; M. K. Krikorian, *Armenians in the Service of the Ottoman Empire, 1860-1908*. London, 1977; B. Lewis, *The Emergence of Modern Turkey*. Oxford, 1969; R. Lewis, *Everyday Life in Ottoman Turkey*. London, 1971; V. Oshagan, *The English Influence on West Armenian Litera-ture in the Nineteenth Century*. Cleveland, Ohio, 1982; K. A. Sarafian, *Histo-ry of Education in Armenia*. La Verne, Ca., 1978; L. S. Stavrianos, *The Balkans since 1453*. New York, 1966; V. H. Tootikian, *The Armenian Evan-gelical Church*. Detroit, 1982.

Chapter XIII - Armenians in Iran:

For the past two decades I have concentrated my research on the Armenians in Iran and Transcaucasia from 1500 to 1840. The following studies have been published to date: *The Khanate of Yerevan under Qajar Rule, 1795-1828*. Costa Mesa, Ca. 1992; *A History of Qarabagh: An Annotated Translation of Mirza Jamal Javanshir Qarabaghi's Tarikh-e Qarabagh*. Costa Mesa, Ca. 1994; and "The Armenian Community of Isfahan in the Seventeenth Century," (2 parts), *Armenian Review* 24-25 (1971-1972), 27-45, 33-50. A study on the history of the post-Safavid khanates of Nakhichevan, Qarabagh, and Ganja is forthcoming. Other primary and secondary sources include: A. Davrizhetsi, *History* (in Russian). Moscow, 1973; N. Garoyants, *Iranian-Armenians* (in Armenian). Tehran, 1968; V. Gregorian, "Minorities of Isfahan: The Armenian Community of Isfahan, 1587-1722," *Iranian Studies* 7 (1974), 652-680; E. Herzig, "The Deportation of the Armenians in 1604-1605 and Europe's Myth of Shah `Abbas I," in *History and Literature in Iran*, C. Melville ed. Cambridge, 1990; I. Ra'in, *Iranian-Armenians* (in Persian). Tehran, 1970.

Chapter XIV - Armenians in the Indian Subcontinent:

The most detailed history of the Armenian communities in India is still M. J. Seth's, *Armenians in India*. Calcutta, 1983 (first published in 1937). J. Emin's memoirs, first published in 1792 in London, was republished by his great great granddaughter as, *Life and Adventures of Joseph Emin 1726-1809, Written by Himself*, 2 vols. Calcutta, 1918. Two recent articles shed light on early emanciapatory efforts of the Armenians in Madras, H. Khachatrian's, "Shahamir Shahamirian's Views on Natural Law," *Armenian Review* 42 (1989), 37-46; M. Tololyan's, "Shahamir Shahamirian's Vorogait Parats (Snare of Glory)," *Armenian Review* 42 (1989), 25-35. S. Wolpert's, *A New History of India*, the latest edition published in 1993 in New York, remains the best brief account for the non-specialist.

Chapter XV - Armenians in the Arab World:

The best work in English, as well as the source frequently consulted for this chapter, is A. K. Sanjian's, *The Armenian Communities in Syria under Ottoman Dominion*. Harvard, 1965. The following are studies concentrating on specific aspects, periods, or individuals discussed in the chapter: A. Lutfi Al-Sayyid, *Egypt and Cromer: A Study in Anglo-Egyptian Relations*. London, 1968; A. J. Arberry, ed., *Religion in the Middle East*, vol. I. Cambridge, 1969; V. Azarya, *The Armenian Quarter of Jerusalem*. Berkeley, 1984; B. Braude & B. Lewis, eds., *Christians and Jews in the Ottoman Empire*, vol.

II. New York, 1982; Nubar Pacha, *Mémoirs de Nubar Pacha*. Beirut, 1983; B. Ye'or, *The Dhimmi: Jews and Christians under Islam*. London, 1985; W. R. Polk & R. L. Chambers eds., *Beginnings of Modernization in the Middle East*. Chicago, 1968; A. L. Tibawi, *A Modern History of Syria, including Lebanon and Palestine*. New York, 1969. M. E. Yapp's, *The Making of the Modern Near East, 1792-1923*. London, 1987, is the best concise account of the region from the French Revolution to the Treaty of Lausanne.

Chapters XVI& XIX - Armenians in Russia and Transcaucasia:

The most comprehensive studies and the sources consulted for these chapters are R. G. Hovannisian's, *Armenia on the Road to Independence, 1918*, Berkeley, 1969 and R. G. Suny's, *Looking toward Ararat*, Bloomington, 1993. Other important works include W. E. D. Allen, ed., *Russian Embassies to the Georgian Kings 1589-1605*, 2 vols. Cambridge, 1970; W. E. D. Allen & P. Muratoff, *Caucasian Battlefields: A History of the Wars on the Turco-Caucasian Border, 1828-1921*. London, 1953; M. Atkin, *Russia and Iran, 1780-1828*. Minneapolis, 1980; J. F. Baddeley, *The Russian Conquest of the Caucasus*. London, 1908; J. Bryce, *Transcaucasia and Ararat*. London, 1896; V. Gregorian, "The Impact of Russia on the Armenians and Armenia," in *Russia and Asia*, W. S. Vucinich, ed., Stanford, 1972; D. M. Lang, *The Last Years of the Georgian Monarchy, 1658-1832*. New York, 1957; A. Von Haxthausen, *Transcaucasia*. London, 1854; H. F. B. Lynch, *Armenia: Travels and Studies, vol. I: The Russian Provinces*, London, 1901 remains one of the best geographical and ethnographic sources; A. L. H. Rhinelander, *The Incorporation of the Caucasus into the Russian Empire: The Case of Georgia, 1801-1854* (Ph.D. dissertation), Columbia University, 1972 and *Prince Michael Vorontsov: Viceroy to the Tsar*, Montreal, 1990; R. G. Suny, *The Making of the Georgian Nation*. Bloomington, 1988; and L. Villari's, *Fire and Sword in The Caucasus*, London, 1907, which vividly describes the Armeno-Azeri conflict of 1905-1907.

Chapter XVII - Armenians in Eastern and Western Europe:

There are few detailed studies in English on the Armenian communities of Europe. Material in other languages include specific studies such as: V. B. Barkhudarian, *History of the Armenian Community of New Nakhichevan* (in Armenian) Yerevan, 1967; V. R. Grigorian ed., *Documents of the Armenian Court at Kamenets-Podolsk* (in Armenian).Yerevan, 1963; V. A. Mikaelian,

History of the Armenian Community of the Crimea, 2 vols. (in Armenian) Yerevan, 1964-1970. The following volumes are of particular interest: R. Adalian, *From Humanism to Rationalism: Armenian Scholarship in the Nineteenth Century.* Atlanta, 1992; G. Amadouni, *L'Eglise Armenienne et la Catholicite.* Venice, 1978; K. Bardakjian, *The Mekhitarist Contributions to Armenian Culture and Scholarship.* Cambridge, Mass., 1976; M. Oles, *The Armenian Law in the Polish Kingdom (1356-1519).* Rome, 1966; K. S. Papazian & P. M. Manuelian, *Merchants from Ararat.* New York, 1979; E. Schutz, *An Armeno-Kipchak Chronicle on the Polish-Turkish Wars in 1620-1621.* Budapest, 1968; L. Ter-Oganian & K. Raczkowska, *Armenians in Poland: A Bibliography* (in Polish). Warsaw, 1990; and "Armenians in Poland," *Ararat* 31 (Fall, 1990), 2-72.

Chapter XVIII - Armenian Question and Its Solution:

The best work on the subject remains R. G. Hovannisian's, *Armenia on the Road to Independence, 1918.* Berkeley, 1969. The numerous articles of the foremost genocide scholar, V. N. Dadrian, are also of special value. They include: "A Textual Analysis of the Key Indictment of the Turkish Military Tribunal Investigating the Armenian Genocide," in *Armenian Review,* 44 (1991), 1-36; and "Genocide as a Problem of National and International Law: The World War I Armenian Case and its Contemporary Legal Ramifications," in *Yale Journal of International Law,* 14 (1989), 221-334; and "The Naim-Andonian Documents on the World War I Destruction of the Ottoman Armenians: The Anatomy of a Genocide," in *International Journal of Middle East Studies,* 18 (1986), 311-360; and The Role of Turkish Physicians in the World War I Genocide of Ottoman Armenians," in *Holocaust and Genocide Studies,* I (1986), 169-192; and "The Documentation of the World War I Armenian Massacres in the Proceedings of the Turkish Military Tribunal," in *International Journal of Middle East Studies,* 23 (1991), 549-576; and "Documentation of the Armenian Genocide in Turkish Sources," in *Genocide: A Critical Bibliographic Review,* vol. 2, Israel Charny, ed. London, 1991. Other sources, dealing with general or specific events outlined in the chapter are: K. Aharonian, *A Historical Survey of the Armenian Case* (trans. By K. Maksoudian). Watertown, Mass., 1989; T. Akcam, *Turk Ulusal Kimligi ve Ermeni Sorunu.* Istanbul. 1992; H. Anassian, *The Armenian Question and the genocide of the Armenians in Turkey: A Brief Bibliography of Russian Materials* (in Russian and Armenian). Los Angeles, 1983; S. Astourian,

"The Armenian Genocide: An Interpretation," *The History Teacher,* 23 (2, 1990), 111-160; K. B. Bardakjian, *Hitler and the Armenian Genocide.* Cambridge, Mass., 1985; E. M. Bliss, *Turkey and the Armenian Atrocities.* Fresno, Ca. 1982; N. & H. Buxton, *Travels and Politics in Armenia.* London, 1914; A. Chalabian, *General Andranik and the Armenian Revolutionary Movement.* Detroit, 1988; H. Dasnabedian, *History of the Armenian Revolutionary Federation. Dashnaktsutiun 1890-1924.* Milan, 1988; L. A. Davis, *The Slaughterhouse Province: An American Diplomat's Report on the Armenian Genocide, 1915-1917.* New Rochelle, N.Y., 1989; J. Derogy, *Resistance and Revenge.* New Brunswick, N.J., 1990; M. H. Dobkin, *Smyrna 1922: The Destruction of a City.* Kent, Ohio, 1988; V. K. Goekjian, *The Turks Before the Court of History.* Fairlawn, N.J., 1984; S. Hoogasian Villa & M. K. Matossian, *Armenian Village Life Before 1914.* Detroit, 1982; R. G. Hovannisian, *The Armenian Holocaust: A Bibliography Relating to the Deportations, Massacres, and Dispersion of the Armenian People, 1915-1923.* Cambridge, Mass., 1978; and as editor, *The Armenian Genocide: History, Politics, Ethics.* New York, 1992; and *The Armenian Genocide in Perspective.* New Brunswick, N.J., 1986; P. Kazanjian, *The Cilician Armenian Ordeal.* Boston, 1989; C. Keyder, *State and Class in Turkey.* London, 1987; J. S. Kirakossian, *The Armenian Genocide: The Young Turks Before the Judgment of History.* Madison, 1992; W. L. Langer, *The Diplomacy of Imperialism, 1890-1902,* 2 vols. New York, 1935; and *European Alliances and Alignments, 1871-1890.* New York, 1939; J. Lepsius, *Armenia and Europe.* London, 1897; and *Deutschland und Armenien 1914-1918.* Potsdam, 1919; O. Mukhtarian & H. Gossoian, *The Defense of Van.* Michigan, 1980; L. Nalbandian, *The Armenian Revolutionary Movement: The Development of Armenian Political Parties through the Nineteenth Century.* Berkeley, 1963; L. Marashlian, *Politics and Demography: Armenians, Turks, and Kurds in the Ottoman Empire.* Cambridge, Mass., 1991; E. W. Martin, *The Hubbards of Sivas: A Chronicle of Love and Faith.* Santa Barbara, Ca., 1991; R. F. Melson, *Revolution and Genocide: On the Origins of the Armenian Genocide and the Holocaust.* Chicago, 1992; D. E. Miller & L. Touryan Miller, *Survivors: An Oral History of the Armenian Genocide.* Berkeley, 1993; H. Morgenthau, *Ambassador Morgenthau's Story.* New York, 1919; A. Nassibian, *Britain and the Armenian Question, 1915-1923.* London, 1984; M. Ormanian, *The Church of Armenia.* London, 1955; R. Peroomian, *Literary Responses to Catastrophe: A Comparison of the Armenian and the Jewish Experience.* Atlanta, 1993; M. Z. Rifat, *The Dark Folds of the Ottoman Revolution* (in Armenian). Beirut, 1968; A. O. Sarkissian, *History of the Armen-*

ian Question to 1885. Urbana, Ill., 1938; Y. Ternon, *The Armenians: History of a Genocide.* Delmar, N.Y., 1981; and *The Armenian Cause.* Delmar, N.Y., 1985; H. M. Sachar, *The Emergence of the Middle East, 1914-1924.* New York, 1969; R. W. Seton-Watson, *Britain in Europe, 1789-1914.* Cambridge, 1938; H. Stuermer, *Two War Years in Constantinople.* New York, 1990; S. G. Svajian, *A Trip Through Historic Armenia.* New York, 1983; M. Tarzian, *The Armenian Minority Problem.* New York, 1922; A. Ter Minassian, *Nationalism and Socialism in the Armenian Revolutionary Movement (1887-1912).* Cambridge, Mass., 1984; H. F. Tozer, *Turkish Armenia.* London, 1881; U. Trumpener, *Germany and the Ottoman Empire, 1914-1918.* Princeton, 1968; Sh. Toriguian, *The Armenian Question and International Law.* La Verne, Ca., 1988; C. D. Usher, *An American Physician in Turkey.* Boston, 1917; V. Yeghiayan, translator, *The Case of Soghomon Tehlirian* (court proceedings). Los Angeles, 1985; A. T. Wegner, *Die Verbrechen der Stunde-die Verbrechen der Ewigkeit.* Hamburg, 1982; F. Werfel, *Forty Days of Musa Dagh.* New York, 1934; E. J. Zürcher, Turkey, *A Modern History.* New York, 1993.

Volumes which present documents on the genocide include: R. Adalian, ed., *Guide to The Armenian Genocide in the U.S. Archives, 1915-1918.* Alexandria, Virginia, 1994; A. Sarafian, ed., *United States Official Documents on the Armenian Genocide, vol. I: The Lower Euphrates.* Watertown, Mass., 1993; *The Treatment of Armenians in the Ottoman Empire: Documents Presented to Viscount Grey of Fallodon.* London, 1916; *The Armenian Genocide*: Documentation edited by Institut für Armenische Fragen, vols. I, II, VIII. Munich, 1987-1991.

Revisionist Works by Turkish and American authors include: *Documents on Ottoman-Armenians*, 2 vols. Ankara, 1983; Y. Ercan, ed., *The Armenians Unmasked.* Ankara, 1993; K. Karpat, *Ottoman Population, 1830-1914: Demographics and Social Characteristics.* Madison, 1985; H. Lowry, *The Story Behind "Ambassador Morgenthau's Story.* Istanbul, 1990; J. McCarthy, *Muslims and Minorities: The Population of Ottoman Anatolia and the End of the Empire.* New York, 1983; S. & E. Shaw, *History of the Ottoman Empire and Modern Turkey*, vol. 2. New York, 1977; S. R. Sonyel, *The Ottoman Armenians: Victims of Great Power Diplomacy.* London, 1987; E. Uras, *The Armenians in History and the Armenian Question.* Istanbul, 1988; B. N. Simsir, *British Documents on Ottoman Armenians, 1856-1890*, 2 vols. Ankara, 1982-1983.

Chapter XX - The Armenian Republic:

The most important and monumental work, and the main source for the information in this chapter, is R. G. Hovannisian's, *The Republic of Armenia,* vols. I-II. Berkeley, 1971-1982 (volumes III-IV forthcoming in 1995). Other sources include: S. Afanasyan, *L'Arménie, l'Azerbaïdjan et la Géorgie: de l'indépendence à l'instauration du pouvoir soviétique, 1917-1923.* Paris, 1981; O. Baldwin, *Six Prisons and Two Revolutions: Adventures in Transcaucasia and Anatolia, 1920-1921.* Garden City, N.Y., 1925; J. L. Barton, *Story of Near East Relief, 1915-1930.* New York, 1930; L. Evans, *United States Policy and the Partition of Turkey, 1914-1924.* Baltimore, 1965; J. B. Gidney, *A Mandate for Armenia.* Kent, Ohio, 1967; P. C. Helmreich, *From Paris to Sèvres: The Partition of the Ottoman Empire and the Peace Conference of 1919-1920.* Columbus, Ohio, 1974; H. N. Howard, *Turkey, the Straits and U.S. Policy.* Baltimore, 1974; J. Kayaloff, *The Battle of Sardarabad.* The Hague, 1973; and *The Fall of Baku.* Bergenfield, N.J., 1976; F. Kazemzadeh, *The Struggle for Transcaucasia, 1917-1921.* New York, 1951; S. Kerr, *The Lions of Marash: Personal Experiences with American Near East Relief.* Albany, N.Y., 1973; F. Nansen, *Armenia and the Near East.* New York, 1928; R. G. Suny, *The Baku Commune, 1917-1918: Class and Nationality in the Russian Revolution.* Princeton, 1972; T. Swietochowski, *Russian Azerbaijan, 1905-1920.* Cambridge, 1985; R. R. Trask, *The United States Response to Turkish Nationalism and Reform, 1914-1939.* Minneapolis, 1971.

Chapters XXI-XXII-XXIII - Soviet Armenia, the New Spiurk, and the Armenian Republic:

The best studies in English are: A. Bakalian, *Armenian-Americans, From Being to Feeling Armenian,* New Brunswick, N.J., 1993; M. Matossian, *Impact of Soviet Policies in Armenia.* Leiden, 1962; R. Mirak, *Torn Between Two Lands: Armenians in America 1890 to World War I.* Harvard, 1983; B. Norehad, *The Armenian General Benevolent Union,* New York, 1966; R. G. Suny's, *Armenia in the Twentieth Century.* Chico, Ca., 1983 and *Looking toward Ararat.* Bloomington, 1993. Other works, more of a political science nature, include: V. Aspaturian, *The Union Republics in Soviet Diplomacy.* Geneva, 1960; R. Denber, ed., *The Soviet Nationality Reader,* Boulder, Co., 1992; I. Bremmer & R. Taras, eds., *Nations and Politics in the Soviet Successor States,* Cambridge, 1993; L. Hajda & M. Beissinger, eds., *The Nationali-*

ties Factor in Soviet Politics and Society. Boulder, Co., 1990; R. Karklins, *Ethnic Relations in the USSR.* Boston, 1986; G. Libaridian, ed., *The Karabagh File.* Cambridge, Mass., 1988; and *Armenia at the Cross-roads: Democracy and Nationhood in the Post-Soviet Era.* Cambridge, Mass., 1991; and *The Earthquake in Armenia: One Year Later. Proceedings of the Conference on Reconstruction in Armenia, December 4-6, 1989 Paris.* Cambridge, Mass., 1990; C. S. Mouradian, *De Staline à Gorbachev: Histoire d'une Republique Soviétique: L'Armenie.* Paris, 1990; S. Shahmuratian, ed., *The Sumgait Tragedy: Pogroms Against Armenians in Soviet Azerbaijan.* New Rochelle, N.Y., 1990; Y. Rost, *Armenian Tragedy: An Eyewitness account of Human Conflict and Natural Disaster in Armenia and Azerbaijan.* New York, 1990; G. Simon, *Nationalism and Policy Toward the Nationalities in the Soviet Union.* Boulder, Co., 1991; G. Smith, ed., *The Nationalities Question in the Soviet Union.* London, 1990; D. T. Twining, *The New Eurasia.* London, 1993; C. Walker, ed., *Armenia and Karabagh.* London, 1991; Parliament of the Republic of Armenia, *Decision '91. Armenia's Referendum on Independence, September 21, 1991.* Yerevan, 1991.

Index